WORKING
AT THE
BALLPARK

WORKING
AT THE
BALLPARK

The Fascinating Lives of Baseball People—
from Peanut Vendors and Broadcasters
to Players and Managers

TOM JONES

Skyhorse Publishing

Skyhorse Publishing books may be purchased in bulk at special discounts for sales promotion, corporate gifts, fund raising, or educational purposes. Special editions can also be created to specifications. For details, contact Special Sales Department, Skyhorse Publishing, 555 Eighth Avenue, Suite 903, New York, NY 10018 or info@skyhorsepublishing.com.

www.skyhorsepublishing.com

10   9   8   7   6   5   4   3   2   1

Library of Congress Cataloging-in-Publication Data
    Jones, Tom, 1950 Mar. 30–
    Working at the ballpark : the fascinating lives of baseball people—from peanut vendors and broadcasters to players and managers / Tom Jones.
        p.   cm.
    ISBN 978-1-60239-226-7 (alk. paper)
    1. Baseball—United States.   2. Baseball fields—United States—Employees.   I. Title.

GV875.A1J66   2008
796.357092'2—dc22
[B]
                                                            2007046508

Printed in Canada

For Jason, Ryan, Caitlin, and Abigail

CONTENTS

Chapter Five: In the Stands and on the Street

Chapter Six: Eyes and Ears

Chapter Seven: Support Crew

FOREWORD

As a young boy growing up in the little town of Alvin, Texas, I learned the meaning of work very early. My dad held two jobs, one as a supervisor with an oil company and the other distributing the *Houston Post*. I remember vividly—as much as a kid could at one in the morning—helping him gather the papers and throwing them out of our car window. Those times taught me about the value of hard work and dedication. I believe it created a strong foundation of commitment and perseverance in me that later in life helped me to pitch successfully in 807 major league baseball games spanning twenty-seven years.

In this compelling book by Tom Jones, you will meet a cross-section of good and interesting people talking firsthand about their lives in major league baseball. Some speak about their upbringings. For example, Ron Jackson, a friend of mine fondly known as "Papa Jack"—a name I gave him when we were teammates with the California Angels—describes how he and his brothers worked alongside their father laying bricks at job sites on Saturday mornings in Birmingham, Alabama, and then playing baseball together in the afternoon. In the book, Papa Jack shares the kind of hitting advice that helped the Boston Red Sox become World Series champions in 2004, and also talks about his more recent work as the hitting coach for my Round Rock Express, the Triple-A club for the Houston Astros.

And there is Jim Fregosi—a solid shortstop who I, along with three other players, was traded for in 1977 and who later served as my seventh big league manager—recalling growing up in South San Francisco where the scout who signed him would, once a week, stop by the delicatessen Jim's dad owned to report on how he was doing in the minor leagues. Fregosi remembers how his dad was a good athlete but never had a chance to seriously pursue a baseball career because he needed to be there to raise his family. These days, Jim works for the Atlanta Braves where he scouts players, looking for men who have the right baseball tools and who conduct themselves as professionals.

Just as my dad worked two jobs, you also will meet Steve Carlovsky, who works as a teacher by day and sells beer by night at Miller Park, and

Chris Hanson, who likewise teaches before changing into his Bernie Brewer costume as the mascot for the Milwaukee Brewers. Similarly, Bob Tayek works full time as a media director for a church organization before traveling across town to his second job behind the microphone as the public address announcer for the Cleveland Indians. And then there is Pete Quibell, who works as a city recreational coordinator during the day before taking on usher duties in the seating area behind home plate for the San Francisco Giants.

Take a look at the table of contents and you will find an interesting collection of names and occupations, including some young and upcoming baseball players like outfielder Eric Byrnes and first baseman Nick Johnson. You'll also find the familiar names of experienced baseball people like pitching coach Leo Mazzone and third base coach Doug Mansolino, and veteran players like pitcher Woody Williams and Gold Glove shortstop Omar Vizquel. They talk about their jobs as well as show the personal side of baseball.

People often say that baseball is only a game. That's true in the sense that baseball—like any sport—has rules, competition, and winners and losers. But it's more than that—much more: it's a way of life. You will read about the long hours people put in at work and how being away from their families is a necessary part of the job. You also will see how passionate they are about their career choices, and how the wins and losses are felt not just by the athletes on the field and the coaches in the dugout, but by everyone in the team's organization, top to bottom. From the executives in the front office to the advance scouts on the road, and from the groundskeepers, clubhouse managers, and trainers to the peanut vendors, mascots, and scoreboard operators—a baseball organization can only succeed when everyone works and plays hard together.

I pitched in my last major league game in September 1993. After throwing only twenty-eight pitches, the ulnar collateral ligament in my throwing arm tore. That was the end of my playing career, but not my baseball career. These days I keep busy with a lot of community and business activities, including being part of the ownership group of two minor-league teams: the Double-A Corpus Christi Hooks and the Triple-A Round Rock Express. I knew during my playing days how important it was to be able to count on the guys playing with me, and how essential it was to play for teams with solid organizations. As a team owner now, I appreciate even more the special kind of commitment among those who work at a ballpark and that I, as do other baseball team owners, count on every one of them to help provide great service to fans. Within these pages, you will see what I mean.

Working at the Ballpark is a different kind of baseball book. It is a wonderful collection of true stories by people who, in their own words, give a peek inside baseball, on the field and behind the scenes. It's almost like sitting in the dugout next to manager Mike Hargrove, behind home plate with umpire Fieldin Culbreth, or up in the press box alongside radio and television broadcaster Lanny Frattare. You don't have to read the book cover to cover. Skip through the pages to find one interesting person after another. You'll never watch a baseball game the same way again.

—**NOLAN RYAN**
Alvin, Texas
January 2, 2008

INTRODUCTION

Three hours before the first pitch on a late August afternoon, Arizona Diamondbacks outfielder Eric Byrnes sat in the visitors' dugout talking about his job:

> *"It's very, very simple. I mean, shoot, it's just really [about] trying to play the game as long as you can, and enjoying every minute of it. It's a grind because you constantly have to produce, you know. You're constantly measured by your next performance. If you don't stay on top of your game, it will wash you out quick. Each day, it's a battle to come out here and perform. If you can do one or two things to help your team win a game, you can continue to have a job. If you don't, the game can turn on you quickly."*

This book is about people, like Byrnes, that work in major league baseball. It is about their jobs—what they do for a living and how they got into baseball. It also is about who they are and what the job means to them. The ballpark is their job site, be it in a dugout, in a clubhouse, in a bullpen, in the press box, in the executive office, on the field, or in the stands. As with other Americans who begin their workday at perhaps a factory, school, hospital, high-rise office building, or farm, baseball people trade their labors for a paycheck and, as the reader will find, much more.

Working at the Ballpark is a collection of candid, engaging conversations with fascinating people that have jobs across the spectrum: player, manager, coach, beer vendor, groundskeeper, usher, clubhouse manager, executive, broadcaster, writer, mascot. Their stories are personal, yet they reflect the experiences of many others that work in similar jobs, at other stadiums. Some of the people you will meet are full-time career employees who work long hours, travel frequently, and often are away from their families. Others make the ballpark their second job of the day.

They speak for themselves, in their words. Most will never get their faces on a baseball card or names in a starting lineup, but they all have stories worth telling. Whether it's a veteran player who is paid millions to work on manicured grass in front of 40,000 spectators on a summer afternoon, or a guy who teaches eighth graders by day and sells beer at night, it's clear their job demands and pressures are as real as they are for other American workers. These are ordinary people, even though some have extraordinary skills. They come to work, of course, for pay, but their jobs can mean more than that. Take it from official scorer Jim Ferguson:

> *"If you're with a team, you have such an attachment that you live and die with wins and losses, just like the players do. Sometimes more than the players because they can do something about it, plus they're going to get paid no matter what. If you're working in the front office with a team, you are up or down mentally, whether you won or lost the night before, and how you won or how you lost."*

I conducted the interviews with the fifty people who appear in the book during the 2006 and 2007 major league seasons, almost all at ballparks. Most were arranged with assistance from the teams' media directors. The interviews with managers, coaches, and players generally took place in clubhouses, a few hours before a game, as they prepared for work.

Interviews were also held in dugouts during batting practice, or at places and times convenient for the interviewees. For example, the first half of a two-part interview with Ron "Papa Jack" Jackson occurred in the summer of 2006, when he was the hitting coach for the Boston Red Sox. We sat in the stands, on the first base side, at Fenway Park. After the Red Sox did not renew his contract at the end of the season, I caught up with him the next year to talk about his new job with the Triple-A Round Rock Express. This time, we sat on metal folding chairs in a parking lot at a minor league stadium.

Boston Globe sports columnist Dan Shaughnessy invited me to his house where he gave the first interview for the book. Eleven-time Gold Glove shortstop Omar Vizquel rested in front of his clubhouse locker as he spoke into the voice recorder about his job and his love of fine arts, while reporters gathered across the room before San Francisco Giants teammate Barry Bonds. When ticket hustler Johnny "from Connecticut" heard someone wanted to talk about his trade, he approached me on Brookline Avenue in Boston during the early innings of a Mets–Red Sox interleague game. While he was on the road, umpire Fieldin Culbreth agreed to meet in his hotel room to talk about calling balls and strikes. Padres CEO Sandy Alderson spoke on the field during batting practice at PETCO Park before a game against the Mariners. Bob Watson talked while we sat in the commissioner's office in New York on a late Friday afternoon. And Philadelphia sports talk show host Howard Eskin took time before his afternoon show, and during commercial breaks while on the air, to describe what he does for a living. All the interviews were held face to face, with the exception of two separate phone conversations with Bob Boone of the Washington Nationals and ballpark architect Joe Spear.

I explained to each person that I wasn't seeking controversy; I wanted only to talk about their jobs and what working in baseball meant to them. I wasn't looking for a story; I was looking for *their* story. Our talks revolved primarily around three questions: What do you do for a living? How did you get into this line of work? What does the job mean to you? From there, we simply talked. Some reminisced about their childhood passion for baseball. Some recalled memorable anecdotes from throughout their careers. And some, like umpire Fieldin Culbreth, wanted readers to know how difficult their work can be:

> "I am absolutely amazed at just how tough it is. I think people think, 'Well, hell, it's just a strike or a ball, what can be so tough about that?' You're talking about the best players in the world. [Randy] Johnson isn't just throwing that thing over the plate just to be throwing it over the plate. He's trying to make it do different things and doing it at 95 to 100 miles per hour, and I'm supposed to tell you if it's a ball or a strike in this imaginary box out in space with this thing that's lying on the ground. And there's somebody in front of me and somebody to the side of me. It's a whole lot more complex than it seems."

Generally, the ushers, vendors, groundskeepers—those who rarely speak with the media—spoke freely. The coaches usually were quickly entertaining, informative, and chatty. Front office staff tended to be guarded initially, seemingly concerned how their words might reflect on their organizations; while players commonly were more sensitive about how an interview might reflect on them personally.

Most of the time, I arrived at a stadium hours before the beginning of a three-game series to obtain media credentials and wander the empty and quiet park, waiting until the media are allowed into the clubhouses. Groundskeepers were frequently the only employees in sight at those times, grooming the field for that day's game. Under the rules of Major League Baseball, clubhouses are open to the media three and a half hours before the first pitch. There, players relax by reading, talking, and playing card games. They're also dressing into their practice or game uniforms, walking in and out of rooms that are off-limits to the press (such as the trainer's room), eating, exercising, watching game film, and taking indoor batting practice. Reporters stand around looking to see which players might be willing to talk, or they wait for a specific player. Clubhouses then close 45 minutes before game time, and re-open again about ten minutes after the final out, sometimes longer to give managers and players a cooling off period or to have a postgame team meeting.

Some interviews flopped, and are therefore not included. For example, when I approached infielder Alex Cora as he was getting dressed for batting practice, he agreed to talk. About three minutes into the interview he said, "This isn't working for me." I understood and appreciated his honesty because he realized that the oral history format of the book would take longer than the brief quote he might typically give to a newspaper beat reporter. There also was third baseman Jeff Cirillo, who initially questioned what I was doing in the Milwaukee Brewers' clubhouse but later stopped on his way to the field to volunteer an impromptu interview about the reason he wears a tattered T-shirt that reads "No More Stinking Tacos" under his uniform top. (It had to do with a time when he joined a team in Mexico under the assumed name of Jake Taylor—a fictional player in the movie *Major League*—so he could rid himself of a toe-tap habit that nearly ruined his hitting career.) Cirillo and I tried again to meet—this time after he signed with the Minnesota Twins—but he was too rushed to complete the interview because he preparing for that day's game, being interrupted by a reporter and other players, eating a sandwich, and trying to focus on the interview all at once. Although not an interview flop, another person not in the book is Don Zimmer, the last former Brooklyn Dodger still serving on the field in any capacity. After Don and I talked about his fifty-eight years in baseball, I inadvertently erased the interview while changing batteries in the voice recorder.

I aimed to accurately preserve the meaning and actual words spoken by those appearing in the book, editing primarily for clarity and brevity. Sometimes fragmented comments are combined. In other places, comments are rearranged to present a clearer sequence of events. The tone, rhythm, and speaking styles belong to them. The perceptive reader will notice questionable grammar and word usage. That's okay. It's how a lot of us talk.

I have been a baseball fan since the spring of 1960, when my dad took me to a Giants-Pirates game at Candlestick Park in San Francisco. As a kid, I often played in our front yard pretending I was Willie Mays, making the kind of over-the-head catches that he snatched off the bat of Vic Wertz in the 1954 World Series. And at night, I fell asleep while listening to radio announcers Russ Hodges and Lon Simmons call Giants games, trying to stay awake during the late innings of a close game—especially if that night's opponents were the dreaded Dodgers.

Each time I approached an interview, I knew I was intruding into another person's daily job routine and was never certain how they would respond. I wanted something from them and hoped they would feel as comfortable with me as if they were sitting across the kitchen table talking to a familiar friend. I think Cy Buynak, the visiting clubhouse manager for Cleveland Indians, can speak for each who appear in the book:

"I look back, I can't believe it's been forty-five years. I enjoyed the job. I always tell my young guys, 'Don't look for money. Look for a job that you can enjoy.' There's tons of people that wake up and dread going to work because they look at the clock. I don't have that. I wake up and I know what I got to do that day, and I go out and do it. I'm very blessed that I have this job. It means the world to me. Baseball has been good to me."

CHAPTER ONE

MOVERS AND SHAKERS

PETER MAGOWAN

Managing General Partner, San Francisco Giants

Peter McGowan's grandfather was Charles Merrill, co-founder of Merrill Lynch and Co., Inc., and his father was chairman and CEO of the Safeway grocery chain, a job Magowan held before buying the Giants with other investors in 1993.

Six weeks remained for the Giants to make a run at the 2006 division title. In his office at AT&T Park, McGowan pulled a notepad from the center drawer of his desk. There are two columns on the page in his handwriting. "I keep something like this out here every day. This shows how many games are played, how far out we are, what we need to do. I wrote this last Saturday morning. If the Giants win twenty-seven and the Dodgers win twenty-three, we would beat them by one game. Until we're mathematically eliminated, I do something like this to try to talk myself into thinking that it still is possible; and it is possible."

*   *   *   *   *

My love affair with baseball started around 1950, and it's been there ever since. I grew up playing the game in New York City. I played stickball in the summer with my friends from sunrise to sunset. There were three great baseball teams in New York at the time: the Giants, Dodgers, and Yankees. My first game was a Giants game. I went with my dad; just fell in love with the beauty of the ballpark at night.

Nineteen fifty-one was the year Bobby Thomson hit his home run to beat the Dodgers. I was in class that day. I was nine years old. Half of the class were Dodger fans; half of the class were Giants fans. It was a very tough school. We were never allowed to listen to the radio, but the teacher let us listen to this game, which he knew was a pretty special game. And the Giants, of course, won it with Thomson's home run in the bottom of the ninth. I went home that day. My dad came through the front door of the house about an hour later and he said, "Guess where I've been today?" And I said, "You couldn't have been there." And he said, "Yep"—he was there.

He went with three people from the office where he worked. The other three all left at the beginning of the bottom of the ninth. So he says, "This is a lesson I hope you never forget about baseball: that it's never over till it's over." He said it long before Yogi Berra ever did. I'd never missed a day of school in my life. I'd been shoved out of the house sick as hell. But in the fifth grade, I'd never missed one day. And he said, "Would you like to go to the World Series tomorrow?" So I went to that game. The Giants beat the Yankees. Monte Irvin stole home. I can remember it all like it was yesterday.

In 1957, the Giants and the Dodgers left New York to go to California. I couldn't believe it. The Giants had won the World Series in 1954. I saw the second game. It's the last time they've won a World Series. The Dodgers won the World Series in 1955. And two years later these two great, historic teams were gone; gone from the biggest city in the country, the richest city in the world. And I just couldn't believe it. I was very depressed, as I think everybody in New York was. In fact the next year, 1958—you could look this up, but the Yankee attendance—their attendance, now being the only team in New York instead of three, went down. And that's a pretty good indication of the depression of baseball fans who had the game taken away from them.

All this background of my getting interested in the game of baseball came back in 1992 when I got a call from Bob Lurie, who was the owner of the Giants. He had been the owner for sixteen years. I was on his board of directors. And he called to say he'd sold the team to people from Tampa Bay, Florida. And I basically said, "How could you do this?" He said he couldn't make any money at it; he couldn't survive at Candlestick Park. The people didn't want to build a new ballpark. He was tired of writing out checks and baseball had no future in San Francisco, and he was selling the team. I wished him well. But I said, you know, I wouldn't be able to live with myself if I didn't do something to try to keep the team here because I had grown up in New York and I had this scarring from what [the Giants and Dodgers moving] did to the people of New York. And I believed the same thing would happen to the people of San Francisco, and the Bay Area would be deprived of the baseball team that they'd rooted for since 1958.

This was very late in the day. He had concluded a definitive legal agreement to sell the team but he had not obtained permission from the new acting commissioner, Bud Selig. He had the right to shop the team, but not to sell the team. And he sold it. We called up the commissioner, and the commissioner said, "If you can put in a competitive offer and do it quickly, then we'll look seriously at keeping the Giants in San Francisco." We were able to put together a group of civic-minded businessmen from San Francisco and scrounged up the hundred million dollars to keep the team here.

I had a pretty good idea what I was getting into. I followed the game pretty closely, and I knew what the economics were. I feel that a baseball owner doesn't really own a team the way he owns another asset. He is a caretaker. He owns something that really belongs to the community. Eventually, he's going to hand it over to someone else. And I think his responsibility is to hand it over in better shape than what he found it in. So he's supposed to nurture this investment, make it one that the community will support, but not try to, you know, make a lot of money—run the thing almost as if it was something like a public utility.

We've had our ups and downs in some fourteen years here. But we've never distributed a check to the partners in the years that we've made money. We've always put the money back into the team. I think that's one of the jobs that I have is to increase the value of the franchise for my partners, for my investors. That's how they get their money back. It's not by getting dividends like they would from a normal investment.

The first issue that faced us was that baseball, I think, was dying in San Francisco. The team had lost ninety-two games in 1992. The attendance was down to a million and a half people. There was a lot of worry that, you know, new people had bought the Giants. But why is their fate gonna be any different than the previous owners? This wasn't the first time that the Giants had been under all this pressure. What we needed to do was to quickly revitalize interest in baseball. We did it by signing Barry Bonds. We signed him even though we didn't quite technically own the team yet, and got ourselves into a lot of trouble with a lot of other people [because of it].

Well, we negotiated the contract with Barry, and it was a unique contract. It was the only one I've ever negotiated in my fourteen years, and it took less than a minute to do. I met at the airport hotel with him and his agent, and I said to the agent, "I think Barry Bonds is the best player in the game." He had just won the MVP in 1992, and he'd won it in 1990. "I think he ought to be a Giant. His father was a great player for the Giants. His godfather is Willie Mays. We'd love to have him. I think the best player on the team—the best player in baseball—ought to be the best paid. The best paid right now is Ryne Sandberg. He's earning $7.1 million a year, and he signed to a four-year contract." This guy's just nodding at everything I'm saying, the agent, Dennis Gilbert. And then I said, "We propose $7.2 million and five years." And Dennis now speaks for the first time. And he says, "He has his heart set on seven years." And so I said, "How about six?" And he said, "Done." That took a minute: $43 million.

Now, Barry Bonds was a Giant, or so we thought. The story starts coming out over the radio that night. And people say, "Can you believe this? The Giants are not only still here, but they got Barry Bonds onto the team. The best player in baseball is going to be a Giant for the next six years." The front-page story, GIANTS SIGN BONDS. Not front page of the sports section, front page of the news section. Everybody's excited as hell. We had planned a press conference for Barry Bonds.

I go to Louisville for the winter league meetings. And we get a message to see the commissioner. And in his office was the president of the

National League; the president of the American League; the lawyer for the National League; the seller of the Giants, Bob Lurie; and his general manager, Al Rosen. There were no smiles in this room. We were told to cancel the press conference. They said, "Who do you guys think you are, spending $43 million of someone else's money to sign Barry Bonds?" And we said, "Who says it's someone else's money?" "Well, it would be if you weren't approved as owners of the Giants. And the way you're acting, you probably won't be." We said, "Well, now, nobody has led us to believe that we aren't going to be owners of the Giants. We have the wherewithal to own the Giants, and what are we supposed to do, watch other people sign everybody in sight?"

The Braves had just signed [Greg] Maddux from the Cubs. We were trying to revitalize interest in baseball. And they said, "Well, you can't do this. You have to unwind your contract." So we eventually said, "Well, it seems to us that Barry Bonds is owed the $43 million that we promised him. And if Bob Lurie ever retains ownership of the Giants, which Bob doesn't want to do, we agree he shouldn't have any obligation to Barry Bonds, so we'll have to come up with some solution that solves both of those problems."

So for forty-eight hours, we thought about it and put together a deal whereby if Bob Lurie retained ownership of the Giants, Barry Bonds would become a free agent again. And anything less than the $43 million that we had promised him we would make up at the end of the six years. You know, if he got $44 million, we were off the hook. But if he got $22 million over those six years, if he was injured in the second year and couldn't play baseball again, then whatever difference between the $43 million that we had promised and that whatever he made, we, the ex-owners, would make up the difference.

We sold a hell of a lotta tickets in the off-season. In that first year, we drew 2.6 million instead of 1.5 million. We won 103 games, which the Giants had never won before, or since. Barry Bonds hit a home run in his first at-bat at Candlestick on opening day. We hired Dusty Baker to be the manager, and he won Manager of the Year; Barry Bonds was named MVP [of the National League].

So the start of revitalizing the interest was Barry; getting Dusty to be the manager was another pretty bold move because he'd never managed before. I asked a lot of people: "Who should be the manager?" And they said, "Don't hire someone who's never managed before." We hired Dusty, and we refurbished Candlestick; cleaned it up, put in a new outfield fence, put in new bleachers right on top of that outfield fence, agreed that we would pick up all the hot dog wrappers that came on to the field, greatly improved the food. We all wore buttons: WE'RE LISTENING. And we were listening to our customers. What are we doing right? What are we doing wrong? How can we do it better?

A big part of what we were trying to do was change the image of the Giants, become more community-oriented. I asked the players the first day in spring training: would they all agree to work for a charity of their choice during the baseball season? They said yes. We were the first team in baseball that could make that statement: that every player worked for a charity.

In 1994, we had our first game for AIDS research; raised money for AIDS awareness. That was the last game we played that year because the strike came along. But our game was reported on the ABC Evening News that night as the most important baseball game of the year. It was controversial then. I got a lot of hate mail over all of this. But the players supported it. And we really were off to a good start with turning around the image. Then the strike came. And all of the goodwill that we had I thought developed in terms of saving the team, putting a good team on the field, getting the best player in the game onto our team, refurbishing our ballpark, I thought there'd be some reservoir of support. But there wasn't. We got kicked in the teeth with the strike. The fans were just very upset, took it out on the owners and the players. Our attendance went down to 1.2 million in '95, from 2.6 in '93; and we went into last place. But we came back and got into first place in '97. And that was the beginning of what became a really remarkable streak of eight years in which we had the third best record in all of baseball.

Every year, you're faced with challenges. We were in the World Series in 2002, and then 2003 comes. What are we going to do about 2003? We parted company with Dusty Baker. Parting company with a manager who puts you in the World Series is not a normal occurrence, and we had to deal with that. So we always have to deal with new sets of problems, whether we're coming off a very successful year, or very unsuccessful year.

Now this year is another unsuccessful year for us, the second in a row after really having eight years of great success. And so there are now lots of decisions that need to be made. This will be a very intensive process that we'll start—well, it's already started. You will begin to see the decision making the day after this baseball season ends. Things are going to have to happen.

The baseball operations report to me. Anything that's important on the baseball operations, such as the signing of a free agent with a multi-year contract, I have to approve of. The basic overall trade strategy I would need to be involved. It doesn't mean that I have veto power, but I expect to know what's happening. And I expect to know what's happening before it's happening.

Generally speaking, we operate the baseball club with a budget for the general manager. He has freedom to take whatever decisions he feels are the right ones within the concept of that budget. If he goes over the budget, he has to get permission. But as a courtesy to me, he knows that any central decisions, even though they're within the framework of that budget, he needs to discuss with me. He doesn't have to get them approved by me, but I want to hear what his thinking is.

I got a call in the middle of the night last week about our chance to sign a sixteen-year-old Dominican player for $2.1 million. This wasn't fully covered in the budget and was a surprise. It was something falling into our lap that we didn't expect. But it's a major commitment. We haven't done things like that historically. So, I get this call: "We could get this guy, we think, for $2.1 million tomorrow morning"—which was in about three hours time down there. "Can we go ahead with these negotiations?" So I asked a lot of questions about this guy. I asked, "Who's the scout that signed him, or that wants to sign him, and what's his reputation?" Well, it turned out to be a great Dodgers scout. And that guy said, "This is the best player at this age I've ever seen in the Dominican Republic." "Well, what's his family like? Does his family understand what's going to happen if he's going to go live in the United States, and not be there? Are they going to be happy? Is he going to be happy? What does he know about America, about English? What are his values? Does he get into trouble?"

If you're spending all this amount of money, you want to know that you're spending it on the right kind of guy because we, as an industry, have a terrible track record of predicting who's going to be successful and who isn't. You know, only 10 percent of all the players who are signed in baseball ever make it to the major leagues, much less have a decent career.

Basketball is much easier to predict. If a guy shoots 85 percent foul shots at Duke, he's going to shoot 85 percent foul shots for the New York Knicks because it's the same environment. But in baseball, are you going to perform differently if there's 40,000 people there as opposed to 400? You just don't know. Statistics can't tell you.

I remember that little pitcher, Billy Wagner, now with the Mets; had great statistics, and we all said, "Yeah, but look who he's pitching against. How can that little guy pitch against major-league players?" Well, clearly we were wrong on that. Mike Piazza—sixty-second round draft pick—and yet you have all these first-round picks. Many times they fail. So football, basketball: they have a much better track record than we do.

Another job I have is some PR responsibilities for the organization. We get a lot of mail here. We try to answer all of this mail directly. Now, some owners take quite an invisible position, and other owners are out there on the field all day long. I sort of try to be sort of in-between these two positions. But, I am the face of the ownership group. We have twenty-five investors, and they have ceded to me the authority and the visibility, both good and bad, that goes with being an owner. I like to describe myself as leading the ownership group, not being the owner of the Giants. But the way it's described usually is I am the owner of the Giants, which I'm not. I'm *one* of the group of partners.

I try to encourage people to make as many decisions as possible, and not be afraid to make mistakes. Businessmen—and I've seen them in my previous life at Safeway—who try to make no mistakes will end up making two decisions a year, and they'll both be right. But they'll get only two things done.

The people that are prepared to make mistakes will get a helluva lot more done, and they'll learn from the mistakes that they do make. On the one hand, you have accountability and responsibility for the mistakes that you do make; but on the other hand, you feel you're going to be a better businessman through what you've learned through your mistakes. For example, I think we all collectively made mistakes this year with our team, thinking that because these players have been great players a year ago, or two years ago, they would still be great players—like Steve Finley. Finley in '04, hit 37 home runs, played in every single game, and won a Gold Glove. In '06, he's hitting .250; he's a part-time outfielder. Moises Alou in '04, hit 37 home runs for the Cubs, and hit about .330 and played 145 games. Now he's playing about half the games, hitting .290, hitting 15 homers. We made the mistake of thinking that they would be able to maintain that in the face of what typically happens to players when they are over thirty-five, no matter how good they are. We all were a part of those decisions.

People say "one shot," but it's been one shot for fourteen years—the third best record in baseball. Only the Yankees and the Braves have done better. When you have as much money committed to Barry as we have paid him, there's a limit to what's left over for everybody else. I mean we've tried to put good players around him. Other people said if you didn't have Bonds, you could've spread that money amongst three or four good players instead of one absolutely great player. But would we have done better?

The wheels began to fall off the wagon last year. Barry got hurt, and Alou didn't play anywhere near as much as we thought he would. And Durham and Alfonzo didn't play as well as we thought they would. So, you know, was it a mistake? Yeah, I'd have to say in retrospect it was a mistake. Are we going to now go in a different direction? Yes, we will. We're going to learn from our mistakes. Are we going to fire Brian Sabean because he made these mistakes? No, because we're all in this together. I would say the good times in baseball are the most fun I've ever had. And the bad times in baseball are probably the worst times I've ever had.

Both businesses [Giants and Safeway] are marketing businesses. I mean, we try to get customers into our stores, and we try to get customers into our ballpark. And how do we try to do that? There are certain similarities, I think, in both situations. We really try to be nice to our customers. If you come to a game here, you get a friendly greeting. You are waited on by knowledgeable staff. They try to be helpful. And to be sure that they're acting the right way, we mystery-shop them with people who ask questions like "Where's my seat?" or "Where's the restroom?" or "How do I find my lost child?" Things like this. And we score our people on the basis of how they do with this mystery shopping. We did the exact same thing at Safeway.

I remember the first game I attended as an owner in 1992. As I was leaving the ballpark, some parking lot attendant said to me, "Did you have a good time?" And another one said, "Please come back." I'd been going to Candlestick since 1960, and I had never heard those words at Candlestick before. I told this story to all of our ushers and ticket takers and concession workers the first day we opened in 1993. I said, "I expect to hear those words, not those words, put them in your own words, but I expect you to understand that it's these customers, having them come back, that pays for your job and pays for my job. And they won't come back, or they won't come as often as we want them to, if they're not made to feel like a real guest in our place." All that is Safeway stuff. Nobody likes to wait at the checkout. Nobody likes to wait getting into this ballpark. We try to have—like I said earlier back at Candlestick—no hot dog wrappers on the field. They still fall on our field here, but we pick them up lickety-split.

There's always pressure to perform. I think that the people would not give me the greatest marks in the world the last couple of years. I don't deserve them based on how we've played. But there's a reservoir of support for me and the ownership group, based on our track record. It wasn't very good last year, but it's been very good over the past fourteen years taken as a whole body. I mean, we've never, ever done as well in fifty years of being here as we've done the first six years of this ballpark in terms of wins and losses on the field. And I think people say, in terms of my image, they said, "We know Peter wants to win. We know, however disappointed we are with these expectations, he's even more disappointed than we are, and he will do something about it. And we trust him to get the job done." I think that is still there. Now, if we have another year or two like this one in which we're a losing team, then that image would change. Anybody's image can change. I remember George Bush, the first, coming into Congress after the first Iraq war with a 92-percent approval rating, and [he was] out of office eight months later. I remember George Bush, the second, you know, "Mission Accomplished" on the aircraft carrier and everyone singing his praises and the Taliban defeated. Look at where he is today. So things can go in a hurry in sports, as they can in politics.

You know, when things go bad, my wife keeps asking me, "Why do this if it's not fun anymore?" And I always tell her that the fun part of the business is doing something that is difficult to do. It's hard for me to see how George

Steinbrenner really can enjoy baseball because he's got a two-hundred-million-dollar payroll; he ought to win. He usually does win. He's not been in last place. He doesn't understand the joy of seeing what happened to us in '97 when everyone expected us to be in last place, winning our division. The joy of getting into the World Series in '02, beating a team like the Braves in the playoffs, and the Cardinals, which we had to do to get into that World Series. Nobody thought we could do those things. And there's tremendous satisfaction when you accomplish that. What I think keeps a lot of us going is not only the competitive spirit, but really the feeling and satisfaction when you can do something that people thought you couldn't do.

You know, when I think back on my years here, that's been a huge part of the whole experience. People said, "You can't keep the team here. They've been sold to people in Tampa Bay." People said, "You can't get Barry Bonds onto the team; you don't own the team." People said, "You can't win an election; the previous owner tried four times, lost four times, to build a park." People said, "You can't build a park privately; it hasn't been done since Dodger Stadium was done." People said, "Even if you build the park, no one will come. This is a football town. There's five Super Bowls for the 49ers." People said, "Even if they come, they won't come for long because you can't put a good team on the field because you've got so much debt service."

The way we measure success in this business is primarily, you know, can you win a World Series? People say, "Well, you've accomplished everything you wanted to accomplish." We kept the Giants here, and we put a good team on the field. We built a beautiful ballpark. We've got a great community image. We've had a lot of success. We've drawn three million fans or more for the seventh year in a row. Only five teams in the history of baseball have done that. We've led the National League in attendance over these last six years. A lot of good stuff has happened. But we haven't won a World Series.

So as long as I have the enthusiasm to try to achieve that goal, not just for me but for the community, I will expend the energy to try to accomplish it. If the time comes when I feel I'm just worn out—I've tried; I gave it my best shot; we came close, but we're not going to come any closer—then that would be the time to get out.

* * * * *

SANDY ALDERSON

Chief Executive Officer, San Diego Padres

"Baseball teams are small businesses. We're not talking about General Motors here. We're talking about $150 million or so in revenue. That's not a real big business. The profile we have is so extraordinary that it's a great platform for representing the city, and leading other businesses in the sense of corporate citizenship. Many people think that professional franchises are one indice of municipal status. So in that sense, I think it's more of a quality of life issue than it is an economic, or standard of living, issue. I think baseball, and other professional sports, do have an economic impact, but I think it's far surpassed by just the psychic benefit that's derived from a city from being associated with a successful professional franchise. It can be an economic catalyst, but more importantly, I think it can be a cultural societal leader."

Alderson and I talked on the field during the Padres' batting practice at PETCO Park prior to an interleague game against the Seattle Mariners.

*　　*　　*　　*　　*

As CEO, I oversee all the operations of the club, which includes baseball, business and finance, community affairs; all of the various activities of the franchise. We are like any business. We have various elements that will either make or break us. We have to have a good product, and that's the team on the field, but we also have to provide good service. We need to be good corporate citizens, and over time, we have to break even otherwise we can't sustain all of the other good things that we are doing. So like any business, all of those things come into play, every day. Obviously, the team on the field has the most cachet, and it's the part of the game that is the most critical and most romantic, but there are a lot of things that go on behind the scenes.

I get involved to some extent in all of the deals; certainly in the major contracts, contract signings, and major player transactions. But you have to be careful not to get too carried away with your own involvement in these things, if you're not spending all of your time doing it. There is tremendous reliance on other people. But ultimately, I have to be comfortable, too, with what we're doing.

I think often the difference between success and failure is leadership. From my standpoint, people deserve an opportunity to respond to new leadership, rather than making assumptions about people's inability to respond to ideas or direction. So I would rather try that. It's like an injured player who rehabs first, until the doctors decide that's not working, and then he has surgery. You don't always go to the surgery first.

Keep an open mind. Be open to new ideas, new perspectives, new ways of evaluating things. I think that's ultimately why we were successful in Oakland because, by necessity, we were open-minded, but it's sometimes harder to do when you have a more established organization. Stability, particularly in leadership positions, is very important to long-term success in baseball. But it has to be a stable leadership, and a stable organization that is nonetheless open to new ideas and new things.

I'm fifty-eight. My dad was in the military, and I traveled around. I've had a few favorite teams as I moved around the country. At the age of nine, I was a White Sox fan, and at age eleven, I was a Milwaukee Braves fan. Hank Aaron was my favorite player. I grew up as a fan, and as a youth I played a lot. I played into college. More than that, it was serendipity. I was a practicing lawyer in San Francisco, and got involved strictly out of the blue. I figured if it didn't work out, I could always be a lawyer. This has worked out, so far.

I happened to be working at a law firm that started doing the outside legal work for the people who bought the Oakland Athletics from Charlie Finley. From that outside counsel position—a guy named Roy Eisenhart brought me over—I moved to the A's full time as general counsel, and then not too long thereafter, as general manager. So getting involved was fortuitous. Becoming the general manager was filling a void at a time when I probably wasn't fully qualified, or prepared, for the position. I'm not sure I ever had a sense, at the time, that I wasn't qualified, and certainly didn't have traditional qualifications or experience. But when you're younger, you don't recognize your limitations. In retrospect, I look back and say, "Well, gee, how did I survive that?"

I think the legal training helped quite a bit because contract negotiation is important, but also because I didn't have the experience in the game that a lot of other people in my position had. I was open to new ideas, and those new ideas involved statistical analysis and a lot of things that have become more prevalent in baseball today in terms of decision making than they were back in 1980. In fact, they were non-existent in 1980. The experience and considerations that form the background to those decisions are very different today.

Then, in baseball, it was more subjective about players. It was more tools-based: Can a guy throw, and can a guy run? Does he have power? Whereas today, there is more statistical analysis; it's not a matter of projecting based on physical qualities. It's a matter of measuring based on more objective metrics and statistics. For instance: What has this person done? How does all of this physical ability translate into productivity? What is it that this person is able to do with whatever talents they have? In 1980, I don't recall having a computer. It was more of a mathematical analysis than [something] computer driven, and it wasn't terribly sophisticated the way an analysis can become with the use of computers. The mathematical formulas have gotten a lot more complicated because computers are able to evaluate a lot more information, and spit out more precise numbers. I rely primarily on experienced baseball people, but with a strong eye also for statistical analysis. You try to merge the two perspectives, and bring both to bear, weighting them according to the circumstances; hopefully appropriately. It's really a balance.

I worked for six and a half years at the commissioner's office. I was in charge of umpires, baseball operations, baseball administration, international baseball, facilities, security—a bunch of different stuff. All the cats and dogs. When I left the A's and went to the commissioner's office, I was interested in taking my club experience, which at that point totaled about seventeen years, and [trying] to apply it at the league level; but also learn at the league level from other people I respected in various other disciplines and benefit from their experience. I can't say that it worked out all that well. It's just the way we operated. It was difficult to get involved in other departments from a learning standpoint. There wasn't quite as much time to do it, nor inclination on my part, or maybe even on the part of other people to provide that. In any event, I didn't miss the baseball. I didn't miss the day to day at all, at that point. Maybe after seventeen years, I was a little burned out on it. But after a period of years, you miss the ability to really get emotionally involved, and root for your own guys and your own team, and all of what that means, at the community level, within a front office, among a group of fans, where everybody is hoping for the same result, trying to make it happen for the benefit of everybody. Experiencing it day to day, like everybody else. That's what I missed.

There is a cyclical nature, and a seasonal nature to the game. Every part of the year has its own peculiar set of activities and priorities: spring training, opening the season, the All-Star break, the amateur draft, the trade deadline, September pennant races, the post-season, winter baseball meetings, free agent signing. It's a chronological rhythm; it's almost a lunar rhythm when you get into the season.

I like the sense of renewal that takes place. When I go to spring training, I feel like I'm going, not for the first time, but it's fresh, and you know what to expect. There's an excitement that comes from that anticipation. But the rhythm is not just seasonal. It's a daily rhythm, too, depending on whether you're home or on the road; depending on whether you've won the day before or lost the day before; depending on what the weather might be; where you are in the standings. There's a range of activity that is dependent on a lot of external forces. As a result, no day is the same, particularly for someone like me who's dealing not just with baseball, but business and finance. There's always something new to consider and evaluate. That's probably true in a lot of businesses, but this has the advantage of being probably less predictable, short term and long term.

I think baseball—and the business of sports; any sport—is very similar, in a lot of ways, to any other business. You have to have a product; you have to service it; and you have to make a profit, or at least be able to sustain the enterprise financially. Probably the biggest difference is the fact that in most businesses the single motivation is profitability. In sports, it's not just making a profit, or breaking even, or taking into account the financial results—it's also about winning. I'm sure that's true in other businesses where the product and the excellence of the product is important, just as the profitability is, but ultimately, businesses are about making money. This business is about keeping an eye on the financial side, but just making money wouldn't make this a successful franchise. In fact the owner, or the management, wouldn't survive very long even if we were a successful business venture strictly on that measure because of the public, or quasi-public, nature of what we're doing.

I can tell you that if you don't win the World Series—and I have experienced both winning and losing the World Series—then you go home unhappy. We all have high expectations. There's only one happy franchise at the end of the season. However, in the aftermath of all that, we know there is relative success; there's a zone within which you are reasonably happy. You're never truly happy in the case of baseball, unless you win the World Series. Yeah, I've won it once—1989—but that was a long time ago, so I'm trying to do it again. Happiness lasted about two months. In fact, I got a call from an agent the next day about a new contract for his player. So it didn't even really last two months. It lasted a few hours.

Sure, I get anxious from time to time. I get elated. But you don't get elated if you haven't previously been a little anxious. You don't become euphoric unless, at some point, you've experienced depression.

Sometimes I'll leave in the eighth inning or so, and listen to the game on the way home. Sometimes it's out of frustration, sometimes it's out of superstition; sometimes it's out of exhaustion. When you realize the difference between a successful season and a losing season is maybe two games, three games, you realize there's a lot of randomness involved. Even if you're going to win ninety games and lose sixty, on any given day what are your chances of winning or losing a game? Well, they're a fraction better than the opposition presumably. But from day to day, you have no idea what's going to happen, so it tends to feel random. And you have this sort of—particularly in my position sitting there watching it like everyone else—a certain helplessness that sets in.

Sometimes I equate it to the tide. You go to the beach, and you watch the surf for a couple of minutes. You really can't tell whether the tide is coming in or going out. You just watch a couple of waves break. You really don't know anything. You have to sit there for a while, until you get a sense of whether the tide is coming in or going out, and that's sort of the way baseball is. You don't really learn anything in one game. There is a tendency for all of us to overreact to what happens in a single game—that's true of the media, that's true of fans, that's true of the executives, it's true of management, it's true of managers and coaches. But what's really important is sitting there for a while, observing, and then acting accordingly.

*   *   *   *   *

PAT GILLICK

Vice President and General Manager, Philadelphia Phillies

Pat Gillick was the general manager of the Toronto Blue Jays for seventeen years, leading them twice to the World Series title. He then moved into the same job with the Baltimore Orioles for three years and then with the Seattle Mariners for four years before signing a contract with the Phillies. We talked four days before the trading deadline.

"The players, this time of the year, are kind of are edgy, thinking that they might be playing someplace else a week from now. I think they're a little bit uptight and tense, but that's part of the business; that's part of what they have to go through. It may be new to some of them, but a lot of them have been through it before."

*   *   *   *   *

I kind of got into it by accident. I finished playing baseball over forty years ago and I was going to go back to the university to get a master's degree. I'd spent my career in the minor league system in Baltimore. I was a left-hand pitcher, and I played all the way up to Triple-A. Had spring training with a big league club in '62. Two of the people that I was in contact with during my minor league period were Paul Richards and Eddie Robinson. Paul had gone to Houston as general manager, and Eddie was in charge of their scouting and player development.

I wasn't looking to get into this business—didn't send out a resume; didn't ask to interview. It was just sort of by accident—just because of my past with the Orioles, and Eddie and Paul going over to Houston. They decided that they wanted to give me an opportunity. Just before I went back to school in September '63, I got a call: They wanted me to come down to Houston to work for them.

At first, I was sort of reluctant about going down there, but I agreed. I went as an assistant in the farm and scouting department. Spent about eleven years there, and had a number of jobs. I was assistant farm director. Then I got into scouting. Then I was the East Coast Latin-American supervisor. Then I was the scouting director. I was there up until '74, and then took a position with the Yankees for about two years, till August '76, and then went to Toronto.

So, it's kind of, you know, accidental the way I got in because I never really had any intention to. Once I finished my playing career, I was going back to school and I was going stay probably involved in athletics, but it was going to be at the teaching level. In fact, I was going back to [the University of Southern California] to be an assistant coach on the baseball team. My pay was going to be tuition and a small amount of money to get my master's; hopefully, get placed in a high school somewhere in California.

I think there's different ways to become a GM. It's kind of changed a little bit over the years. There's a very good sports administration course at Ohio University. Dave Dombrowski, and Danny O'Brien—who was up until recently the GM at Cincinnati—and Andy McPhail, the president of the Cubs, they all went to Ohio U. But there are some guys that are in it who are ex-players. When I got into it, there were more guys that were ex-players doing this job than there are now. It's kind of a, I don't know—it's not a mishmash—but they come from different areas.

It's a sort of a difficult game to explain to ownership because it's probably one of the only businesses—it's actually a business—the only business where you can fail seven times [in ten tries] and be successful. Sometimes you try to explain that to ownership and they can't put their hands around it. What's happened is that owners can put their arms around statistics so, consequently, I think there's more decisions now made with the help of statistics; more so than there used to be. It's something you can quantify, and so there's, I think, more young people in it now who are more administrators than there are people that really came out of baseball. I think that's one thing that's really changed.

Going back to when I started—really started out, I mean—my strength was not in the office. My strength was in the field because I had a scouting and player development background as opposed to administration. But that's kind of changed, you know, over the years—free agency, player representation, collective bargain agreements. So, consequently, there's a lot more things on a daily basis, from an administrative standpoint, you have to take care of than you did thirty years ago. When I got into it, you were concerned more about the players. Now, on a daily basis, there are other things to be concerned about.

Patience is one thing that I think has really changed over the years. I think a lot of it goes back to ownership. When I went over to Toronto in '76, which was thirty years ago, we paid seven million dollars for the franchise to get into the league. These guys now are paying three hundred fifty to four hundred fifty million dollars, so you can't be as patient as you can spending seven million. Ownership needs to generate revenue to service debt. So consequently, I don't think the owners are as patient. You know, it takes a player x number of years to develop. I don't think ownership wants to hear that. I think, just like society, people want something to happen instantaneously. They want it to happen right now.

I think society has sort of changed, too. I used to go to a baseball game and have a conversation. You'd kind of relax and kick back, and really not miss anything. I don't think the public really is as patient, or is relaxing, as they were thirty years ago. I mean, I don't know, it's almost like they can't find time to relax. All these things, whatever you want to call it—all the added value that supposedly goes with a baseball ticket—it's basically an event; an experience going to the park. You get about the same thing going to an NBA game, or going to National Football League game—the way it is marketed, it usually doesn't mention too much about the game. It just mentions the experience you are going to have. I think everybody thinks they've got to have some sort of hook, or hype, to stay competitive with the other sports. I think that aspect has really changed.

I think the pool of players here in the United States is shrinking. What's really happened over the years, I think, is that basketball and football are revenue producers in high school, whereas baseball isn't. The other thing is that ten kids can play a full-court game with one basketball, where if you go out to buy equipment for baseball for ten kids—you've got the glove and shoes, and all that—it's out of the question. You get a football, and you can play touch football or flag football. So consequently, kids these days are more drawn to the sports that you can play: you get a football, you get a basketball, you get a soccer ball, you can have a game. In baseball, I think it's changed a lot. We used to play games with three guys on a side, but I don't think that goes on that much anymore. Consequently, that provides more opportunity for a Hispanic player; for the player from the Far East. I think that probably in the next ten years, I'd say the major leagues is going to probably be 60 to 70 percent international players as opposed to American-born players. I think it's headed that way.

We use physical evaluations. The scouts go out and evaluate the players on a physical basis. Then we try to get to know as much as we can about them from a mental standpoint. Then we use statistical data to give us some sort of a track record of what the player's done in the past. Same thing as you look at on a racing form for horses. You know what they have done in the last ten or fifteen races. It gives you a pretty good idea what the history is. I think you've got to look at players, and you have to look at their statistics, and throw that into the whole package. You have the physical evaluation [where you] try to find as much mentally about the players as you possibly can, and then you add statistical information. Then you try to make a decision that makes sense.

Mental aspect? Say, a high school player: you try to talk to the kid; you try to talk to his parents; you try to talk to his high-school counselor; you try to talk to his coach; you try to talk to his classmates. Get as much as you can just to find out. We do psychological testing, too. Consequently, through psychological testing and meeting and talking with people, you try to get background and [determine] what kind of a person is going to be your employee.

On a professional level, you try to talk to people in the business who know the player. Again, what kind of a teammate is he? How he is in the clubhouse? What, exactly, are his pluses and minuses? This is aside from really what your scout gives you. You try to do as much background check as you possibly can on an individual.

If you're getting a rental player for a couple of months and you don't have a long-term plan for the individual—a stopgap type player—probably it's not important. But if you want to get involved with a player longer than a couple of months, then the complete dossier on the player is quite important.

We have twenty-some [scouts] employed. At the major league level, we've got seven or eight. Today, we will talk on a call for an hour to an hour and a half. We talked last Thursday for an hour or so. We've pinpointed particular positions that we need to fill, or we have pinpointed certain players that we want to make sure that we have as much data on as possible. They've gone back on some players the last five or six days that we have interest in; making sure that they are physically healthy; that there hasn't been a major change in their evaluation. And then we'll discuss anything else that they might have seen that might prove valuable to the team.

We have a pretty good idea of what the other twenty-nine clubs' needs are, and what our needs are. Then we try to match up, and see who out of those clubs makes sense for us to talk to. There are some clubs that we don't match well with—we don't have what they want, and they don't have what we want. So, consequently, that narrows it down, and it's probably five or six clubs that you can seriously sit down and discuss what might be their excess, and what might be our excess, and what fits for them, and what fits for us. By the end, you might come out with two or three clubs that you might be able to dance with.

In a trade, try to get a situation where both clubs come out satisfied with what they got. I mean, we are happy with our players, and they are happy with their players. Come up with something that's creative that works for both clubs. They might be people we want to do business with again. I think you can win, and the other club can win. You don't have to have a grand slam every time.

We made a deal last night; a small deal with the Yankees. We got a player from the Yankees' Double-A club in the Florida State League for a backup catcher: Sal Fasano. Most of the negotiations were carried out by my assistant, Ruben Amaro, and by the assistant GM of the Yankees. We gave up Fasano and received a second baseman back by the name of Hector Made. Basically, this was just a straight trade. This wasn't one where there was a lot of hoops to go through. Fasano didn't have a no-trade, so, consequently, we could trade his contract. Waivers didn't have to be in effect because it was before July 31, so there was nothing that prevented us from making this trade. After the deal was agreed upon, the Yankees sent a message to us announcing that they wanted to announce the transaction in the morning after their game, because they were playing in another time zone. Then there was a confirmation of the agreement: "The Phillies will assign outright to the Yankees, the major-league player-contract of catcher Sal Fasano dated the sixteen of December of 2005, and the Yankees will sign outright to the Phillies, minor-league player Hector Made from the Tampa Yankees to the Clearwater Phillies." It's just the general the nuts and bolts of what we agreed to.

This is a very simple transaction. Usually, if it's a simple deal like this, we will call the agent; just let the agent know that we are making the deal. You can get into more complicated transactions where you got to have waivers involved; where one player might be at a different compensation level than another player, and there might be cash going into the deal. If there are some other hoops that we have jump through, then we call the agent, and try to work through those. If it's a situation involving cash, then we have to call the commissioner and get an okay from him regarding the amount of cash that's in a particular transaction. It just depends on the situation.

This is really the first time we have been out of it for a long time, and we are kind of out of time at the moment. We are not playing well. That's how I kind of gauge where we are. But I have always been a buyer, so this is going to be a little different. Probably, we are going to be more of a seller than a buyer. It's just, when you are a seller, you probably got more clubs to deal with, which is good from a negotiation and competitive standpoint. When you are buyer, you've probably pinpointed a couple or three clubs that probably have what you are looking for. When you are a seller, it's like you've got a house up for sale, and you've got to listen to all the buyers. I've got an open house: "Anybody, come in and take a look and see what you like." When you are a buyer, you look at a house, and then you say, "Yeah, I like one or two houses, and I am going to concentrate on those two houses." It's the same way in baseball.

We've made some transactions that didn't work out. I kind of think buyer's remorse, or seller's remorse, is something you feel within a twenty-four hour period when you wish you hadn't done—wish we could take it back or something. I don't think I've ever experienced that. At the time we made the deal, I thought that we've done the right thing. Sometimes they don't work out, but at the time—I'm really thinking back—I don't think I've really had, you know, buyer's remorse.

I'm pretty open about the players. I don't really view any players as untouchable. I've never had any untouchable players. The reason for that is that you never know. Some players have higher values than others, and maybe those values that we place on them are a bit unrealistic. That kind of makes them untouchable to the other clubs, but if somebody was willing to go to that level, which we think would be the top of the market, then we move that player. I mean, I don't like to rule out anything, because there might be somebody willing to pay the top of the market. I like them to feel they can suggest anything. I like to feel I can suggest anything. Just because you suggest, doesn't mean you have to do it.

In Toronto, we traded Tony Fernandez and Fred McGriff for Joe Carter and Robbie Alomar. We ended up winning a couple of championships over there—'92, '93. Joe and Robbie were a big part of that. We made another deal in '92. We got David Cone from the Mets, and we gave them Jeff Kent in the deal. We won, but the guy didn't pitch very well for us. Then we made another deal with Oakland, in '93. We gave them Steve Karsay for Ricky Henderson, and that just worked out fair. Kent has gone on to be one of the better offensive players in baseball, and the other guy—I mean Ricky—Ricky did a decent job for us. Cone did a decent job, but probably we gave a little bit more than we should have.

It's like any other business. You talk to all the clubs. Do your due diligence. Basically, do your rounds; talk to them every week or ten days. You can't rule out anyone. What makes the situation a little bit different is this: It's my opinion—Kansas City, Pittsburgh, Milwaukee, Tampa Bay—those clubs can't afford to make a mistake because they are low-revenue clubs, so consequently any deal they make they want to make sure that they got an extra gap in there if something goes wrong. I mean, they want an extra player, or they want a better quality player, just in case things don't work out as they anticipated. Whereas a higher-revenue club such as the Yankees and Boston, they can spend more money, and cover up that mistake. For instance, the Yankees, right now, they've got Sheffield on the DL; they've got Pavano on the DL; Matsui, DL. Consequently, they've got probably thirty-five million sitting on the DL over there. That's more payroll than some clubs! That's more payroll than Florida. It's more payroll than Tampa Bay. But that doesn't stop them from going out—and I am not saying those are mistakes—but low-revenue clubs sitting with thirty-five million on the DL, they can't go out and spend more money to take the place of those players. They can't do it because they don't have the revenue.

We're probably in the upper third revenue-wise, about ninety-five million. We have some weaknesses on this club that we have to address. Right now, our club is sort of in a catch-22 situation—we've got some outstanding talent here, and what we need is to build further support for those players. We're looking to do some things that are going to change the culture of this team. We have had this group for a period of time, and up to this time, they haven't won *the last game*, so consequently, I think we have got to kind of change some faces. I think this team is a little too comfortable, so I think that we need to change that a bit.

I think the fans generally in all the sports here, are a little frustrated. It's a nice city, with nice people. They haven't really had a world championship for a while. The last time the Phillies were in it was '93, and lost in the World Series. I think, overall, the sports fans here are—they say they are a little rough; I don't think they are rough—I just think they are pretty frustrated that there hasn't been some sort of championship brought here in the last ten to fifteen years.

It's a good city. Got really great ownership here. We've got a new park. The fans, as I say, are a bit frustrated, but I think the fans are good fans. I think there are a lot of positive things going on here.

It's a challenge. You know, my history—going back—I guess I'm more of a builder. It's a good challenge to find ways to build clubs and redesign clubs. Keeps your mind active thinking of different ways to get it done. It's my fourth club as a GM—Toronto, Baltimore, Seattle, now here. Overall, as I said, we have got some good talent. This is a good team. We are just trying to get support around them to put this thing going in the right direction.

Yeah, I read a little bit. I think all news is good news, except there are degrees of good news. There is nothing to me as old as yesterday's newspaper. As far as what we do, or transactions, or how we go about our business, it doesn't have any effect. I talked about how the game has changed—it's more of an event, an experience now. Basically, the electronic and the print media have changed, too. I mean, there are more opinions, instead of writing about the game, and what transpired on the field. No matter where you go—be it on television—I mean, you go on a sport show, and it is one person debating another person, or whatever you want to call it, arguing with another person. You look at Tony Kornheiser—his show—they just debate, argue, discuss back and forth. And I think the print media, and also radio, to be competitive they have to change their style, and so consequently they've all got different shticks that they are doing out there to keep their circulation up, or keep their ratings up. So I don't think you can listen too much to what they have to say. I think you've got to go on, make the business decisions that you think are the correct ones, and let the cards fall however they may.

*　　*　　*　　*　　*

JOE SPEAR
Founding Senior Principal, HOK Sport

The architectural firm of Hellmuth, Obata + Kassabaum (HOK), based in Kansas City, is the nation's leading designer of major league baseball fields. As a senior principal, Joe Spear led projects for the White Sox, Orioles, Rockies, Giants, Tigers, Padres, Reds, Indians, Phillies, and is leading the design for the new ballpark for the Washington Nationals.

"It's gratifying to see people come in and enjoy the park. The first opening day I went to was at Pilot Field [in Buffalo]. You had gotten accustomed to seeing the park empty, or see construction workers. There's poetry in that image too. An empty baseball park can be a very poetic thing. But it was just, you know, this riot of color and noise and activity, and you realize this is what we did. This is what we all worked so hard to make. Memories are going to be made here. Families are bringing their children. You get an enormous sense of accomplishment—it's probably a mixture of relief sometimes. That's payday for us.

I don't ever worry about the Orioles or the Indians or the Rockies wanting to move out of their ballpark. What we're trying to do is design something you can fall in love with. Yeah, they're going to want to modify the park and they're going to want to respond to market forces that change, but once you get that emotional connection, I don't ever see these clubs wanting to build a new one."

*   *   *   *   *

I'm an architect. I was born in 1952. I'm from Parsons, Kansas. [The population of] my hometown would fit three times in most baseball parks.

About a year out of school, I went to work for a firm here in Kansas City. It was a small firm, about twenty people. And as luck would have it, one of the guys had this idea that there could be an architectural practice that specialized in sports work. I think it's kind of bizarre, now. You know, you ask someone you meet, "What do you do?" "I work for so-and-so." "What do *you* do?" "I design baseball parks." It's kind of a strange thing to hear yourself say. I've spent the last twenty-three years basically doing that.

Pilot Field, a Triple-A park up in Buffalo, New York, was really my first project. Oh, gosh, that would have been in the early eighties. That project took five years from conception to the political process to raising the funding, and three years to design and build. Sometimes we'll work on these projects four or five years. San Francisco was fifteen years. Once the funding gets in place and the politics are aligned, that makes a project happen. It's a lot of work.

After Pilot Field, I worked on the design of [new] Comiskey Park. Then Camden Yards. The early seventies was a time when major league sports were really taking off. And people were understanding this meant a great deal emotionally to a community. The Pilot Field project was very important for the city's own self image. I mean, for example, they had come through a very tough time economically. The steel industry up in that neighborhood of the world had literally collapsed. I think they had a 25-percent unemployment rate. Johnny Carson was telling snow jokes on television.

When we first started going to Buffalo—where you usually took a twenty minute taxi from the airport—I'd ask the taxi driver, "I hear you guys are going to build a baseball park here." Typically the taxi driver would say, "Yeah, they'll probably screw that all up, too." Or, "Yeah, we'll see if they get that done or not." It would be sort of almost a defeatist attitude.

I'll never forget the day the park opened—this emerald green baseball field sitting out there. It made the front page of *USA Today*. It meant something. It seemed to give the community a lot more confidence. I think there's a lot of cities that see the value in that. You can get into a good debate if you want to talk about the economics of it. There are a lot of economists who feel that a Major League Baseball franchise is about equal to a good quality regional shopping center. I've heard that argument a lot. I don't know of any study of the economics of the impact of Pilot Field, but it certainly made a difference in the way people felt about their community.

I'd call it an evolution. The White Sox played in the old Comiskey Park. It was very run down; had seen a lot of miles. They were interested in a modern facility that would have all the revenue-generating features people could think of at the time. And they made it clear they'd like to have a concrete structure because they were interested in low maintenance. And when we were hired to do the work in Baltimore, the Orioles expressed a clear preference for a steel structure. Most of the classic parks were steel structures. It adds to the feeling of a nostalgic place. It brings back memories of some of the old classic parks.

And in Baltimore, we were able to use the old B&O Warehouse. It's a brick structure; a unique structure. It's about 120 feet tall, 50 wide, and a quarter of a mile long. It creates a sense of place. The scale of that building is very compatible with the ballpark. It's kind of like finding a site with a waterfall, or a limestone bluff. It was a feature that was very memorable. The team was looking for an icon. When you turn on the game in the third inning, you know instantly that you're watching the game from Oriole Park [at Camden Yards], in Baltimore.

As a designer of these projects, you want to do anything and everything that you can so that the community feels like this is *their* hometown; this is *their* ballpark. You want them to fall in love with the thing that you're designing because if the fans fall in love with it, it's going to endure. It's going to be another Wrigley Field or a Fenway Park. That's the home run.

I think in the sixties and seventies a lot of communities needed homes for baseball and football franchises. And it was a failed economy. Their thought was, "Well, I could build a baseball park and a football stadium, or I could build one and save money." I don't think there are too many multipurpose stadiums that lasted past one lease.

The multipurpose stadiums were not romantic enough. They weren't good enough that the fans would fall in love. If you'd been to a game in Three Rivers Stadium, you knew what it was going to be like to watch one in Cincinnati; what it was going to be like to watch one in Atlanta. It just wasn't about those communities. And so when we picked the site in Pittsburgh one of the things that we said was, "This site would have a spectacular view of the Golden Triangle"; and it does. Some people think that's the best view in baseball. Some people think San Francisco is the best view.

The City of Pittsburgh just can't buy advertising as good as evening games. At seven o'clock you get this rosy pink glow of the sun setting shining on the Golden Triangle, out there, beyond the scoreboard. If Disney made a movie, that's the kind of image that they'd want.

You can't orient the ballpark towards the west. The rulebook says that the sun will never be in the batter's eye, and it should affect only one set of fielders at a time. What that means is, generally, you orient the field towards the east. For example, in San Francisco, if you stand at home plate and look at second base, you're looking almost due north. There's a similar orientation for Yankee Stadium. Most of the other new ballparks, if you stand at home plate and look at second base, you're looking northeast. And some of the ballparks, if you stand at home plate and look at second base, you're looking to the southeast. Anywhere in those ranges of orientation you can usually make something work. In Washington, D.C., everyone would have loved it if we would have been able to put home plate in the southeast corner of the site because then the majority of the fans would be focused back towards the Capitol dome and the Washington Monument. Unfortunately, at about four o'clock, the sun would be in the batter's eye.

There's a lot of thinking about the efficient movement of people that goes into laying out and designing a concourse. We have to think about when the fan, coming to a ballgame, becomes a pedestrian. And what that means is he's parked his car or gotten off the city bus or off a metro line. We need to know where that happens because that's going to tell us where he's going to enter the ballpark, and we want to put entrance gates and turnstiles where it's convenient for him. We don't want to have to have him walk on the street outside past his seat to an entrance on the other side of the ballpark, enter the ballpark, and then have to walk back in the direction from where he came to get to his or her seat.

If the Orioles could change one thing about their ballpark, I'm pretty certain that they would want to have the concourses have views of the playing field. Baseball has a quite relaxed pace. You can sit at the park, keep a scorecard going, have a conversation going, and still feel connected with the game. What that means is that people socialize more: They get up. They walk around. "I'll meet you in the third inning, by Boog's BBQ." And why they choose to meet by Boog's BBQ in Baltimore is they can see the game from Utah Street. Utah Street is—I think most people would agree—a success; and part of the reason is that you can see the playing field. So what we see today in Cincinnati and in Philadelphia, even the upper decks have a view of the playing field because we find that people at a baseball game are willing to get up, mix with other people, take a stroll. You don't really get that in a football game or a hockey game. You couldn't get a fan out of his seat at a hockey game with dynamite, I don't think. And it's because of the pace of the game. I mean, if you get up in an NFL game and, you know, go buy a hot dog or whatever, you might miss the only touchdown. Baseball has inning breaks, change of pitchers—you have all sorts of things. I think people enjoy it. You get tired sitting in one spot after three or four innings. We see a difference between a concourse with a concession stand with a view of the playing field, and one without. The difference is people, as they're getting up to socialize they're much more willing to have another hot dog, or buy a beer, or whatever.

Baseball is a very traditional game. A lot of people feel that it is more timeless than a lot of the other sports. I think, frankly, baseball benefits from the fact that it has so many games and the season is so long. You tend to see a lot more children at baseball games, I believe, than you do at a football game. It seems to be a little bit more family-oriented.

Used to be a baseball franchise would consider itself successful if they drew over a million people a year. Today they're trying to draw three million people. When I started in this career, if you had the basics right—the sight lines were where people could get into the park, into their seats, enjoy the game, see the scoreboard, see the line score, be able to see all the action on the field—for the baseball purist, that was what you needed. But when you try to triple the attendance, particularly in years where you may not be that successful on the playing field, you really need to think about reaching past that purist demographic, and trying to get families with kids; trying to get people in the park.

Baseball, I believe, has done a great job as an industry trying to respond to that. They're very sensitive to the overall price of tickets. A family of four can come to a game and get in and out for two hundred bucks or something. They pay attention to that. You take young children to a game. They get a little restless in the fourth inning. That's when it's good to have things for them to go see and do. You know, go get some ice cream or go get a funnel cake, or go have your face painted. So I think it's more about all-around entertainment today than it was [before]. I can remember telling teams: beer, soda, popcorn, hot dogs—that's what you need. If you want to have a pizza oven somewhere and sell pizzas, fine. Now, people are eating crab cakes. There's sushi bars. You have wine. Customers have spoken, and these are the things they want.

I tell clients that the most important decision is the site. You want each one to have its own unique identity. So much of what we do, as a designer, is try to relate to that site and that community. You know, the Giants had a conversation with the mayor's office when [Peter] Magowan's group purchased the team, and they knew that if they were going to keep the franchise in San Francisco they needed to have a new ballpark. So they proceeded with purchasing the team. The mayor said, "We have three sites that we could make available for a baseball park." China Basin was one of those sites. They asked us to help them analyze the three sites. We did a thirty-day study. They were all small. Basically I told them, "None of these sites would make our generic list for a baseball park. None of them are really big enough. So whichever one of the three we select, you're going to have to make compromises, but China Basin would be worth it because of the water." You have to know the community you're working in, and what their values are. The way I described it: if they had an out-of-town guest in San Francisco, obviously you're going to show the Bay. That's the image. And, you know, I think in San Francisco one of the things people show visitors is McCovey Cove because during the game people are out there on kayaks and boards with nets and they're amongst these big, huge cabin cruisers trying to catch a home run ball.

Baseball is the only game that an architect gets to affect. All the other sports have very prescribed field or court dimensions. You wouldn't be allowed to play on a ninety-five-yard NFL field—although Halas did it when he played at Wrigley Field. A hundred-yard football field would not fit. We work with a team to define the playing field dimensions. And Major League Baseball obviously has input into the design because, while they don't have hard and fast dimensions, they don't want to see a park design where it's unfair somehow. Some teams say they want a pitcher's park. Some teams say we want a hitter's park. We work through that with them, and show them how the dimensions can respond to that.

There's a lot more freethinking about it today than there was twenty years ago. As an architect, what you look for is something that doesn't seem artificial. A good example of that is the short rightfield dimension in San Francisco. The site was so small that to get everything to fit, we needed to pull the fence in. Major League Baseball said, "Can you get us a tall home run fence there so that it tends to balance." If we had an eight-foot fence at 308 feet, you could get a check-swing home run. So it's that kind of thing.

It's actually pretty hard to create a balanced park. I mean, if you want a hitter's park, you have short fences; if you want a pitcher's park, you have long or tall fences. I think a lot of baseball purists argue questions like, "Would so-and-so have had that many home runs if he didn't play five years in Coors Field?" I think baseball fans enjoy debating things like that.

I think people appreciate what we do. Baseball is a special sport in America. I think it's more special than any of the others, frankly. As an architect, I have friends who work on quote-unquote real buildings. I remember one of them said, "Why would you want to spend your career designing stadiums? There's never enough money to do great architecture. The structural engineer really does most of the designs." I said, "I don't see it that way." Buildings, too, have limitations. I'll tell you what, it's a pretty rare experience that you get the chance to design a Major League Baseball stadium. It's a very sweet thing. I mean it's not something that you get complacent about. When we started this, in the pre–Pilot Field days, the expectations were just so minimal. It's changed. People's expectations are much higher now about a ballpark, or a football stadium. It's a different game.

Baseball is very big. It's a wonderful sport. It's just so special in American society as a game. A newspaper usually has seven or eight pages on sports, and three or four on business. That's what people are interested in.

*   *   *   *   *

BOB WATSON

Vice President for On-Field Operations, Commissioner's Office

"Baseball chose me. I played more ball as a kid than most. I grew up in Southern California and I played on four teams at one time. My grandmom would take me from ballpark to ballpark, and I would change uniforms in the back of her car. It was one of those things that I knew at ten years old: I was going to be a big league baseball player. I was five foot eight, one hundred eighty pounds. At twelve, I was probably six foot, two hundred pounds. So all these teams wanted me to play with them. Schedule permitting, I'd play two or three games a day."

Watson played nineteen years in the major leagues, finished with a .295 lifetime batting average, and scored the millionth run in Major League Baseball history. We talked in his New York City office.

* * * * *

I'm vice president of standards and on-field operations. What does that mean? The "standards" part of the title means I am in charge of all types of things from the lighting, grounds crews, safety issues, to on-field signage of all thirty ballparks. The "on-field operations" part of it is anything that happens on the field. I'm in charge of discipline.

Before all the safety gear and body armor find their way to a major league game, I have to sign off. All of that comes through this office. The vendors submit it to me, and I go through a checklist of things I've come up with over the years. They have to meet them, and if they do, it's approved for major league use.

Things have evolved over the years. If you remember back in the fifties era the catcher's mask had one bar across it, and a little padding around it. But as you see sitting here, we have a hockey-style mask, where it's a helmet all made in one piece. It's like a nice wire cage. There's a lot more protection. With the little mask, there was a number of catchers that got hurt pretty bad from hitters with the long back swings. The hitter would come back, and hit them in the back of the head, or in the ear. This new style of catcher's mask will protect catchers. The padding has to be a certain standard, and the wire cage itself. Also, the type of plastic has to withstand somebody throwing at least 100 miles per hour. And some vents to let the heat out, so the guy doesn't pass out.

What happens is there's almost like a fair the first week in December. There's a big exhibition hall, and all the booths are set up. All the vendors go. That's when the bulk of the orders are taken. Anything and everything to do with baseball—from scoreboards to Astroturf, to helmets, to bats, to balls, gloves, anything in the concessions, uniforms, undergarments—everything is sold there.

Same thing with the ballpark. I don't get into designs. You want your own nooks and crannies and quirks, but it's got to be safe for the participants on the field. A big example: Wrigley Field is the only field that doesn't have padding on the outfield walls. There's padding down the sidelines, but a signature part of Wrigley Field is the ivy on the walls. I don't know how we're going to be able do it—it's got to be done during the winter time—but we're going to have to take the ivy off, put padding up, then have the ivy grow back. We try to work with not only the club, but also the player's union. They are heavily involved in this also. The union would love to have it because it protects their players. We're trying to come up with a solution to the problem, and like I said, I don't know how we're going to do that. Everywhere else we have padding.

This is my forty-second year in baseball, and I've seen a few ballparks. You know what's safe, and what's not. You go around and look. Myself and an ex-ballplayer from the union also goes around. If he sees something he'll bring it to my attention, and we'll go check it out.

I signed as a catcher in 1964, with the [Houston] Colt .45s. My first year, we were playing in Greenfield, South Carolina, in the Mets farm club. I had caught something like 115 games in a row. We had just signed another catcher and I was hitting well, and they said, "Hey, can you go play the outfield?" I said, "Sure." There wasn't a warning track, and a brick wall. I ran into the brick wall, broke the tip of my right shoulder, and broke my left wrist. I was eighteen and that was the end of my catching career. I played for nineteen years. I wouldn't have caught for nineteen years. I couldn't throw as well, but it didn't hurt me to swing. But it was probably a blessing in disguise because I ended up playing first base for the bulk of my career.

I went to Boston for a half a season, which was in 1979. In those days they had a June 15 trade deadline; I got traded on the fourteenth. I joined the Red Sox and had a real good second half of the year. I hit .340 and had fifteen winning hits for them. I wanted to stay there, but the Red Sox had just been sold. The new owners had just enough money to buy the team. They didn't have enough to keep free agents. So I went to the Yankees.

In 1980, the Yankees won the division and we lost in the playoffs to the Kansas City Royals. We had the best team: we won 105 games. And we lost three in a row to Kansas City in the first round. In that playoff, I hit a ball that ended up getting a third-base coach fired, and our manager ended up quitting because of the incident. Willie Randolph was on first, two out in the eighth inning. I hit a ball off the left field wall. The wall had padding, but the padding didn't go all the way down. The ball hits concrete and bounces right back to Willie Wilson, who turns and overthrows the cutoff man. But it takes one bounce right to George Brett, who throws a strike to home. Third-base coach Mike Ferraro waves Randolph in, which is what he's supposed to do, and he's out at the plate. George Steinbrenner, who is sitting in the stands, erupts like Mount Vesuvius. He goes off. He's yelling and screaming. The reason why he got mad? He was saying hold Randolph at third and me at second so that Reggie Jackson has a chance to hit. I was hitting fourth that day. Reggie Jackson was hitting behind me. In those days Reg was swinging the bat pretty good, so I don't think the Royals would've pitched to him. I think they would've put him on. Of course that didn't occur to Steinbrenner. So we come in. He says, "We lose because Randolph's out at the plate," and he's yelling and screaming, and he tells Ferraro he's fired. Right there in front of all the media and everybody. Dick Howser, who is our manager, takes George by the coattails and pulls him into his office, slams the door, and you hear them yelling. He says, "You can't do this in front of everybody, and if you don't go out there and apologize and get him back, I'm out of here at the end of this thing." He wouldn't do it, so Howser leaves.

I retired at the end of '84. Then I went to Oakland. Sandy Alderson interviewed me and said, "Hey, we'd like you to be our organization's hitting coach." During that interview he asked me, "What's your ultimate goal?" I told him, "Sitting in your chair." He said, "I'll help you." So I was the hitting coach during the season, and during off-season I went with him to winter meetings and worked on trades. Three or four years down the way, Houston called and said they wanted me to be their assistant GM. So I went back to Houston for seven years.

Then I come to New York as the GM under Steinbrenner, and I put together the '96, '97, '98 teams. Just before the '98 spring training I had one too many blow-ups with him and I said, "I'm going home." It was just the straw that broke the camel's back. He wanted me to trade for Chuck Knoblauch, which I didn't have a problem in doing. But he wanted me to give away three top players, and I wouldn't do it. That's my fault. He's the owner. But I had a real good sense that I could give two broken bats and a bag of batting practice balls, and I'd get Knoblauch. But he said, "Give him number one picks. Give them another outfielder and another pitcher." I wouldn't do that. He asked somebody else to do it, and I said, "If you do that, then I quit." I'm serious; the Chuck Knoblauch deal could have been made for, maybe not a broken bat, but a good bat.

The commissioner's office started doing special assignment work in '99. I put together the first professional team to play for the Olympics. Pat Gillick and Sandy Alderson were also involved. We went to Sydney in 2000 and we won the gold. Then I came to work for Frank Robinson, doing special work for Frank. Then Frank goes and manages, and he says, "Hey do you want to be my hitting coach, or do you want to sit here in the office and take care of this until I come back?" I said, "I don't want to go back on the field. I'd rather sit here." Here it is six years later.

Alderson wasn't a baseball guy. His strong suit was that he surrounded himself with baseball people. Smart guy, and it just so happens when I came here to the commissioner's office, it wasn't something that I was looking to do. But he said, "Look, we need some help. We don't have anybody in the office who's been on the field and who's coached it." So that's why I'm here.

When I played, the league presidents handed out all discipline. You had your American League president and your National League president. When they combined—what we call "central baseball"—the commissioner's office created this position. They gave this office the powers of the league presidents on discipline. It made it a little [bit of a] tougher job because the league presidents only dealt with their league, so you only had twelve teams or fourteen teams [to oversee]. Now it's sixteen and fourteen to deal with. I've got all thirty [teams].

There's a ton of history here of things that have happened on-field. There's been ejections of all kinds. There've been fights. There's been fan interference. There's been fan-and-player fights. There have been fan-and-umpire fights. Anything that has happened from a disciplinary situation is up on my shelf here. There's a room down the hall that has tons of videos. We have the capability now to get every game. If anything happens during any ballgame, umpires call in on those two phones right there. My assistant takes [note of] what the situation was, and within a couple minutes—depending on where it is in the country—I will have a DVD on my desk, or I could pull up the infraction on my laptop, and within twenty-four hours there will be an umpire's report on whether it was an ejection, a bumping, a fight, whatever.

Let's say you're Randy Johnson. You're pitching for the Yankees and the Atlanta Braves' pitcher hits your guy even if it wasn't intentional. Well, words or looks happen, so you go back out and you feel it's your duty to retaliate. Okay? The umpires, to keep the peace, now come out and say, "We are warning you. If something happens, you are out of the game and your manager is out of the game." In this case it's a warning issue. You weigh the situation: my catcher just was hit, so I've got to retaliate. So *bam*, he threw at a batter. He didn't hit him actually, but the umpire had put the warning in and he felt that he threw at him intentionally. You're automatically out of the game, and the manager goes, too. That's it. It's cut and dry:

You throw at somebody after a warning it's a five-game suspension and a fine from one thousand dollars to ten thousand dollars. If you throw it at his head, now that's a whole different situation. You're talking ten games to fifteen games, and the dollar amount ratchets up. The other side of this is the hitter. If he wants to take matters into his own hands and he charges you for throwing at him, then he gets suspended for three to five games himself. The money goes to the Boys and Girls Club, and there's also another charity called Baseball Assistance Team.

I get video. I get reports. Then I look at it to see if the video matches the reports. Sometimes they don't. Then we go through books of cases that are similar, or exact. See if a precedent is set. You've done something in the past and you do it again, we say, "All right, that's a five-game suspension with a five-grand fine." I decide. I'm it. There's only a few times the commissioner has stepped in—the Kenny Rogers situation. He hit a cameraman and pushed down his equipment. Even though it happened on-field, the commissioner felt that it was high profile enough that he should handle it. Most of it is on me.

The most I've ever handed out was, I guess, the Francisco Cordero thing where he threw the chair and hit the lady in the face. Remember— the Texas Rangers in Oakland? The fine was the rest of the season—seventeen or eighteen days—and thousands of dollars.

The manager and coaches don't have the right to appeal. The players do because that's part of their collective bargaining rights. We try to get out an appeal within ten to fifteen days, but it could be thirty to forty-five days, or even longer. I will get on a plane and fly anywhere to get it done, rather than the old way when you had the league presidents who handled all the discipline. They would wait until you came here so they wouldn't have to travel. But the New York teams got the advantage of that system because say they are heard on Friday morning; well, Friday afternoon they uphold the appeal, or even reduce it to the game that starts that night. The Yankees or the Mets had an advantage over the team that had their guy lost during the appeal process. So to keep that from happening, we get on a plane and go. I think there is a strong possibility that we will use video conferencing. But that has to be collectively bargained, and that's coming up after the season when the contracts are up, so we'll see if we can get that.

The commissioner hands out anger management; that's something that my office doesn't hand out. He's probably done that five or six times. I recommended Milton Bradley have anger management. But the commissioner did the Ozzie [Guillen anger management] thing. It just so happens he was being disciplined by this office because his pitcher hit a St. Louis guy after the warning, and he got a one-game suspension and a fine. The bases were loaded and it was 13–2, or whatever, and the St. Louis pitcher hits two guys. Now do you think they were throwing at those guys at 13–2? No. But what happened is the umpire says, "Look, you guys are just blowing out the Cardinals, and I want to put in a warning just to make sure nothing else happens." Lo and behold, the White Sox pitcher comes in; the first guy he sees, *bam*, he hits him in the back. And the umpire says, "You're out of the game." So Ozzie goes too. Like I tell ya, it's automatic now. For the manager it's a one-game suspension; relievers it's three games; the starter it's five games.

The other side of this is fans see that Major League Baseball does not condone guys throwing at each other. On top of that you can get hurt, and hurt bad. Don Drysdale and Bob Gibson would have difficulty pitching today. Those guys didn't care if they hit you. I won't say they'd throw at you, but they didn't care if they hit you. A lot of times, if they gave up a home run or if someone took a hard swing at them, you find out the next time the guy is dusting himself off. In today's rules, the umpires will issue a warning or eject the player off the mound right then and there. I think it's the safety of the players that really came about. There's also the mentality of ownership. There's been an escalation in salaries. Drysdale was probably the highest paid pitcher of his era at $250,000. Now we got pitchers who get what, twenty million dollars? So owners say, "I don't want my guy getting thrown at because they're an extremely valuable asset."

I got kicked out of a ballgame once for offering my glasses to an umpire. It was the first inning. I was playing for Houston. We were playing Cincinnati. César Cedeño was on first base, and he's a base stealer. The count was like *one* ball, two strikes. Pitch out. Cedeño's going. Johnny Bench was the catcher. Throws down. He's safe. I'm knocking the dirt out of my spikes getting ready to hit, thinking the count is *two* balls and two strikes. The umpire was a fellow by the name of Dick Stello—he's passed away now. He says, "Why are you still here?" I was stunned. I said, "What do you mean? It was a pitch out! You called that a strike?" He says, "Yes, the ball was on the corner." I said, "On the corner of Fifth and Main. If you call that a strike, you need these." I handed him my glasses, and he kicked me out of the ballgame. Johnny Bench was rolling. He's laughing. That was the only time I got kicked out of a game. I didn't curse him. I didn't show him up. But I said, "You definitely have issues with your eyesight."

*   *   *   *   *

BOB BOONE

Senior Director of Player Personnel, Washington Nationals

Bob Boone is a four-time All-Star catcher, a former manager of the Cincinnati Reds and the Kansas City Royals, and played a central role in leading players in the 1982 baseball-strike negotiations. He is the son of the late third-baseman Ray Boone, and the father of major leaguers Aaron and Bret Boone. We talked in late September.

*   *   *   *   *

The baseball season never ends. I mean, it's actually more busy right now. I just got back from D.C., and I've got to go back to Arizona next week.

My title is senior director of player personnel and assistant general manager for the Washington Nationals. I took this job when Jim Bowden got hired as a general manager. I got fired as a manager, and then I went to work for the Phillies as a special assignment scout. The Nationals asked permission from the Phillies to talk to me, and offered me a better position.

The franchise was owned by Major League Baseball when it bought the Montreal Expos. We were moving it to Washington, so at that time we had a skeleton crew. I went to work basically as an assistant to Jim, and was involved in every department. Then [the team] was sold to the Lerner Group, and we are currently trying to get up to speed as far as hiring staff in positions that take a load off of me. We're starting to do it a little more professionally, I guess. Putting together a team is much more difficult than it used to be because you don't have control over the players for that long. There are so many variables, money being the biggest one. If you've got the money, you can build a competitive team real quick. If you don't, you are going to lose players.

This past season I oversaw the minor leagues, but not very efficiently because I was in so many departments. I wasn't able to see nearly enough games, and we just kind of ran it by the seat of our pants. It's been a tough go from that standpoint: you want to do everything right; it's just [that] my job is pulled in too many directions.

Everybody has four teams: Triple-A, Double-A, high A and low A. Then you have a rookie team that starts in June, after the draft, and most teams have a lower rookie team that's mostly high-school guys. I go to spring training. I'll do a little bit of teaching, and talk to the pitchers and catchers. And as soon as spring training ends, it's my job to organize all of the minor leagues and see amateur free agents. That's my all-encompassing job from the end of spring training until the June draft. Then we have minor league free agents that are coming up. We're going to have to sign quite a few on the Triple-A club. You try to align your sights on what possible free agents fit your system, and then figuring trades. All of that takes time.

Our first draft, we had the number-four pick in the nation, and we didn't have a second round pick, so my job was fairly easy. I had to narrow down the field of the top guys, and was able to spend a lot of time seeing them. We arrived at Ryan Zimmerman, who was certainly my favorite pick—a real aptitude for hitting, using the entire park, great swing mechanics, a tremendous defensive third baseman. My involvement in getting Ryan and getting him to the big leagues, that's very gratifying. I mean, a Ryan Zimmerman comes along once, possibly, in a career.

When you're going to make your draft pick, you better be right—you're spending a lot of money. Character is probably the number-one issue. It's something that ultimately transcends skills because there's always going to be somebody that's got comparable skills. If you have people without character, getting through the minor leagues is tough. The game is too tough. You get to know him: you watch him; you follow him; you meet the family; you talk to coaches, managers, and the area scouts that have seen him more than anybody. What kind of competitors are they? We see it every day, guys getting in trouble in professional sports. You got to have somebody that will really compete and that will live his life right. In the end, you're selling tickets and a product people will see. You can't see bad-character people; you'll never sell any tickets.

Only 3 or 4 percent of your players that you end up putting in this machine we call Major League Baseball will ever come out the other end. I've had to release a lot of players, and in my current role, I still have to release players. In my role, I usually don't talk to them directly, but I'm the guy that orders it. Baseball is hard. When you have people that won't compete but have a lot of skill, you'll pick the guy with skill that will compete *harder*. All the major leaguers that we watch on TV that have ten and twelve- and fifteen-year careers—certainly the starting players—nobody unseats them. Sometimes the guys under them at that position go to find another job somewhere else. Or go away, because ultimately that's who you are competing against as a minor-league player: you are competing with that level of guy in every organization. It takes time in our sport to go from college to the major leagues. You need time to hone your skills to get to there.

I played football, basketball, and baseball in high school. Turned down a football scholarship at the University of Washington. Went to Stanford on a basketball scholarship, and got out of basketball my freshman year when I found out that I really couldn't play that. There was always baseball.

I played third and was a pitcher. I was an outstanding pitcher in high school, but when I went to Stanford I went to third base full-time until my senior year. I had the second lowest ERA in Stanford history. Oh, I don't even know—like 1.70. When I signed, I asked the scout, "Did you sign me as the third baseman or one of the pitchers?"

"Third base."

"Okay, I will sign." I just didn't care for pitching. But then catching came. I always kind of figured they were going to move me. When they asked me to move, I was hesitant because I didn't want to be a utility guy. I told them if catching comes to me real quick, I will do it. It did, and the rest is history. I had really good hands, a very strong arm, and I was tremendously fast for about two feet. That means your range at third base was going to be below average, but your range of catching is going to be far above average. So that's how the move was made.

I went to high A at Raleigh Durham. It was, first of all, kind of a cultural shock because you're in one of the major schools where you've got a brand new uniform and you're traveling in airplanes, and then you go to the minor leagues. At that time, all the uniforms were hand-me-downs. I could see my leg through my pants. We had four helmets. My first game I was going to play, I'm all fired up, and the lights on a few of the poles went out. And they didn't have enough to light the field, so we got lighted out.

It's much different now from when I started—better stadiums and new uniforms. The minor leagues have really taken off, but a lot of the parks are still old and got crappy little clubhouses. After the game, you shower before you get on the bus. There is no hot water, and you're traveling overnight to get back home or to the next place. If you're in Triple-A, you are flying, but you fly the day of the game because they don't want to pay for another hotel room. So you fly in and get to a hotel; it's eleven o'clock and you find out none of the rooms are ready until two. You camp out in the lobby or go have lunch. And then you play every day, with very few off days. You know, it's a tough life. And it's a fun life.

The money certainly is the carrot. If you do this right and learn your lessons, you may never have to work again the rest of your life. Unfortunately, money gets played big to the public. None of us relate to the millions of dollars that some players make, but you know what, for each one of those guys that make that kind of money there's thousands and thousands of guys that don't. Like in my case, I got five hundred a month when I signed. That was top pay, and you're only paid for four-and-a-half months. It's not a lot of money. I had an apartment. I had a family. It wasn't like we were rolling in dough. And at any point, you can crash and not make it.

Minor-league pay has increased, so guys at Triple-A can make a decent wage, but you can't save anything. You can't buy a house where you have payments year-round. You're risking years of your life trying to get to the major leagues, and you are not really getting there because of the money. You're getting there so you can say that you're a major leaguer. If you're not going to be one of those guys that really makes the money, you're risking possibly ten years of your life. You've got a good chance of coming out of high school or college and being twenty-eight, twenty-nine years old, and really have no skills for the job market.

It runs the gamut at Triple-A, from probably $3,000 per month to some top guys making $20,000 who are kind of career Triple-A people that are valuable. We call them "Four-A" players. You have them so if somebody gets hurt in the big leagues, they can go up, and back. And they're putting up big numbers in the minor leagues to help your Triple-A team win. So, once you get to Triple-A, you've got the guys that are coming up that are stars, and you got the guys going backwards who aren't going to get back.

Baseball is my life. Baseball was in the family. My dad, you know, played in the big leagues. I was raised in that environment. We'd travel every year to wherever he was playing, and get taken out of school. Go to spring training, get taken out of that school. Go to Detroit or Cleveland or Chicago, and be put in another school.

All three of my boys signed professionally. My youngest played six years in the minor leagues, and Aaron and Bret have had great baseball careers. When my dad was alive, it was my dad, myself, my kids, year-round talking baseball. I understand how unique it was with my dad playing. We were the first three-generation family, and we were the first three-generation family that started an All-Star game. Three generations is really remarkable. While statistically that's unbelievable, for us that's just what we did. It's no big deal.

Nobody cares, when you are facing Roger Clemens, whether your dad played or not. It's how you tote the bat up at home plate. It's whether you are going to get a hit or not. They had been around stars; they had learned from them. While other people, once they get to the big leagues, are kind of awed by it, I was not; my kids weren't. They grew up in it. They understood it.

I'm blessed. I'm involved in every aspect of baseball, a game that I love and a job that I love. It's a lot of work, but it's not like a job. If you haven't had a day off in three weeks, working sixteen hours a day, and getting a little tired, I'm not thinking, "Gosh, it's a bad job." There's always some-body to help, and there's always something to do to make your team better. Everybody is trying to outwork everybody else. If you don't, you're left behind.

I knew how to play, and I trained diligently for fifteen years of my life. I didn't miss a day. I was very serious about it. I don't miss playing. I've basically done every job there is in the game. I love every one of them; they're all different. But I don't love one particularly better. It's the rela-tionships that you cherish.

*   *   *   *   *

CHAPTER TWO

IN THE DUGOUT

LEO MAZZONE

Pitching Coach, Baltimore Orioles

Leo Mazzone's pitching staff with the Atlanta Braves, led by Greg Maddux, Tom Glavine, and John Smoltz, had a cumulative earned run average of 3.53, the lowest in the major leagues from 1991 through 2005. In 2006, Mazzone joined the Baltimore Orioles. Over the years, television viewers have watched him sitting in the dugout, rocking slowly. "I don't even know I'm doing it half the time, but my wheels are turning when you see me rocking. I did it when I was a kid; I rocked in a highchair. I've done it my whole life."

He was leaning back on a chair in front of his clubhouse locker reading a book, *Saving the Pitcher*, before a game in early September against the Oakland Athletics. This interview had not been scheduled, but he was eager to talk about pitching anyway. He says, "They think there's gotta be a secret. Well, the secret is doing two things really well: commanding a fastball and changing speeds."

*   *   *   *   *

From the time I was nine years old, I loved the game of baseball. Everything else had to drop way off. I've loved baseball my whole life.

I turned down a college scholarship to sign out of high school, because that was what I wanted to do since I was this high. The scout says, "We can't give you a lot of money because you're not real tall, but don't worry; you'll make it all when you get to the big leagues. A four-hundred-dollar bonus and incentive bonuses." No problem. Right away, I eat that up.

I pitched in the minor leagues and then became a coach. Spent twenty-three years total in the minor leagues—ten as a pitcher, thirteen as a coach. Sometimes, if you were on the verge of getting an incentive bonus and you had equal talent as another guy and he didn't have an incentive bonus, you were sent down so they didn't have to pay you. You start learning that end of the business too.

I wasn't very smart. I thought I could blow guys away. I had that "little man's syndrome" and I thought I threw harder than I actually did. I was a strikeout pitcher in my minor-league career. I struck out over 750 hitters in 1,000 innings. Ten years later, I still hadn't made it. I got close, but no cigar. But that's okay. I have no regrets.

Someone said, "Mazzone, you're lucky." I said, "Yeah I'm lucky, but how many people would've spent twenty-three years in the fucking minor leagues? They would've quit." But I loved it there. I loved it when I was pitching and I loved it when I was coaching. It was all I knew. Then, the perfect situation for me was when Bobby Cox became the general manager in Atlanta. He says the guys in the minor leagues were healthy and developed, and he saw my connection with Johnny Sain. Hell, that was then pretty much a no-brainer.

I met Sain in '79 in my first years as pitching coach in the Braves system. He was in charge of the pitching. He took me under his wing and I figured, you know what, I better pick this guy's brain because he had more twenty-game winners than any pitching coach in the history of the game. He's the one that put the pitching coach on the map in baseball. He was basically the first great pitching coach.

No coaches in the Hall of Fame; only managers. The first one that should go in as pitching coach is Johnny Sain. They don't know what the fuck we go through down here, and in the minor leagues. It's tougher to be a coach in the minor leagues now because when I was a coach in the minor leagues, I didn't have any restrictions put on me. I didn't have somebody telling me, "You can only throw this many pitches, or you can't use this guy." I could do what I wanted, and it worked! I always had healthy arms from rookie league all the way up.

Hank Aaron was my boss then, and he said, "I hired you to take care of the pitching." Hell, now you gotta go through the front office; you gotta go through all these different channels to get something approved. Why hire the guy then? I hadn't talked to Hank in three months, and I'm thinking, "Oh, boy, he must be pissed at me." So I called him up and I said, "Hey, is everything all right? I haven't heard from you lately." He said, "Leo, if I have to call you all the time, then something is wrong. I ain't had to call you at all. You just keep doing what you're doing. That's what I hired you for."

We had a big meeting when Bobby became the general manager in Atlanta. He had all the entire farm system there, the major-league people there, everyone. He says, "I'm going to turn an offensive-oriented organization into a pitching one. Who's going to take care of the pitchers?" Naturally, I said, "I'll do it." There was another pitching coach there. He said, "I don't believe in Leo's programs. As much as he has them throw, they'll be dead by August." I thought, "Well, this son of a bitch." In front of everybody, I said, "Can I ask you a question?" He said, "Sure, you can ask me anything." I said, "What do you do that extra day when you don't have 'em throwing?" He said, "Well, I take them out in the outfield and have them play catch." I said, "Why don't you explain the difference to me between playing catch in the outfield and getting on a mound at sixty feet, six inches going downhill to a catcher and playing catch?" He said, "Well, they have a tendency to throw too hard." I said, "Well, that's what the fuck they pay you for is to regulate the effort." That was it!

I spent fifteen years in Atlanta and now my first year here in Baltimore. I come in, go over the pitching charts from the night before, keep certain notes on our pitchers. I have the notes on the opposition, but I'm more concerned about our pitchers and what they do; then get ready for the daily programs of the other pitchers to get ready for their next starts. You do that every single day, and then you go back in and get ready for the ballgame.

For seven months out of the year, seven days a week, you're going to the ballpark—after lunch if it's a night game; getting home at midnight. If it's a day game, you're coming out here at 9 a.m. and getting done about 6 p.m. You're either going back to your home or you're getting on an airplane, and that's a constant for seven months; hopefully eight. That's not counting spring training.

I always get out early and watch the other team hit. I remember one time we were in Chicago, Shawon Dunston and Mark Grace were stretching behind the cage, and they said, "Here comes Leo with a smile on his face. Leo, you're always smiling. Who you got pitching today?" I said, "Maddux." They said, "How about tomorrow?" I said, "Glavine." They said, "How about the next day?" I said, "Smoltz." They said, "No wonder you're smiling. Christ Almighty!" You know what I'm thinking right there, "We're already halfway through. We were already in their head."

I had the privilege of coaching Greg Maddux for eleven years, and he said there isn't anything more to pitching than locating your fastball and changing speeds. He said, "Everybody thinks I'm the smartest guy in the world, but you'd be amazed at how smart people think you are when you can put your fastball where you want." That's what you pitch off of. Every pitcher's fastball is the most important pitch they have—and the command of it. It doesn't have anything to do with velocity. It's where you put it.

Radar guns are everywhere now. I hate them. Too many people get enamored with them. Pitching is a touch form—an art form—a craft; not a bully out there who just blows the damn thing as hard as he can. I think baseball is getting off track in not signing people or not looking at prospects that have a chance to pitch if they can't reach a certain number on the radar gun. I think they're missing the boat. I think if you try to pitch to a radar gun, you raise the risk of arm injury because you're trying to do more than you can with a pitch. Bobby Cox didn't want it coming in, and we didn't want it coming in, but the fans love them. They like to say, "Oooh . . . aaah." I wouldn't be surprised if there's some ballparks that don't jack that up just so the fans can say, "Oooh, aaah, oh my, he's throwing 97 miles per hour." I'm not so sure that's not about four miles an hour faster than what they're actually throwing. I always subtract four from any number I see.

Putting the pitch counts on the board, that's another joke. I can't stand looking up and seeing pitch counts. All you're doing is talking the pitcher into getting tired. I used to keep a clicker, but hell, now I don't even need it. All I have to do is look up at the board, and there's the pitch count. I used to cheat on it. If Maddux or Glavine or Smoltz were pitching real good and their pitch counts are getting high, I'd just say, "Oh, well, I won't count that one, or I'll let that one go." I'd always have them a little lower than they what actually were if I felt it was a good thing.

This game is very simple as far as pitching is concerned. You have to command the fastball and change speed. There's no more to it than that. If there's anything after that, it's cake. But those two things have to be done in order to be successful. For example, the game that Glavine beat Cleveland 1–0 in the sixth game of the World Series: After the first go-around, the Cleveland hitters moved up the plate on him to take away the down-and-away strikes. Tommy came in and said, "Leo, they're moving up on the plate; they're crowding me now. I guess I'm going to have to go in more, right?" I said, "Well, wait a minute; now you've got two options. When a player moves up on the plate that doesn't change his vision of the ball coming to the strike zone. They move up on the plate, so go out a little farther and see if they follow you out. If they follow you out, you're still in the same boat as if they were off the plate. But, if they follow you out and they're shooting you to right center, then you're going to have to go in more to open it back up." They followed him out. If I can tell another pitcher that, they can't execute it. Glavine had the ability, and the thought process, and the control to go farther out and they followed him.

Strike zones are smaller now. I know they base the strike zone by the rules, but in my sixteen years here, the strike zone has become smaller. It started in '98 or '99. Pitchers were getting calls on the corners and off the edges, and they wanted to have technology make sure that everybody's strike zone was the same. And in doing so, it shrunk. I'm a pure traditionalist, okay? If Maddux or Glavine or Smoltz is out there pitching, they have pinpoint control. If they can hit a target that's the width of the ball off the plate, the umpires were calling them strikes. They were rewarded for having control. By the same token, if Barry Bonds or Wade Boggs or Tony Gwynn were at the plate, we couldn't get a called strike on them because they had earned that right of having a great eye and a great knowledge of the strike zone. They got the benefit of the doubt. So, on both ends of the ball, you were rewarded for your high standard of excellence. Now, somebody can be wild all over the place and happen to hit one border-line pitch. If they hang a slider now, they call it a strike if it's not too high, so he's being rewarded for making a mistake.

But seeing the evolution of pitching since my first year in the big leagues in 1991 until now, there's heavy favor towards the hitters. The pitchers are at a disadvantage because of smaller gaps in the alleys, lower mounds, smaller strike zones. You go back and look at some of those old World Series games or see some of these guys pitching and get a called strike. Now you don't get that pitch. When that strike zone changed, that was the first time that Maddux and Glavine, in their careers—in the same year—gave up more than two hundred hits in a season. But they still won.

Umpires are graded now. You know damn well if you have somebody looking over your shoulder while an umpire is trying to make a split deci-sion if it's an inch off or not on a 95-mile-per-hour fastball they're going to end up tending to be more conservative, or make sure that this damn QuesTec machine that's now in is grading them right. You cannot take the human element out of this game. And that's taking the human element out. Umpires were great until that shit came out.

Now it's almost like everybody in sports wants parity. Nobody has an individual strike zone. Everybody's strike zone is based off technology, not the individual. You used to enjoy it if you knew what the umpire's strike zone was going to be. You could pitch accordingly. You'd know who was umpiring, and you knew their strike zones. Some were more liberal; some were more conservative, but that's being a human being. Every pitcher is different. Machines can't win ballgames.

I just tell them to walk more guys. The hell with it; we're not giving in to the strike zone. Here's something that I don't understand: The smaller the strike zone, the longer it is for the games to go. Well, baseball is doing all this stuff to speed up the game—you know, "Pitchers get on the mound; throw the pitch; get in here from the bullpen"—they do everything except bang strikes, and the one thing that will speed up the game is banging strikes. The borderline strike used to go to the pitcher. Now the border-line strike goes to the hitter because people want offense. Every move since 1968, when they lowered the pitcher's mound, has been toward offense. They promote it more.

We had a saying in Atlanta that we're still developing here in Baltimore: "We're going to quietly stick it up their ass and leave." Don't bring any attention to yourself or start jumping all over the place hollering and screaming and all that. I think the admiration I had for guys like Maddux, Glavine, and Smoltz was their professionalism and the way they went about their business. Glavine was a real strong-minded individual, so you could be a little more firm in your conversation with him. With Smoltz, you could say the same thing, only you'd have to have a lighter presentation because he was a little more emotional. With Maddux, [I had to] be very businesslike: have something that means something, or don't say anything.

If something isn't going quite right in the game, don't dwell on that because the most important pitch is always your next pitch. Sometimes a guy will walk a leadoff hitter, and they'll dwell on that. Well, that carries over into the next hitter, and that carries over to the next hitter. Don't dwell on something. You're going out there to give them support.

Here's the other thing: Someone might say, "Oh, how can he throw that guy that pitch?" Well, guess what? If he had put it where he wanted, nobody would be asking that question. Remember Mark Wohlers giving up the home run to Jim Leyritz in the 1996 World Series? The pitch was a hundred miles per hour. "How could he throw him a slider?" Well, if the slider was in the dirt, he was going to miss it by three feet. After that home run, I told Mark—he was pretty upset; it's the World Series and we had blown the lead—I said, "Don't ever second-guess yourself on that pitch. If you'd thrown it in the dirt, he'd have swung and missed." So everyone says how can they throw that; well, guess what? Tell the pitcher: "Make your selection; throw with conviction; simplify your game so that you're locating your fast ball; and then don't second-guess."

I never called a pitch in my career. The catcher puts down the signs, and the pitcher has the option of accepting the sign or shaking it off and going to something else because we try to have the pitcher take full responsibility for what happens. I can see fatigue; I can see strength; I can see mechanics; I can see all these things with my eyes, but I can't feel what he's feeling on a particular pitch. It's always nice to be in sync, but my preference is for a catcher to make a good presentation to the pitcher on his target, a good presentation to the umpire, receive the ball quietly, and when he puts his fingers down, he's making a suggestion, not the decision.

I have a theory: Get on the mound as often as possible and make the ball do something without maxing out their efforts. One of the things I'm most proud of is my track record of healthy arms. I'm more of a rebel. I'm not conservative as far as I want the pitchers to throw more often with less exertion. You're teaching touch on the ball, which translates into better control. I've always had two sessions in between starts, so on the two middle days they do practice off the mounds. So you have a regular routine for them and then [a different one] for your relief pitchers. If somebody hasn't warmed up or gotten in a game in a couple of days, I like to take them down before a game and give them a little five-to-ten-minute session off the mound, throwing downhill to a catcher. It's a constant every single day.

Now, your arm injuries occur from over-exertion and over-extension. In other words, if I told you to run seven miles in a week where would you feel better: running one mile every day for seven days, or running your seven and then taking three or four days off, and doing it again? I believe the same thing is true with arms.

They even have pitch counts in Little League. There's so many people who are worried about arm injuries that they give the pitcher restrictions, which don't allow them to develop. I think that raises the risk. You've gotta have good mechanics. You've gotta be able to pitch without maxing out your effort all the time and acquire touch on the ball. That's how you stay healthy. It isn't a certain number that you put on shit.

I gave a big talk in Atlanta for youth in the area, and a Little League coach asked me, "How many [innings] do you think the Little League pitcher should pitch?" I said, "Well, do you guys have a limit?" He said, "Well, yeah, they can pitch six innings a week." They asked me how many, and I said, "Twelve." They said, "Why twelve?" I said, "Well, six on Monday and six on Saturday. That's two starts." They said, "Well what would your pitch count be?" I said, "Here's what I would do. If the pitcher that's out there is pitching good, I'd leave him in. If he's getting his ass kicked, you take him out. If he's pitching good and you think he's getting tired, then take him out. If he's out there pitching good and he's not getting tired, you leave him in. If you need a number to tell you that, you shouldn't be coaching."

The lowest batting average in the history of baseball is [against] the down-and-away strike. All the great pitchers own that part [of the strike zone]. When you own down-and-away, that allows you to go to all the areas of the strike zone. I think it's important to know where to attack with the fastball and what the guy will chase, but if you go strictly by that, then I think you're defeating the purpose. Bottom line is you can read all those reports you want, and it always comes to down-and-away and in. No matter how you word it. So, in other words, it's more important that the pitcher execute what he can do as opposed to who he's facing. Too many pitchers worry that the hitter knows what's coming. Watch the reaction of the hitter, get a read off your fastball, and pitch accordingly.

I spent fifteen years in Atlanta, and then Sam Perlozzo was named manager of the Baltimore Orioles. Our families grew up together in western Maryland, so when the opportunity came to go to Baltimore, I felt it was time. You can't be afraid of change. It was a very emotional and difficult decision for me to leave Atlanta, but the timing was right. It's been a difficult change, but I'll be better adjusted next year. The first two days I felt awkward in Baltimore because, you know, it's an entirely different situation. But now I feel real comfortable, and there's some good things that we can develop here. My own expectations are the highest they can possibly be. I felt that it would take a turn for the good quicker than it has, but I also see some building blocks for Baltimore's future that could put us in position, with a few acquisitions, to make a run at the pennant.

With one year left on a three-year contract, Mazzone was fired by the Orioles after the 2007 season.

*   *   *   *   *

MIKE HARGROVE

Manager, Seattle Mariners

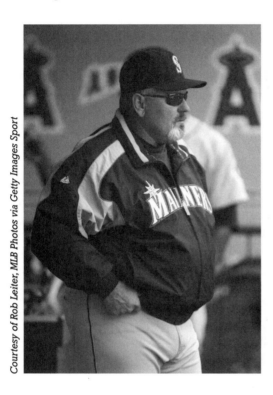

Courtesy of Rob Leiter, MLB Photos via Getty Images Sport

Hargrove was a first baseman during his twelve-year career as a major-league baseball player, which included being named the American League Rookie of the Year in 1974. He batted .290 in 5,564 plate appearances, and finished his playing days with the Cleveland Indians. In 1991, he was hired mid-season to manage the Indians, a job he held for nine years before managing the Baltimore Orioles and later the Seattle Mariners. Sitting behind a desk in the visiting manager's clubhouse office before an afternoon game in Arlington, Texas, he talked about his career.

"Yeah, I think I've changed over fifteen years. The biggest change that ever happened was when I was managing the Indians. We had a boating accident in spring training where we had two pitchers killed. I came out of that with a lot more compassion than I had going on at the surface. You know what I'm saying? I mean, I guess the compassion was closer to the surface than it had been before the accident. I changed. I noticed that change immediately.

I am a little more tolerant now than I used to be; no less aggressive, but I think I realized that there are human frailties. If their desire is there and their effort is there, then I can be patient to a fault. It is a real fine line that you have to walk as a manager between

being patient and being foolish, and sometimes it gets difficult. You find yourself being a little foolish every now and then."

*   *   *   *   *

The job is kind of hard to define. You are in charge of twenty-five players. Then you've got trainers and coaches that you have direction over, and your job in a nutshell is to keep the mental and physical efforts of everybody in one area, and that's winning baseball games. You're everything from confessor to a dad, a brother, a boss, a jailor. You are really all of those things. The easiest part of a manager's job is managing the game.

My job as a manager is to prepare for the worst and hope for the best, so I choose to look at the glass as half full instead of half empty. In all of baseball, it's real easy to see that glass half empty all the time. I learned a long time ago that in this game, when it is over, you review what happened that night, how effective this one way was or the other, and you say, "Okay, that might have made a difference or I could have done that. The next time we get to that situation, we will do that next time." Then you let it go and look ahead to the next game. If you dwell on the negatives for too long, you're never ready. A bad loss is a lot more sour than a really good win is sweet, but you tend to forget the victories quicker than you forget the losses. I sleep about the same. Maybe a little worse at times.

You have to have the right kind of mix of discipline and compassion to get it to go. With a young team, you are going to be more of a strict disciplinarian than you would be with an older club that knows how to do things and knows how to win. You give them more leeway and latitude, but it is different from team to team. You can have an older team that needs a lot of discipline; you got to be over them all the time and check to make sure everybody is doing what they are supposed to do at the same time. But you can go to another team that is a veteran team, and you have veterans that police themselves. You don't have to worry about guys being where they are supposed to be or doing what they are supposed to do. I mean, you still check on it obviously, but it's not a constant concern.

In the whole scheme of things, we get the benefit from team effort—the Mariners do, the Mariners' fans do, I do, and the coaches do. But when you come down to it, I can sit there and tell a guy on this team a hundred times, "You know, that's not the way. We want to do it this way," or take him out of the lineup, or cause him some playing time, whatever. But if a teammate comes up and says the same thing to him, it just makes all the difference in the world and it has been that way since Abner Doubleday invented this game.

There are team leaders—different kinds. They're important to a team, and some come naturally; some evolve into it. I don't know if we have anybody here that will get in teammates' faces. I don't want to name names, but there are quiet team leaders who lead by example and quietly tell a teammate, "That's not the right way to do that. We don't do that here." We've got a couple of those guys that will do that. In any successful situation I have ever been in either as a player, coach, or manager, the players police themselves because when you come down to it, they're not playing for the Seattle Mariners, they're not playing for Mike Hargrove, they're not playing for Mike Hargrove's coaches. They are playing for each other and their family. That's who they are playing for.

From 95 to 99 percent of the players in the big leagues today had to work like a dog to hone a talent, to get to where they are, so they understand the work ethic; they understand the importance of structure. But then there is the other 5 percent, or 1 percent, that is the tallest guy in high school. He's the best basketball player. He didn't really have to work at it. He goes to college, and now all of a sudden, he is not one of the tallest and did not work out, and now he is lost. I think it's kind of that kind of thing where there are people who skate through because they are just more gifted than other people, and they never really had to put the work in. I don't think it's generational. It was that way when I played. There are guys, who if you give an inch, they'll take a mile. Then there are guys, who if you give an inch, they'll only take a half-inch. It's just who they are.

I think night-in and night-out, talent wins games. There may be a series of games—two games, three games, ten games—where a break will go your way and it wins the game for you. You just have to be in the right spot at the right time.

I think the biggest separator in our game today is mental toughness— mental preparation. There are some people that do it really well. There are other people who don't do it at all. You see players of the same talent level that have a good work ethic. They have a good mental approach to things, and their talent just takes off.

I learned early on in my career from Billy Martin. He made a statement that I use today. Billy said, "I'll accept this error because physical errors will happen. You get to a ball and it takes a little funny hop, and hits off your glove or off your arm, and you are charged an error. Those things will happen, and I'll accept those. But mental errors are unacceptable because that's the one thing in this game that is controllable." I think you just have to preach about it all the time.

You know, as a hitter, I can control sometimes how hard to hit the ball. I can't really control whether it is caught or not. But if I am not in the right spot where I should be and I don't know I should be, or I go up to the plate and in an at-bat I swing at pitches that I normally don't swing at because I wasn't mentally focused, that is my fault. That's something I can control. I tell our players that you should never ever find yourself in a situation where it beats you mentally. Physically, yeah, it's going to happen, but nobody should ever beat you mentally. I think that's the thing that separates the good teams from the mediocre teams.

How do you cultivate that? You just have to talk about it a lot, especially in extra-innings games where you get into a tough spot, then you really see guys bear down. They get through it and come out on the other side and win the ballgame. Then you point to it and say, "We were mentally tough tonight." It becomes a part of the culture.

I think you just have to preach about it all the time. In this game, at this level, everybody is looking for an edge, and even the slightest edge you get can make the difference because the talent is so equal. We talk about, you know, mound presence or body language. If a pitcher on the mound is out there like he is apologetic for being there, or walks around like he didn't really want to get up on the rubber and pitch, that gives a slight psychological edge to a hitter, and a lot of times that is all you need. That's how fine the line is. We talk to our people all the time about their mound presence and the image they are projecting to the other team. It's something we call a swagger, but it was not necessarily sluggish. It is how you carry yourself and project to the other side that *I'm good. And if you blink, I really probably will beat you.*

Baseball is a game of statistics and it's a game of percentages. It really is, but I think that if it comes to the point to where percentages become the deciding factor in every one of your decisions, then I think you are not using all the tools available. Everybody calls it "I went on gut instinct." That was not a gut instinct. It's your baseball experience telling you this is the thing to do rather than going with the numbers. I've watched a lot of really good successful managers over the years, and the ones that play the percentages most of the time are the ones that won, and that gets back to talent. I watched Earl Weaver. I played for Billy Martin. I watched Gene Mauch. Talent prevails. That's what it comes down to. There are times that you won't go to stats and that leaves it open for second-guessing, but baseball is built on second-guessing; everybody second-guesses the manager—everybody. Everybody and their dog knows when it's time to bunt and when it's time to hit and run, when it's time to squeeze and when it's time to steal, and all those things. I mean that is not rocket science. An owner, Dick Jacobs in Cleveland, told me one time, "Mike, there are two things in this world that every man thinks he can do better than anybody else: cook a steak and manage a baseball team."

There are a lot of factors that go into a ballgame. You would hope a pitcher would complete each inning with fifteen pitches or less. If he can get it down to fifteen or less, he's got a good chance, number one, of obviously throwing a complete game; but point two is that if he's lower than fifteen pitches an inning, then he's throwing pretty well, that low pitch count allows you to keep him in. You get to know your pitchers and realize that pitcher A at the eighty-five- or ninety-pitch mark starts losing his stuff, and he is not nearly as effective. Well, what's the score of the game when he gets to that pitch mark? Are you five or six runs ahead? If you are, then go ahead let him go try to save the bullpen because you had three guys out there who pitched three days in a row, and they are not available. You don't want to fry everybody else. But if it's a close ballgame and you say, "We've got to win today," you go to those guys—use them again, which means the next day you're going to be short.

Or, you get a guy on first base who's a decent base runner. The coaches have the stopwatches out checking the release time from the pitcher to the catcher. If it's 1.3 [seconds] and above from the time he starts his first move to when the ball hits the catcher's mitt, then he has got a better than even chance of stealing that base, unless it's a guy like Pudge Rodriguez who has a really good arm. So, I mean, there are a lot of things that you have to factor in, and is it at a point or time in the game before you are willing to risk that out? How important is that runner? Say you are two runs down; there is no real sense in stealing a base if it's that close because if he gets thrown out and the next guy hits a home run, you're still one run down. I think any time that you start managing to cover your ass, you probably should go do something else.

You have to maintain an even keel in this game, playing 162 games. I mean, you can't get too high or too low, or you would just be absolutely burnt to a crisp by the time the season is over. The one thing that got us all through that 0-and-11 stretch with our sanity is there's good team chemistry on this club. In July, we went on our West Coast swing, and we were like 14 and 4 in contention; then we went 0 and 11 and came out of it out of contention. We didn't pitch well, we didn't swing the bats well, and we just did not catch a break. There were games that we just absolutely played terrible. Not many, but some. And there were other games where we had leads and we'd give up a bad-hop base hit that would cost us two runs, and we'd get beat by one.

When your team is in contention, you have the stress of trying to finish it off and clinch a spot. When you are not in contention, you have the stress of finishing the season off well for your fans and for your own pride—different degrees of stress, but still the same stress level.

Your role as a manager is to let everybody know everything is going to be okay. We are all still breathing, this thing will end, and the only way it will end is we stay mentally tough—we play physically hard and stay focused on what our jobs are. Then we'll come out of it, and we'll be better for it. It's no fun. If you had your druthers, you'd druther not do it, but you find yourself in it, and the last thing you want is for your team or coaches to start looking for excuses or to, you know, start saying "Ah, this is just the way it is," and start feeling sorry for themselves.

You focus on the chance that there is always tomorrow. Tomorrow is our next best chance to finish this thing. One time, when I was a rookie and I was going through a little bit of a tough time and I was in a little bit of a slump and I hadn't got a hit in 10 or 11 at-bats, Billy Martin saw me stewing one day and said, "You're 0 for 12. Just think, those are 12 at-bats you don't have to experience until you get your next hit." I thought: you know, he's right. So that's kind of the way I always looked at it: that the longer it goes, the closer you are to the end of it.

I think winning comes before chemistry will come; not all the time, but most generally. Yeah, it's important to have, but it's almost like the chicken or the egg—which comes first: team chemistry or winning? It can really mean a lot. It's real hard to have good true team chemistry when the ball club is not playing up to its potential.

I played for eleven managers in twelve years in the big leagues and every one of them told me their door was open, but there were some, we go talk to them, you know, it might have been open, but they sure didn't want you in their office, so they'd tell you what they thought you wanted to hear to get you out. I say, "My door is open. Just be sure you want to know the answer before you come in because I will tell you the truth as I know it that day." I think honesty is all-important. The one thing that I learned playing for so many managers is if I could believe the manager I played for to treat me like a man—tell me the truth no matter what— I certainly was in their corner, and I enjoyed playing for them.

We've got rules like any other major league team; you know, show up on time. We've got dress rules; we've got curfews; we've got nothing out of the ordinary. Timing has to be right on team meetings because you hold too many of 'em, players will stop hearing what you are saying. They will listen, but they won't hear what you say. I have an old theory that every player has a button behind his left ear. If you yell at him too often and too loudly, he turns the volume off. He knows that you're saying something, but he's not listening to a word of it. So you have to pick and choose your time, and that may be different from when I played. When I played, there were more in-your-face type managers: "My way or the highway." That was back, you know, before free agency, and it was easier to manage that way. Now it has changed to where you can still tell people very forcefully that they are wrong and correct them, but you can't do it as constantly as the people that I played for used to.

When we talk to a player about, you know, being released, traded or returned to the minor leagues, we call them into the office. I don't have a stock speech for all of them. It's different with each individual. I've worked for a couple of organizations where I did it by myself. It depends on the organization, and it depends on whether you really care or not. This organization here, [General Manager] Bill Bavasi always comes down. There are some players you're glad they're leaving, but you try to be compassionate; not be an asshole to him. I really don't want to make it harder for them than it is. In some instances, it's real tough because you really like the player, you really hate to see him go, but for the good of the ball club this has to happen, and that's just part of the business. That's the tough part.

I was the kind of a player that if you paid to come and see the team I was playing on—I don't think anybody paid to see me play—I gave you your dollar's worth. You bet. That's the kind of player everybody would like to manage: a guy that busts his butt, and is there physically and mentally every day, and does not offer excuses.

When I was a player, you knew which writers were out to create stories and which writers just want to report stories. You knew who to be careful with, and what you said or how you said what to people, but that got real old real quick as a player. So I started coming up with all the old tired clichés, and after about a year they stopped coming around to me. That was good.

It has always surprised me, since the first game I ever managed in the big leagues, what writers don't ask. There usually are two or three instances in the game that the game really turns on, and to this day, I haven't had a writer ask me about any of those instances. I mean, the first game I managed, I came off the field thinking, "Oh, I'm going to talk to these guys now, and they are going to ask me this and this, and the game really turned on this play here tonight." They didn't. I guess it's not important to them, or they figure it's not important to their readers. They're just like anybody else. I mean, in baseball 99 percent of the guys are great guys; 1 percent of them you'd waste a bullet if you shot them; same way with writers. You know, 99 percent are great people. It's that 1 percent that you could just do without.

The thing I most genuinely like about this job is that I get to be around the world's best baseball players, and I really mean *the world*. I was one once—not anymore—but I do love being around them and watching how they go about their business, how good they are in their job, how good they are in their hearts. They are really good people.

I'm around some very intelligent, creative good people here in Seattle. I enjoy that. I would hope I am not at the age yet where I say it keeps me young, though I suspect I probably am, but it's fun to compete. I mean, it's fulfilling to compete. Obviously, it's my entire life, but it doesn't define me. It's a great way to make a living.

When I was a player, you'd go out and compete, and if the team lost, you felt really bad about it. But if you got a couple of hits, you thought, "Well, at least I did my job." You've got to take something positive [out of the experience]. As a manager or a coach, if the team doesn't win there's nothing positive to take away from it. There really isn't. That was hard early on in my career to come to grips with, but it's a very fulfilling profession, and I feel very fortunate and honored to be able to have one of only thirty jobs in the world.

Editor's note: In July 2007, Hargrove resigned his position with the Mariners, releasing the following statement:

"Over the past several weeks, I have come to the realization that to be fair to myself and the team, I can not continue to do this job if my passion has begun to fade. I want to stress how much I respect, and love, the players in the clubhouse, and the coaches and staff that we have in place here, and I cannot stress enough what a tremendous place this is to work because of the people who work above me. I am very proud of the work we've done to turn this club around in three years, and I have high expectations for the team this season."

*   *   *   *   *

TODD HUTCHESON

Head Athletic Trainer, San Diego Padres

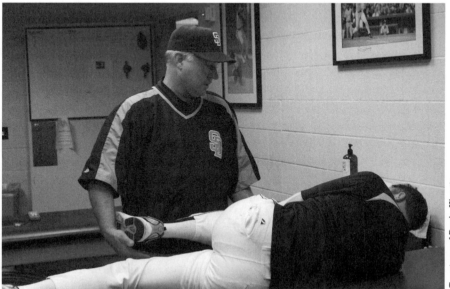

Hutcheson took time away from his pre-game preparations to describe how he helps Padres players avoid injuries and gets them ready to play.

*   *   *   *   *

My job is the head athletic trainer for the San Diego Padres. My job mainly is the prevention and care of injuries to our players, and that doesn't just mean I take care of them when they get hurt. It means we do a lot of maintenance. Whatever we can do to keep them on the field.

A typical day would be to get to the ballpark about twelve thirty or one o'clock for a seven-o-five game. Get the training room ready. Fill the whirlpools. Stock our counters from the night before. Roll any Ace wraps that we have used from the night before. Taking care of e-mails or bills, or whatever happens to come in from the administrative side. Doing some inventory work. Ordering supplies. Making sure that we go over what happened the day before, not only treatment-wise, but if anything happened during the game that we need to address that day during treatment.

We had a couple of things. Our second baseman complained about some pain in one of his hands. He had surgery a few years ago on his left wrist, but his pain last night was somewhere up in his hand. We took an X-ray after the game. That looked good, so we didn't really have to worry much about that.

Scott Linebrink, one of our relievers, has been in three of the last four games, so he came in a little bit sore today—sore shoulder, sore elbow. He's the guy that's generally tight that we do maintenance on every day to keep his range of motion. We do a lot of deep-tissue work with our thumbs or our hands. We dig into the posterior rotator cuff, into his lat, his armpit, his trap, and basically have him move through a certain range of motion that makes tissue tighten up even more and to release it so it returns back to its normal resting length. Once we get the tissue to return to it's normal resting length, any spasm or pain that he has usually subsides, and his range of motion comes back, and he is able to go out and throw relatively pain-free.

Our philosophy in the training room is that if we can do something to help these guys feel better on the field, we feel like they've got a better chance to perform well or better. So we are very proactive in doing a lot of maintenance work. The majority of guys out here are playing every day. Even guys that aren't playing every day, they're still going through batting practice, hitting in the cage, or taking ground balls. They're making sure they stay in pretty good shape. Even if they're not getting into the game, they're still working their butt off pretty much, so those guys need attention as well.

Today was one of our busier days. I think we treated almost eighteen guys—eighteen out of twenty-five. We always work on most of our starting pitchers. Jake Peavy pitched last night. Today he came in to do what we call "thumbing," where he lays on his stomach, we put powder on the back of his shoulder, take our thumbs and just go straight into the tissue because the posterior shoulder and all the musculature—the deltoid, the posterior rotator cuff, and the lat—are fatigued. Some of those muscles may be in spasm and we just go in and we push straight into the tissue, to try to get the tissue to spread out. We are also hyperstimulating nerve fibers to try to get the fatigue out so they don't cause as much pain; try to get the whole area to relax. Once we do that, then we will do some manual release techniques to make sure he gets his range of motion back. We'll stretch him, and then let him come out here. He'll come back in after batting practice for some muscle stimulation.

Tomorrow, he will probably get some ultrasound stim to start to increase the blood flow in the soft tissue to try to keep muscles lengthened out again. Because of the nature of the throwing motion, most of the pitchers are going to lose internal rotation. So we are constantly working on trying to release the posterior cuff and posterior capsule to make sure that they get their internal rotation back.

We see a difference when Peavy comes out and throws. A couple of years ago, he faced the New York Mets. The Mets put a lot of right-handers in the lineup, and he threw a ton of cutters and sliders. He was a lot more sore in his forearm than he would have been had he faced another team that had some lefties where he was throwing more fastballs, or sinkers away, or changeups. So depending on what type of pitches are thrown, and how many of them are thrown during the game—like the game in which he faced the Mets—his forearm was real tight and sore the next day. The day where he's facing a team with a lot of left-handers, he's going to throw more fastballs and changeups so he may have more posterior shoulder soreness. We address that with him: take him through manual exercises, PNF patterns—proprioceptive neuromuscular facilitation—which are resistive patterns where the player goes through resisted motion in three planes; usually in flexion, extension component, an abduction-adduction component and a rotational component, which is basically the way the human body moves. So we will take him through PNF patterns, again stretch him, and then he will go out and throw his side session. That's the second day. Third day: Depending on how sore he is from the side day, he'll do a set of dumbbells. We'll also do ultrasound stim again, and then we will pick and choose what we need [to do], depending on what the tissues feels like.

The day he starts—and this is just Jake—we will do ultrasound stim on him, basically the same thing we do on a side day: soft tissues, some manual release techniques, some PNF patterns. That's done closer to game time. And off he goes to warm up in the pen.

Somebody like Chan Ho Park, who is pitching tonight, has a couple of issues: some stiffness in his back; some tightness in his calf, which we will address; and then we will do a lot of deep-tissue and manual-release techniques on him. Then he will warm up in the weight room, get stretched, and come back and get his shoulder and elbow stretched. Then he will go out. Each pitcher is a little bit different.

I don't know if there is a difference between young and old. I know that a lot of the older players who come from other organizations may not be used to everything that we're doing for them, and they sometimes don't allow us enough time to do what we feel like we can do to help them out. After a month or so, or after something happens to them, they start coming in and they see what we can do.

I feel pretty confident in saying that, at some point time in time, we are going to see all of them in one way or another. Khalil Greene is probably one of the best-conditioned athletes we have, and we never see him unless something happens to him. Last year he dove and broke a toe. He also took a short hop throw at second base. It fractured his fingers on his throwing hand. So we'll always end up seeing the players for something.

The other day Josh Bard, our catcher, fouled a ball off the top of his foot, and he was really concerned that he had fractured one of the small bones in his foot. Got an X-ray on him there in Texas. It wasn't fractured. We did a couple of hours of work on him; used some soft tissue techniques. He missed the next game. Just stretching it out, he was able to play the following day.

Concussions are a real bad problem. We had a catcher—Wiki Gonzalez—run over at home plate by Adam Dunn a few years ago. It was one of the more violent collisions I've seen. Wiki hit his head on the ground after he got thrown back about ten feet. Everything flew off. He had a regular helmet. Even if he had a hockey-style mask, I think that would have flown off as well. Wiki seemed to be okay. Stayed in the game. After about two hitters, the pitcher was having a hard time trying to figure out what Wiki was trying back there, because he was just throwing fingers down. Took him out of the game within about twenty minutes.

Once he came out, they brought him up to the clubhouse where I saw him—I was inside working on Trevor [Hoffman], which I will tell you about in a minute—started attending to him, brought our doctor down, and Wiki asked me the same question four times in a matter of two minutes. We ended up sending him to the hospital. Got a CAT scan, which was negative. He felt tired and sluggish, and his thought process was a little bit slow, which presents a problem in itself in that Wiki, being Latin, couldn't communicate with us. He spoke pretty good English, but for us to be able to tell that he wasn't processing stuff quite the way he normally does was very difficult because for him to try to translate everything, and then tell us in English, was hard enough. But now, to be able to determine whether he was slower than normal was very difficult. Well, between us and having a doctor here that speaks Spanish, we continued to watch him over the next two-week period. Gradually had him go out and just play catch, and see how he reacted to that. He missed about two-and-a-half weeks, and finally got back and started playing [again].

Trevor Hoffman? Hoffy is a guy that we do maintenance on every day. He usually comes in before batting practice and gets something done on his shoulder or elbow, depending on what needs more attention that day. He comes in every day. Hoffy hurt his shoulder after the '94 season, right after the strike. We developed this program because his shoulder was bothering him. Came back in '95 and pitched all year.

He probably had a slight rotator-cuff tear. But we bring him in, we knew he was pitching that night. We were ahead. He comes in like the fourth inning. We do an ultrasound stim on him and I go through his shoulder. He'd go from there into the shower, let the shower run on his shoulder; heat it up. He'd get dressed, come back into the training room; we will do some joint mobe and take him through PNF patterns. And then once we got done with patterns, he will go onto the counter, rub heat balm on him, go finish getting dressed; he'd stretch, go out to the bullpen and he'd be out there in the eighth just in time to warm up as we needed him to get ready to come in the game. Everything was planned based on how the game was going, and when he needed to be out in the bullpen to get himself ready.

He also had another rotator-cuff problem that was debrided. Debrided? They go in with a scope, and they look at frayed ends. They clean everything up. He also had a problem with his AC joint. Well, they did the surgery after the 2002 season. We rehabbed him all winter. Came into spring training and he still couldn't throw. Then we found out it was his AC joint. So they did a Mumford procedure on his AC joint, where they took off about two centimeters of the clavicle to help that joint function properly.

We rehabbed him all year. He pitched a couple of times at the end of the year, and then came back the following year to continue his quest for the saves' title. We knew, after he had that surgery, we needed to be able to get him to that point where he was able to do manual patterns. If he couldn't do the manual patterns, then he certainly wouldn't be able to go out and throw. We had to work until we could get him back up to that point, and now our program has developed a little more with new machinery. He will get a twenty-minute HIVAMAT® treatment—a machine—which is a vibration-type therapy that we started using the last two years. We'll do an ultrasound stim combination on his shoulder and on his elbow, which is another ten minutes. So we are working thirty minutes already, and then I will do deep tissue on his shoulder and elbow, which takes another ten minutes or so. Then he will go into the shower, come back, and we will do joint mobe. He goes and gets his hot stuff on.

The problem here is we don't have a tunnel over to the bullpen, so he's got to be ready to go by the top of the eighth so he can run across the field between innings and get to the bullpen. Otherwise he gets stuck in the dugout. There is no tunnel to get there. At Qualcomm [Stadium], we had a tunnel that could go all the way underneath the stands and he could go out whenever he was ready. Now we have to time it.

I've watched the way we take care of our players evolve from when only two athletic trainers were our entire staff to adding a strength and a conditioning coach. We've had a couple of chiropractors come in part-time to help us out. Now we have a full-time massage therapist, Kelly, who is another pair of hands in the training room that can get to players we can't always get to. She can take care of guys that have tightness—lower back or hamstring tightness—guys that we normally wouldn't be able to get to 'cause we're taking care of guys that are injured, or pitchers that need daily maintenance. She actually works on quite a few of our starters that aren't hurt.

Back when I started back in the eighties, and even before that, players would come into spring training and that's what it was: "Spring training. Let's get our bodies ready to play this season." Players can't afford to do that now. They've got to come into spring training in shape, ready to go, and then they fine-tune their baseball skills to get ready to go for the season.

If you look at the way players' salaries have risen, the players have understood how important it is for them. There's money to be made out there. They know that if they get on a real good off-season conditioning program, and they get their bodies in the best shape that they possibly can to withstand the grind that we go through for seven months of the season, they're going to be better off in the long run. And that's kind of where our philosophy comes in: We feel like if there's something that we can do to make them feel better on the field, they've got a chance to perform better. If they perform better, they are going to be paid more money.

Nutrition is extremely important. These guys are burning a lot of carbohydrates out there, so we make sure that they get a lot of carbohydrates. We always get in arguments with the high-protein diets. There are certain times when you need a lot of protein, or extra protein, in the off-season when you're working out trying to build muscle tissue. During the season, we want to make sure that we get their energy levels peaked at the time when they go out on the field, and not having them eat something that's going to bog them down and make them feel sluggish: the chips and cookies and candy and crap that they might eat. Try to have light meal—pasta, salad—that their body will be able to turn over into fuel fairly quickly.

Electrolytes are pretty important. We were just in Texas. We lucked out because it was only like 85 to 90 degrees, with only 40-percent humidity. It could have easily been 90 degrees, with 90-percent humidity. Our guys would have wilted in that. Some positions are more susceptible than others—the catcher with all his gear on. It's hot enough without the gear on. You put that gear on, his body temperature is going to go up. The guys drink an electrolyte drink during the game, along with water. We try to get a mixture so they are not increasing their sugar levels too much.

How can they enhance their performance? Legally, or illegally? I'm not going into that.

*   *   *   *   *

RON JACKSON

Hitting Coach, Round Rock Express

In his ten-year playing career, Jackson compiled a .259 batting average, 56 home runs, and 342 RBIs. Since retiring as a ballplayer, 54-year-old Papa Jack has had a twenty-year career as a minor- and major-league hitting coach, including stints with the Chicago White Sox, Milwaukee Brewers, and the Boston Red Sox.

I interviewed Jackson twice: first when he was the hitting coach for the Red Sox, and later as the hitting coach for the minor-league Round Rock Express. On the day of our first interview, the Red Sox were batting .339 during an eleven-game winning streak. We sat in the stands at Fenway Park, on the first-base side.

*   *   *   *   *

Back in Birmingham, Alabama, everybody called me "Pops" because I looked like my dad a lot. When my first kid was born, Nolan Ryan said,

"You're Papa Jack now." I was twenty-four. It stuck, and everybody started calling me Papa Jack after that.

I'm from a family of fourteen. I learned my work ethic from my dad back in Birmingham. My dad was a brick mason. We would lay bricks and help him, and when it came time on Saturdays, he would let us get off at one o'clock to go play baseball. I was seven, eight years old. He had one of my brothers take us and drop us off, and then he would come and watch the game.

I always said that I couldn't play forever, so when I was sitting I started watching the good hitters and I started watching the bad hitters to see what they were doing. All the good hitters are doing the same things, and the bad hitters are doing the same things, so I started picking up on a few little pointers here and there. And I always wanted to be a major-league hitting coach once I retired.

I was working in the front office with the California Angels in 1986, and Larry Himes, the general manager of the White Sox, called me up and said, "I would like for you to be the minor-league hitting coach in Triple-A." I said, "I don't have any experience with anything like that." He said, "I'm looking for good people willing to grow with me," and I said, "What kind of money are you paying?" He told me about the money. It's like $18,000 at that time. No way I could take that, but I found that's what the minor league's coaches were getting. I couldn't believe it was that that low, but it worked for me, and so I ended up coaching. That's where I started.

Years later, [Boston's General Manager] Theo Epstein and [manager] Grady Little called to say, "We want to hire you to be our hitting coach. We don't need an interview. We heard nothing but good things about you." We've led the league in hitting three years in a row since I've been here, and the year before last we led all of baseball in everything almost.

I think the thing is that I learned how to get everything I can out of each these guys. The biggest thing that Theo wanted me to do is make sure I would be there for the players. In the past, I heard rumors that some of the coaches weren't there for the players. You know, they're playing cards or playing golf, or whatever. You're tired when you get to the ballpark. I feel like it really takes a lot away from the players when you do that.

I remember in Triple-A, we didn't have a batting cage, so I had to do my extra work out on the field. I used to do soft toss on the field to players every day. If you wanted, I was there. I always said to myself that I'll never have a player waiting on me to come down to the cage to do extra work. I beat them there every time. I've made it a point to do that.

You know, back in the day, our hitting coaches really weren't there working like we work now. I have what I call a "maintenance program." Each and every one of these guys come out, they do their soft toss, hit off the tee before batting practice. That's when I do my teaching down by the cage, like between three thirty and four o'clock. Then we take them out to batting practice. I don't like teaching when they're taking batting practice. I may say a couple of words here and there—"You're not loading up," or whatever—but that's their time. They want to shine; they want to show everybody what they've got. But they do most of their work underneath, in the cage.

Back in the day, I didn't get that opportunity to do that type of stuff. I didn't have coaches that give you soft toss every day to keep your game intact. Plus, I didn't know some of the stuff I know now. I didn't know anything about loading up. Loading up is getting ready to hit. Everything you do, you got to go back before you go forward. What I mean by that is when you shoot a basketball, you go back before you go forward. When you're getting ready to backhand a tennis ball, you go back before you go forward. See, when I was hitting, I used to just go attack the ball. But you've got to load up, like getting ready to hit somebody. Same thing with the hitter and the pitcher: you've got to be loading up, getting ready to hit. I used to get out front and didn't load up like I should have—get that rotation of the hip and come out like a rubber band. That's where you get your power from.

[Soft toss] slows everything down. The player can see where his hands are going; you can see if he's got the right route through the baseball. You're going to see if he's standing inside the baseball. Sometimes when everything is going real fast, you can't pick that up. That's big for me: teaching guys how to get that right route through the baseball. If the head [of the bat] comes through first, you're going to hook it foul. But if the knob comes through first and then you extend through the zone, everything's working out front.

There's a lot of absolutes in hitting. When the front foot hits the ground, everybody should be in the same position. I don't care if you hold your hands up high, or if you hold your hands down low, or if you hold your hands back, or whatever. Once the front foot hits the ground, everybody is pretty much the same. And when you make contact, everybody is pretty much the same. But what I noticed with some of the bad hitters is they aren't doing that. They're not getting their foot down in time enough. They're hitting and swinging at the same time. You can't wait till the ball gets halfway. When that pitcher is turning his behind to you, you should be turning your behind to him. I would rather for you to be early than late.

When that pitcher is on the mound, you want to stay focused. It's in a cocoon; you're in a tunnel vision. Keep your head on the baseball. That's a very big key. Practice that. Do it every time. Don't try to watch and see how far you hit the ball; just keep your head down and make contact first. I think with a lot of kids they see a Reggie Jackson or Dave Ortiz or Jason Varitek—they see the beginning and they see the end. They don't see what happened in between. The most important part of it is what happened on contact. They don't see what got 'em there. Load up and then down through the baseball. Once you get that little rotation of your wrist, oh, the ball is gone. *Wham!*

Watch the pitcher warming up. They've got a little window there where they've got to release the baseball. You want to look in that area. You pick the baseball up there. When you get to home plate, you pick up something on his uniform; like his uniform shirt. You don't look him straight in the eye. You soft focus, you know what I mean. You then look in that little window where he's going to release the baseball. You're going to lose that baseball for a second, and then you are going to pick it up again. You think you can just follow that ball all the way when it's that quick? It gets here, *boom*, then you pick it up quick. All your good hitters see the ball longer than everybody else. They load up early but they let the ball travel longer. Guys like Manny Ramirez, David Ortiz—they can hit the ball to all fields because they see the ball longer.

And we teach [hitting the ball] gap to gap. That kind of enables you to stay on the baseball longer. We don't think about pulling. Once you start playing with only 25 percent of the field, that's what that pitcher wants you to do. Your job is to get that guy in from third base and let the next guy do his job instead of trying to hit a three-run home run. There's a big hole up the middle. Be thinking up the middle. The thing we're trying to do is hit the ball as hard as we can through the infield. No matter where it goes after that, we don't care, but we're going to make sure we see the ball longer than everybody else. That's what makes you a good hitter.

We can sit here and talk about it. We can do it in batting practice. We can say we're going to get a guy in from third base. You've got to make the commitment to do it. That's what these guys are doing now. They've made the commitment to do that. When you get a man on third base, drive the ball to straightaway centerfield. Think up the middle; not to pull. That's going to make you stay on the baseball and not get fooled. You're going to hit the ball hard somewhere. That's the only thing I am trying to do. Sit with me, and I will make them hit the ball up the middle.

I love the word "adjust." I never talk to my guys about "changing," okay. One of the reasons is that change is negative. When you're working with a guy, never say, "Hey, we're going to change this." Say, "We're going to make some adjustments." An adjustment is not negative. I tell them: "You got to make adjustments when you're at A-ball, Double-A, Triple-A, the big leagues, because the pitchers are going to find a way to get you out." You've got to continue to make adjustments. All these players here work every day to make some little adjustments.

It's repetition, over and over again. It's muscle memory, over and over again. This game will humble you so quick. You think you've got it, but you don't have it. Batting practice prepares you to keep it. I've seen a lot of guys who are like, "I got it; I got it; I got it," and the next thing you know, they don't have it.

The Red Sox did not renew Jackson's contract after the 2006 season. We met up again while his new team was on the road. We sat in a parking lot, near the clubhouse.

Right now, I'm with the Houston Astros' Triple-A team, the Round Rock Express. It's my first year. Nolan Ryan is part owner of the ball club, and one reason why I picked this team out of other teams that were calling me is Ryan and I played together for the California Angels. I had a few other big league teams call me, like the Chicago Cubs, the Oakland A's, and even the Colorado Rockies, but they ended up going in another direction. I also picked this team here because I coached under Phil Garner in the Milwaukee organization for a good little while.

We got a lot of ballplayers that are trying to make themselves better. I can't sit around here and say I'm helping them try to get back to the big leagues. No, my job down here is to make these guys better; to help out the major-league club up there. And by doing that, I will get back to the big leagues some day, but that's not a worry for me. I don't want the big league guy looking over his shoulder thinking that I want a job, you know. I just want to do a good job down here.

I remember Phil Garner mentioned to me one time when I was in the minor leagues with him, "It's unfortunate that you guys in the minor leagues don't get enough credit because you guys do a lot in getting guys up to the big leagues and making us look good." So that's just the way it is. That stuck in my mind. I'm not looking for any credit. All I want to do is help the organization win on the big league level. That's what it is all about: trying to get them to the World Series and get that ring again. I have mine with the Boston Red Sox.

The talent is different [down here]. A lot of these guys are not as consistent as the guys up in the big leagues. The difference is that in the big leagues the guys make the commitment to stay within themselves all the time, and guys here are inconsistent when it comes to that. You might tell them that for a week or so, and all of a sudden they go back to their old ways. But it's not that big of a difference, to be honest with you, because they're all human and they all have needs. Guys like David Ortiz and Manny Ramirez and Varitek, all the way down to Coco Crisp—they all need help; they're human. Sometimes we forget that because they make a lot of money. You know, we could talk about anything. You're not just only a hitting coach, you got to be a people person. You got to be there for them no matter what.

My biggest thing here as a hitting coach is I try to manage it just like I did in the big leagues. That's just the way I teach, no matter whether it's A-ball, Double-A, Triple-A, or the major leagues. The only way I can help them is to spend time with them. They get to know me. I did the same thing up in the big leagues with the Boston Red Sox.

I have an edge as a coach over maybe another guy coming up from

Double-A or A-ball. You know, I earned that. In spring training, everybody says, "That's Ron Jackson, a world champion batting coach in Boston, and they broke all kind of records. This guy's got to know something." So, they pick your mind, and it means a lot to them.

You know what? I learned that it doesn't matter what you do in the big leagues these days. It's not about your talent anymore as much it should be. I am disappointed by what happened to me. Yeah; a little shocked. I miss being around the players, and just mingling. But I've got to go on. I can't live on it.

You know, if you interview Johnny Damon, he'll tell you who dragged him down to the cage against the Yankees [after the fourth game of the 2004 American League Championship Series]. He and [Mark] Bellhorn were struggling. We won the first game back at home and Bellhorn and Damon didn't hit at all. I couldn't sleep at night. When they struggle, I struggle. When they hurt, I hurt. When they don't get a hit, I feel I didn't get a hit. I don't give a dog if you struggle 0 for 50, I'm still there.

So we got to New York. I talked to Ellis Burks. He said, "What you need, Papa Jack?" I said, "I need to get Damon and Bellhorn off the card table and get their butts down to the cage because I know what they are doing wrong. They need to do a little early work. Will you help me out?" The rest of it is history: both of them hit. Johnny hit a grand slam and another home run. Bellhorn hit two home runs. But see, that's overlooked. I don't like to say I did it; I was just part of it. A lot of people never gave much credit to that. They don't know about it for one thing, you know what I mean? You ask Johnny Damon about it, he'll tell you. I got it on tape. I [was] going around to all the players videotaping, and asking them to say what it feels like beating the Yankees four straight and going to the World Series. I remember Johnny Damon saying, "Papa Jack, we wouldn't have won it without you. I want to thank you for dragging my butt down to the cage." I got that on camera. That means a lot to me.

I have been here before. You know what? I feel like I'm here to give back, you know. It's all about making sure you go back before you go forward. Sometimes in life you got to go back to understand where you came from before you go forward. I'm here to help somebody else to get to the big leagues. I'm not being selfish. You can't worry about trying to get back to the big leagues. You're disappointed, but you can't take it personally. You've got to believe in yourself and move on. I believe I didn't do anything to get fired, you know what I mean? I can't let anybody else tell me what I didn't accomplish there in Boston. I feel good. Nobody can take that away from me. We will always have that reunion—bringing people back in and reliving it. But I don't give a dog about the second one, third one, fourth one. That first one, after eighty-six years, means so much. I was there.

*   *   *   *   *

STEVE LIDDLE

Bench Coach, Minnesota Twins

Courtesy of Minnesota Twins

Liddle played seven years in the farm systems of the Angels and the Twins. He later became a minor league coach and manager in the Twins' organization and was a hitting coach for the Angels' Triple-A team. He has been the Twins' bench coach under manager Ron Gardenhire since 2002.

*   *   *   *   *

I grew up on the outskirts of Nashville, Tennessee. I am forty-eight years old.

My name is Steve Liddle, and I have been Ron Gardenhire's bench coach for the entire six years that he has been the manager here in Minnesota. We have had quite a run.

My job as a bench coach, I guess if you looked at it from a military standpoint, would be information officer. I have to make sure that I can gather as much information as I possibly can, and let Ron and the other coaches have an idea about what the other teams are doing.

We have an advance scout who goes out and sees teams prior to us playing them. He tries to sees their starting pitchers that are going to be facing us, and he will e-mail me a report about how to play players, how to pitch certain players, where their holes are, what their tendencies are, what their pitchers are going to try to do to our hitters, and who is hot and who is not; if they have any trick plays, their base-running strategies, their bunt defenses, their first and third defenses, any type of fancy pick-off plays that they might use, and how they play the game.

We are fortunate that our advance scout knows the game of baseball. I don't want any statistics from him. I want him to watch what they are doing. I don't care what percentage of strikes are thrown or what they are doing with two outs. I want him to watch the game and see if he can pick up any idiosyncrasies because we play tendencies a lot.

When we get to our first game of the series, I print out the information and give it to the pitching coach and the hitting coach. We put that together with the video that we have, and we give ourselves a plan of attack. We want the defense and the pitchers to be on the same page so that we are pitching and playing people the same way. We want our hitters to have an idea of what pitchers are going to do to them not only in certain situation but in certain pitch counts. You want to give your players as much information as they can handle; you don't want to overload them. They still have to go out and play the game. We have been blessed here in Minnesota to have players with the ability to execute a plan.

It is important that I try to keep Ron appraised of everything that is going on. That way, when the game comes he will know what their bullpen does versus our bench, and what our bench does versus their bullpen in case of late inning adjustments. Good managers play the game a couple of innings ahead.

During the game, I try to steal signs. That's my job. I steal signs. I look at the dugout. So many things come from the dugout that never get to the third-base coach. A manager will give hot signs to coaches at first base that the third-base coach will never see. He will give a sign to a runner at second base that a coach will never see. Signs coming from the dugout might not be from the manager; it might be the trainer crossing his legs, or somebody else taking a hat off.

They try to steal our signs, and we try to pay attention if other teams have our signs. The White Sox had Joe Nossek for many years as a bench coach and believe me, my job got easier when he retired. Not to take away from anybody who is bench coaching now for any of the other teams, but he was something else. There was one occasion where he and I had the same set of signs, and we just smiled at each other.

You can only do so much with a set of signs. They've got to be complex yet simple, and you've got to be able to change them. If you're sitting in the dugout, most of the signs are from the neck up. We have certain players who have had a tough time with signs. It is up to the coaches to spend a little more extra time with those guys. We have to execute the fundamentals to win up here. We don't have guys who are just going to hit the ball over the fence every night. We have some guys with power, but our game is to execute the fundamentals—hit and run, bunting people over—so it's very important that our players know what we are doing, and that everybody is on the same page. In any business, communication is the key. Your players' signs are a form of communication, so it is very important that the communication does not break down.

I also keep charts during the game of when they hit and run, when they pitch out, when they steal, what counts, how many outs. Ronnie lets me control the running game. I tell the pitcher when to throw over; when to pitch out. He delegates a lot of responsibility to his coaches. A lot of managers might not do that. I sit right beside him. We bounce things back and forth, and try to be prepared for anything that comes up.

I am the computer guy. We have a portable scanner on the road. We look at our spray charts and see where we need to play. We will scan that, copy it, and hand it out to each position player so that thy know where they should be when every hitter comes up.

Sometimes, during the game, I will go in and look at certain situations on a video, just to make sure that what we are seeing is really what's happening. Sometimes it's not the case. If a guy goes, "Steve, are those strikes he is swinging at?" The hitting coach may be somewhere else. I can get on the laptop during the game and look at that pitch, and then come back to the bench and say, "Yeah, those are strikes. He is just missing them."

I check the line-up card over and over making sure that it's printed out right. That's another thing that I do.

I am constantly on the stopwatch making sure our pitchers are getting the ball to our catchers in a timely manner so that the other teams, if they want to take the extra base, they've got to hit and run—they can't steal it. I think any time there is a pitch out and we get the runner out on a hit and run, that's a good feeling because you know you have gotten your team out of what could have been a tough predicament. Our pitchers do a great job of holding the runners and getting the ball to the catcher in a good time. The average runner can go from first base to second base in 3.35 seconds. It takes 2.00 seconds from the time the ball hits the catcher's glove to the time it reaches the second baseman's glove on the throw down, so your pitcher's only got 1.35 seconds to get the ball to home plate.

The speed of the game is what separates their ability to play. From high school to college to the minor leagues, the game gets faster, faster, faster. Then to play up here every night—to have the fundamentals to where you can do certain things at this speed, and do them well—that's what keeps you here. The guys that are really good, they have the ability to slow the game down between the ears. Everybody has the physical tools or they wouldn't be here. The guys that can handle the game mentally are the guys that move on. It's the same thing with us coaches. We have to be on an even keel daily. We can't have our ups and downs. You keep an even tempo on the bench. I think the players feed off Ron's style of aggressiveness. They know that he is a solid rock. You try not to let them see you sweat.

What we try to do is never forget what it's like to be a player. The good coaches don't forget because it's easy to blame things on players. You have to evaluate yourself as a coach, just like players are being evaluated. Am I doing the right thing? Did I give him all the information he needed to go out there and be successful? Did I hit him enough groundballs to make that play? What could have made him make that play, or understand that situation a little bit better?

Players need to be able to look to you for reassurance whenever they are faltering. If you don't let them see you sweat, and they know you are going to go down with the ship, then that gives them some piece of mind. We started off poorly last year and we started off poorly this year, and you didn't hear any yelling and screaming and berating from the manager. We all feed off of that. If he is not panicking, why should the rest of us panic?

Every day at work is a good day. I am very thankful to have my job. Only thirty people in the whole world have this job, and I am very fortunate. I didn't get to play in the major leagues. I got hurt, but I think people realized that I had a love for the game, a knowledge of the game, and more important, I had a feel for the game. I can anticipate certain things. I study the game and other managers' tendencies. Sometimes—a manager that used to be an infielder—he has a tendency to manage the game like he played. He might hit and run a little more than guys that were power hitters. For instance, Joe Torre manages the game differently in the play-offs than he does during the season. He is more aggressive in the playoffs. They hit and run more. They bunt more, when they might not bunt during the season.

I feel very fortunate to be in this organization. We have an organization that promotes from within. All of us, on this coaching staff, came from within. It's really a team-teaching type of deal. I mean, everybody's opinion is wanted and everybody's opinion is heard. It's not a one-man show. We have been with each other through battles. We have argued the game back and forth with each other, and it's really a unique situation where you can go to work and everybody wants to succeed, and still be very good friends. We love the game.

I don't aspire to manage. Ronnie says it's because I like being wrong and him taking the blame for it. If I make a mistake, if something doesn't happen right, or I give him the wrong advice and he goes with it, he gets the blame. I see how much non-baseball-related stuff he has to do, and I don't think I would enjoy that. I'm a realist.

I have a wife and three children, two boys that are twelve and eight, and a little girl that's five. I talk to all of them every day. Sometimes if I am gone for a long time, we will videoconference, and I can see them and they can see me. We homeschool our children during the off-season so that they can be with me full time. We have been very lucky so far. My wife and I both were schoolteachers. I just got stuck in this pro-ball thing; now my classroom is the baseball field.

I try to make up time that I miss with my children. Instead of having one house, we have two condos, in Tennessee and in Minnesota. We found that the two condos work for us. They are with me in Minnesota during the season, and during the off-season we go to our condo in Tennessee that is sitting empty, waiting on us. We got the three bikes in Tennessee, we got the three bikes in Minnesota; the pots and pans in Tennessee, the pots and pans in Minnesota. It's really a crazy life.

I have sheltered my children from this life. I don't want them to aspire to do this. I think it's a crapshoot. I want them to be more balanced in their education because that's going to take them a lot further than sports.

I tell you what, I don't see doing this more than five more years. If I do it more than five years, it will really surprise me. I really worry about my children more than anything else. My wife is a single parent for the most part during the season. I get to see them briefly in the mornings, and when I come home at night they are asleep. It's just not enough quality time. I don't think you can make up for that even though I am with them every day during the winter. You miss first steps; you miss teeth; you miss birthday parties, you miss funerals: you miss everything. There's a lot of sacrifices you make being a professional athlete. Money is not everything.

*   *   *   *   *

CHAPTER THREE

FIELD OF PLAY

JEROMY BURNITZ

Outfielder, Pittsburgh Pirates

Burnitz finished working in the indoor batting cages early on a Sunday morning. Sitting in front of his clubhouse locker and still wearing a sweat-drenched practice uniform, he talked to me about his life in baseball.

Courtesy of David B. Vernon

"I have to be straight and tell you that it's been very, very satisfying and rewarding, but it hasn't been fun," he said. "It's been hard. It's been very, very hard. I've had to push every single inch of the way. I've never showed up and been able to coast because if I tried it, I stunk. I had to really, really push to keep a job. I was pushing hard at all times, and it was never fun or easy. Satisfaction is a good word, and I think that with my personality type, that's all going to come after it's all over."

*   *   *   *   *

We're each different in why we're here. For me, doing it as long as I have, it just seems like it's all I ever did. I wouldn't know what else I would've done. I have no idea.

I'm thirty-seven years old. I've been married for like eight or nine years, and I have three kids. My life is at home. When they're with me during the season—which isn't often because I live in the West—it doesn't even cross my mind until I leave the house, then it's work. It's a basic eight-hour day job for the most part. It starts for me just like everybody else: when you leave the house; once you get in the car. It's basically a 24/7 job for seven-and-a-half months a year, throughout my whole adult life.

In trying to answer your question about what it's like, I honestly don't feel like the life is a whole heck of a lot different than most people's lives who are working people. There are outside circumstances that are different—things like fame, people knowing me on the street—that the normal person doesn't experience. And the money is different than most every other person. You know, a few things like that. But as far as what it was like, it was work.

It's like a hurry up and wait–type of job. You have to be somewhere, then you don't for an hour, and then you have to be somewhere, and then you don't. It's all a process leading up to the game. I get my uni on pretty much immediately. I like to be suited up. A lot of guys will hang out in their clothes or whatever, and then practice. Then a lot of dead time, hanging out in the clubhouse. Then batting practice. Team stretch. Team batting practice. If you have any problems, you have to deal with the training room. The whole treatment scene is a whole other story. For those guys it's constant. I didn't have to deal with that, thank goodness. I was lucky.

I've been lucky. I've been hurt only twice. I got hit in the hand. Broke it and missed a month. A lefty named Rosado. Another lefty, Billy Wagner, hit me two years ago and broke my hand; different hand. Cost me a month. That's my injury history.

I hit hardcore every single day of my career until these last couple years. Looking back, I'm not sure it was the right decision. But that's how I did it. I hit because I wanted to get better, but it's also because I enjoyed it. But now I can't do it; there's no need to do it anymore. It doesn't make me any better at this point. I love doing it. It's my favorite part of my job; even the practice. I like to swing the bat. It's always been my gig. That's why I hit. That's how I went about it. I would show up and really practice my craft every single day of my whole career. I just got older and I knew I couldn't do it anymore in order to stay being an everyday player. It was wearing me out. This is who I am.

I never cared at all who was pitching. I knew who they were and I was conscious of it, but I didn't care. I was worried about feeling good with the bat in my hand, and getting a good pitch to hit. I didn't care who it was and what their reputation was. Maybe I could've been a different player with different preparation. I showed up and hit. The good ones kicked your ass no matter what. So it doesn't matter. I'm not really into caring what he's throwing. I'm just watching him throw the ball and watching the guy's on my team hit. That's it. Nothing special. I'm just waiting my turn, honestly.

When I walk up to the plate, my plan is simple: I look right at them in the eyes just until he gets to where his arm comes up, and your eyes shift to the release point. I'm just looking for a good pitch in the strike zone to take my best swing at. That's about it. Hit the ball on a line drive through the middle. That's what I'd like to do. That's the idea. Once again: very, very simple. All that simplicity has come from years and years of overanalyzing. It's a full-circle type of philosophy. You start out as a kid: see it, hit it. Then as you progress, you go through the whole analytical stage. It's all in good faith. You're trying to get better with the mechanical aspects, trying this and trying that. Now, 100 percent of my focus is only about the focus itself. Everything I'm trying to do now is bring all my energy and focus to bear down on the baseball. Just like a kid. You progress, just like we all do—in a big circle.

I use the old-school Louisville Slugger. My bat has changed two or three times over the years, but most of the time ash, which is the old-school bat. I like the way it flexed, the way it felt better. I could feel the flex. I swing a 33.5-inch, 31-ounce T141. I swung a 34, 32, then I went to 34, 31-ounce bats. The sound is definitely a big part of it. Hitting the ball good and really pure has its own sound. That's another reason I like ash bats, because I always thought they sounded a little louder.

It's the same in any kind of ball-striking sport, for me. Where the joy comes from is all about the pureness of trying to hit it right. I like to hit, but the end-all is the feeling of when the ball is hit perfect—just like a golf shot if you smoke one right down the middle of the fairway with your best drive. That's the physical feeling. What that feels like is the same in any sport: same with a tennis racket, same with any ball-striking sport. What that feels like is what it's all about. That's what I'm after. A home run is the one that is the ultimate. But the fact is if you strike it, it feels the same on a home run as it does when you strike it square on a low liner. That feeling is indistinguishable to me.

I'm a guy who made my whole living in this game off the home run. That's what I did. But that's not what I always wanted to do. I would've rather hit the ball harder more often than fewer and farther between.

I try as often as I can to not wear gloves. Lately, I haven't been at all but it just hurts too much. About the third, fourth at-bat you can just feel it. That's just *my* hands; most guys can take it. Now I don't take very many practice swings or nothing. I just go up in the game and not take a bunch of swings. You have to realize I'm an old guy, and I'm in that stretch in my life and my career where I realize it's not going to make or break me to try and relax. I've tried every angle and kind of done always the same shit, no matter what.

For me, there was never any coasting. I tried with every ounce of everything I had every single day. Sometimes you taste success, and some of us can't deal with it at this level. Success brings on a whole other thing—not necessarily a problem—but pressure, money, expectations upon yourself, and what other people put on. They expect you to be good all the time. Just to be good one year means you're capable, but it damn sure don't mean you'll be great the next year, too. You've gotta keep pushing with all your might to do that, or at least I did. Every good year I had I was trying so hard to be that good or better the next year. At the highest competitive level of the game that is not an easy task. This is the highest; there's no level above it. There's only going to be a few people with abilities at these highest levels that it's easy for them, whether they are athletes or in the top of any field that you can think of. Therefore, in order to compete at the highest level, you have to get after it.

It's been my whole life—my *whole* life. It means everything. It's all I've ever done from a young man to now, and it's given me the opportunity to not have to have any other type of job in my life. When I'm done, honestly, I don't want to work at all. So it's hard to describe what it means. Guys wear that shirt BASEBALL IS LIFE. It pounds whole life lessons as many as three or four times a day with the at-bats and mistakes and successes. It's so repetitive that it keeps pounding, even for guys who consider themselves slow learners. I consider myself a Southern slow learner. I've felt like my ability—what I hope is a good job to just be a man, a father, a husband—has all come from this job. I'm not sure there are too many other things I could've done with my life that would've pressed upon the value of how to go about things as this job did. It's everything.

The financial part of it, you can't leave that out. For some reason we have problems talking about the money. I find it amusing, even though every dime we make is in the fucking paper. I understand that I walked into an absolute lucky situation. I realize it isn't because I'm a special guy or a good person. I was a ballplayer, and ballplayers make money. To me that has a huge benefit in a society where it matters. It matters. Period. It makes life better, and I plan on taking what it gave me and enjoying it, hopefully using the time to do a good job with my kids. I consider *that* my next job: to try to do it right. I'm going to have to dedicate as much time as I gave to this to them, which I've never been able to do before because of the nature of the work—"Good-bye. See you later, Dad." You're not part of it. I understand it's not going to be easy, the same way this wasn't. It's not, "Oh, I have all the time in the world." It doesn't work like that. It's like what we were talking about: coasting. There's no doubt I could go home and coast, but if I want to look up five or six years from now and I'm hanging out with my kids, and they're like being nice to me and they are good kids, well, I bet I didn't coast. If I coast, I'm probably going to see them, and they'd be a smart-ass or rude, or whatever, and that would be my fault. That's how I'm looking at it.

I always made decent grades. I was fairly insecure. I felt like sometimes I was a little mean as a younger man. I wasn't into talking to people that much. I'm still not into groups or meeting new people for the most part. I was like that as a kid. That's carried over. But basically everything went pretty good for me. My family's together—not too close-knit late in life, but still no problems; but a together family for my whole life.

I was really lucky, man. I had pretty much no issues, just normal. Came up doing sports, and ended up rolling with baseball, and kept going and going. It's unbelievable it's been this long; it's hard to believe. When you've been in it this long, it's rare. You look around. There's maybe three or four guys in here who've been around like this. It's different when you're in your twenties. It changes as time goes on. It's all I ever knew, and it's all I ever done.

Five or six years ago, I couldn't sit here and have this conversation because I was still at my peak—trying to get there and stay there. Now, all of a sudden, you did it and it's like, wow, there's something about to happen next. But it's been a great run; a great life. I did keep it simple. I was lucky like that. I kept it very, very simple. It was a daily grind for me. I didn't have to deal with much of the outside crap, being hurt. I maybe didn't let myself get as good as maybe I had the ability to get, not because I didn't want to, just 'cause God only knows why.

The Pirates declined their $6 million option on Burnitz after the 2006 season and bought out his contract for a reported $700,000. Burnitz announced his retirement in March 2007, after fourteen years in the major leagues. He was a lifetime .253 hitter with 315 home runs and 981 RBIs in 1,694 games.

* * * * *

DOUG MANSOLINO

Third Base Coach, Houston Astros

Courtesy of Houston Astros

Mansolino and I talked in the Astros' clubhouse before a night game against the Milwaukee Brewers.

"I have little reminders to myself: let the game come to you. For example, we haven't scored runs in like four or five days. About the sixth day, all of a sudden, I'm going to make something happen. I'm going to force the envelope today. Don't get caught in this trap. You will end up getting your ass burnt because you went to the game and the game will chew you out and swallow you whole. I mean, there isn't nothing left of you. A lot of young guys get wrapped up in that. They think they are going to make the difference. No. You let it come to you."

*   *   *   *   *

I was coaching at a college, and Jim Lefebvre, who at the time was the farm director for the Giants, flew into southern California where I was working. I didn't know Jimmy from you. We talked a little bit about base-ball, and he asked me if I would be interested in being the Giants' roving infield instructor, which means basically oversee all the infielders in the entire organization. You go from affiliate to affiliate and you work with them.

I said I would be interested. However, I also told him that even though I was an assistant coach I didn't want to go to spring training because spring training was right in the middle of my season. He said he would get back in touch with me. Sure enough, he called me that night and said he was going to manage the Triple-A club and be the farm director at the same time, "So I was wondering if you would be my third-base coach and handle all my defense." That was in 1985, with the Phoenix Giants. I made like eighty-five-hundred dollars for the whole year to coach third base in Triple-A, and that didn't include my living expenses. We didn't make any money.

My first big league job was '92 with the Chicago White Sox. Got fired after the '96 season, and took a job in '97 with the Mets managing one of their [minor-league] clubs. That winter, the phone rings. I pick it up. It's numbnuts. [Mansolino points in the direction of the Astros' manager's office.] "Phil Garner? What the hell? Last time I talked to you, I had my hands around your throat." And I did. The White Sox had this deal going on [with the Milwaukee Brewers] for like six years. I mean, we were like unbelievable rivals. We were fighting every other series.

There is a huge fight in '93. We were playing them in old County Stadium. I was coaching first that year. I'm standing there at first. They hit Robin Ventura. They had hit us all year. We never retaliated. We were good; they were shitty, to be honest with you, but we never retaliated. Gene Lamont was the manager at the time. Gene had already been thrown out of this game, so I am standing there at first and they hit Robin. [The Brewers' John] Jaha leads off the next the next inning and we drilled Jaha. JJ comes down to first like a pro, nothing happened. So the next half inning, I go out to first and I am talking to JJ. He is playing first. And JJ goes, "Shit, Manso." I said, "JJ, you know somebody is going to get it sooner or later. Hell you hit us like six times this year." I've known JJ a lot of years. Good guy. No problem. All of a sudden, I hear some fucking obscenity, and it's like coming from behind me, in their dugout. I turn around and I look. And it's Garner standing in the dugout. He's looking right at me, and I'm reading his lips. I go, "Are you talking to me?" I start walking a little closer. He gets on the next step and he gets more animated, and I get a little closer and he gets on the next step, and off I go. About the time I got my hands on his throat, I got the living shit kicked out of me. I was the only guy in their dugout—me against the Milwaukee Brewers. All hell broke loose. So I got thrown out of that game and he didn't. And we got into more fights after that.

Anyways, then the phone call. When he called, I said, "You've got to be shitting me." He goes, "I have a position open. Do you want to go to work for me?" I said, "I would love it." He goes. "Don't get too happy until you find out what the Brewers pay because they don't pay shit." So, anyways, off I went. Coached third for him, and have been with him basically ever since.

He got fired halfway through the season in '99. I stayed and coached third. He got the job at Detroit, called me, and I went there. I was coaching third the first year. Next year, he asked me if I would be his bench coach. I told him no. And he goes, "I got to find a bench coach." I said, "I ain't doing that job. That's a stupid job."

Coaching third base, you have to show up for every pitch. I mean there could be nobody on base. If a guy shoots one down the right field line, I've got to make a decision. I've got to pick this guy up. That's what I like about it. I think it's the closest from a coaching perspective that you get to still being a player. I mean, like tonight, I've got to be locked in when [Craig] Biggio hits a ball down the right field line. I've got to make a decision, right now.

Third base is about angles too. For example, if you've got a guy on first, you want to go down behind the third-base bag because after the ball is hit to right field—as he's running—he can look directly at you. That angle helps you see runner and ball at the same time. I got ball and player in front of me. With a guy on second, you will see a lot of times we are down the line closer to home plate. I get way down there a lot of times, more so than anything, because the farther I get down, the farther I can bring him if I have to stop him. The closer I am to that base, my decision process is shorter, because once he gets to me I can't stop him. When a runner runs through your signals then you probably did something wrong. This guy is coming around, and all of a sudden I throw my hands up; too late.

There's a lot of old rules in baseball: Don't make the first out at third. Don't make the first out at the plate. Don't make the third out at third. You go by them rules to some degree, but there's a lot of times you can't preset your mind. You can't say, "Well, this guy isn't going nowhere because you don't make the first out at home plate." I mean, if you do that, then all of a sudden a guy kicks the ball. You've already made up your mind; you've stopped the guy. What a lot of people don't understand is—especially the fans—anytime a ball is in front of the runner, he is on his own. He isn't looking at me. For example, let's say a guy hits the ball in left center. There is no way that I can have an angle and see runner and ball at the same time. I can't do that. The runner sees the ball and he is a better coach than I am because he knows where the ball is. He knows how hard he is running. He knows where he is out on the field. Anytime there is a ball in front of a runner, you will see us—the base coaches—will do nothing. We just stand there and watch, and see what's going to happen. The only time we help guys is when the ball is behind them.

I am a firm believer that if you have bad base runners, you're a bad third base coach. If you have good base runners, you are a good third base coach, period. It's cut and dry. I don't think there is gray. It's black and white. A good base runner checks his outfield. They got to show up for every pitch, even when they are on the bases. They don't all do that, so you will see us do a lot of reminding: freeze on a line drive; check your outfield; all kinds of different stuff. I will tell him that the shortstop is playing right behind him, or the shortstop is off. These are all reminders.

I preach you have to show up for every pitch. For example, if the pitcher throws 120 pitches in a game, and you show up for 118, that's pretty damn good. Well, there's two pitches you didn't show up for that you might have got a bad jump on that ended up being hit that should have been outs. It's very difficult to show up for every pitch. These guys got family problems; they ain't hitting; you got the press. There's a million problems out there. Very hard to do. Very few people can do it.

A lot of times, a manager will have signs. He will have going on contact, make it go through. He will have all kinds of stuff. We relay that, "Listen, we are going on contact, or make the ball go through the infield." If, for example, the infield's in, I will tell the guy at third what he is doing. I have the sign for the guy at the second, so he knows what *this* guy is doing. So for example, *this* guy is going on contact, he knows the ball's on the ground, he is coming. If he knows this guy is making the ball go through, he isn't going to come with the ball on the ground. There are a lot things going on.

Sometimes the manager doesn't signal. That's the beauty of me being with him for so many years. This is my eighth year as a third-base coach in the big leagues. I know what he's thinking even though he doesn't give me anything. I mean there are a lot of things going on in a very, very short time. There's so much information going on, it's unbelievable.

There is a little saying: If you send a guy and he is safe, you are supposed to send him; if you send a guy and he is out, you shouldn't have sent him. The best description that I have ever heard is we are like air traffic controllers. How many hundreds of thousands of safe landings are there a week? You ever pick up the paper and say this is a guy that did a nice landing? But as soon as one goes down, it's on the front page for weeks, okay? But they never talk about all the safe ones because they are supposed to be safe. It's kind of the same deal. On the road, if he's out on a close play, the fans will be cheering. At home, they are booing. You got to have thick skin.

Let's say we have a guy with a tender hamstring. Fans don't know that. So now the ball is hit and he is on second base, and you stop him. Damn, this guy scored eight out of ten times all year long. They see I stopped him. Well, there is a reason why I stopped him: it's that tender hamstring, knee problem, or lower back pain. The fans don't know that. There's a lot of little things there.

Then again, these guys are trying to make to a living, all right? And the only way they make a living is by putting up numbers. Period. Bottom line: It's a game of numbers. More numbers for them, more money. So there is a fine line too. I mean, "I cost this guy an RBI. Do I take a shot?" I don't want to cost this guy an RBI either, and this guy knows what's going on. See what I mean? So there's a lot of things that factor in the decisions; not only the wins and loses. Like last night, it was 11–2. I was out there thinking, "Okay, this guy is on second. If it's going to be close, I might be taking a shot here because at 11–2, if it's close, you usually stop him. It's going to be bang-bang. But then I said to myself, "You know what? Hell, he needs the RBI. There's two out. Hell with it, he's going." I said to myself, "I don't give a shit, he's going." Now, they wanted to jump my ass and fight over it because this guy needs the RBI. His numbers go up. See what I mean? If it's the pitcher hitting it, I don't care about the RBI. Hell, he's making a living—and this is cold—I'm stopping the guy. All this stuff happens like that.

If a third base coach never gets a guy thrown out, he is a horseshit third base coach because he is not aggressive. Probably 99 percent of the time with two outs, the guy will be sent home. Most of the guys are thrown out with two outs. You'll see a lot of third-base coaches almost on autopilot with two outs. Now, grant you, if you are down by eight runs and it's a one hop to the left fielder, you're probably not sending the guy. I mean, that would just be stupid because he'll probably get thrown out. A lot of times you're sending a guy, you know he is going to be out. You know that if he catches the ball, executes a throw, this guy catches it, makes a decent tag, he's out. Now, this guy could bobble it, this guy could throw it just off the base, the ball could hit the ground, and it could skip by the catcher. A lot of things can happen.

There's a lot of different things that happen so fast in the course of the game. I will check the score; I will know the situation; I will see if we got someone throwing in the bullpen. I know how they charge the ball. I know how they throw if they've got to move a step to the left versus if they come straight in; I know how accurate they are; I know what kind of release they've got. Do they have a great arm but take a long time to release it? All that factors in. It happens like that. You kind of do your homework prior to that, you know, but then again there's times, too, where you get your ass burnt.

You can't think that you determine the outcome of a game. If you have that attitude as a third-base coach, you will get burnt. You've got to let the game come to you; you can't go to it. I remember Larry Bowa—when I was in Detroit—he was coaching third for Seattle. A close game: they were down by one. He gambled; he chose to send the guy with less than two outs. The next day he said, "It's my fault; shouldn't have sent him. I was trying to make something happen. We haven't been scoring runs." He's *trying to make something happen.* That's Bowa trying to go to the game. It will eat your ass. It happens to all of us. We ended up throwing the guy out.

You never make a decision with the idea that, well, he will probably make a bad throw. Maybe in high school you could make the decision—this guy is probably going to make a bad throw and they ain't going to catch it—but not here. They are too good. They *will* make a good throw, and they *are* going to catch it. That's what they get paid for. That's why they are in the big leagues. Toughest part, to be honest with you, is that every level you go up—high school, college, rookie ball, A-ball, Double-A, Triple-A, big leagues—every level the speed of the game changes. Guys run faster. Guys have better bat speed. Guys throw harder. The ball comes off the bat quicker. Guys cover more ground. Every level you go up, the speed of the game changes, and at this level this is as fast as it gets. When you first get up here as a coach—even though you might have *x* amount of years in Triple-A—you think, "I'm feel pretty good at it." All of a sudden, "Whoa. Big difference!" I mean, this level is unbelievably different. I guarantee, when I first started, there were times when I would think to myself, "I wonder if I can adjust to the speed at this level." Things are pretty fast. But the more you do it, you have the ability to make adjustments; you adapt.

My guys run the bases well; run hard; give me everything they've got. If I make a bad decision, it's my fault. It's not their fault. Even if a base runner does something bad, you never say he did anything bad. Never. Never. In other words, a guy's on second, a ball's hit, he forgets to check his outfield, and you can't send him. Remember, I am down the line. I've got runner and ball in front of me. Everybody else follows the ball. They don't see that the runner never looked where the outfielder was. I see that. So if a base runner does something bad, you never ever—this is just my opinion, some guys think different—say a guy did something stupid on the bases. I never say the guy shut it down before he got to third. I never say the guy was stuck. I might say to one of our coaches, "Dang, what is he looking at," but I will never say it in the press because when you start doing that, then your players won't trust you anymore. They don't give you everything they've got. I'll wear it: "My mistake." I will just wear it. I mean, as hard as I hate to say it, you've got to wear it. You can never point the finger even though his teammates know. You can never let the fans know, because to those fans that's their hero.

Mansolino left the Astros after the 2007 season and was later hired by the Philadelphia Phillies to be their minor-league infield coordinator.

*   *   *   *   *

ERIC BYRNES

Outfielder, Arizona Diamondbacks

I caught up with Byrnes in the visitor's dugout while the Diamondbacks were playing on the road. He was bantering with a female fan, and signing autographs for fans who were leaning over a railing, before he sat to talk about playing big league ball. "What fun am I having? Talking to fans; talking to players; talking shit to her. I think there is so much stress that goes along with the game, and so many expectations, and I think the only way to counteract that is by having fun; enjoying yourself in the process because if I sit back and worry about stuff, it just doesn't help. So, I mean, the biggest thing is just to, you know, just be yourself, enjoy what you are doing, and enjoy the ride as long as it lasts."

*   *   *   *   *

It's very, very simple. I mean, shoot, it's just really [about] trying to play the game as long as you can, and enjoying every minute of it. It's a grind because you constantly have to produce, you know. You're constantly measured by your next performance. If you don't stay on top of your game, it will wash you out quick. Each day, it's a battle to come out here and perform. If you can do one or two things to help your team win a game, you can continue to have a job. If you don't, the game can turn on you quickly.

Yeah, I collected autographs as a kid. I used to collect baseball cards and stuff. I enjoyed it and I understand where these kids and a lot of the fans are coming from. We are all people. Oftentimes, they will look up to us or look at us in a different light, but I think it's important to the fans to know that we are just exactly like them, and there is nothing different about us than them.

Facing Jason Schmidt today. Yeah, I will look at video. I looked at the last time I faced him; I looked at his last start; looked at maybe trying to pick up any sort of tendencies he has. I think the thing is—more than results— you don't actually look at it like, "Well, how did I do against him last time?" Oh for 4. That doesn't matter. If I have a good swing at a pitch that he threw, then you know, I'm not going to have a problem taking the same swing again; hopefully, catching it instead of popping it up.

Lead off? Yeah, I love it. I like when it's on me to get the team going; trying to jump-start the team; get us going right out of the gate. It's nice to have that responsibility. It's nice to be in charge of kind of rallying the troops.

Stealing? Yeah, love that too. I love playing the game. I love all facets of the game. I mean, maybe I'm not great at anything, but I consider myself to be pretty good at everything. Whether you're making a play in the out-field, or throwing a runner out, or stealing a base, or legging out an infield single, or drilling a ball in the gap, or hitting a home run, I mean for me that's what makes baseball fun. It can be something new every day. You go out there, and you get your fix; feeling that need to get out there. It's a rush. I have fun. I enjoy myself, and I'm passionate.

Why baseball? It's something that I was good at, and just kept playing; T-ball, Little League, wherever they could hide me—shortstop, second, third, catcher. I played every position except for first base. I played all different sports growing up: football, baseball, basketball, tennis; did karate. Baseball, I guess, was the one that I just kept playing, and ultimately got me a scholarship to college. It panned out to make a pretty good living for myself. I didn't become a good outfielder until probably my first or second year in the major leagues. I finally did stick to the outfield. I became a good outfielder, but it took a while. I love centerfield. You are freer. Ultimately, you are in charge. I like it a lot.

Everyone's always kind of looking ahead; looking to get to that next step. If you're at Triple-A, you want to get to the big leagues. If you are in the big leagues, and you are on the bench, you want to get into the starting lineup. And if you are in the starting lineup, and if you're playing well, all of a sudden, then you want to start playing at an All-Star caliber. And then once you get to that All-Star caliber, I imagine those guys want to become Hall of Famers. Me, I'm still trying to get to that All-Star caliber first, and then I will worry about the other stuff later.

The job? It's something that I prepared for my whole life. Yeah, it means a lot to me. I mean, I put a lot of time and energy into it. I'm not sure how many people working other jobs start to prepare, you know, at nine years old. So in that sense, you spend a lot of time, and a lot of effort, and lot of emotions are invested in it. But I think as the years have gone on I have kind of established myself a little bit in the major leagues. I had a lot of ups and had a lot of downs. I just kind of realized that it's a game—it's still the same game I played when I was nine years old. There's no difference.

The clubhouse? Tough to describe. It's our office. I don't think people understand that. We come to the office every day. This is where we work. We have a lot of people watch us work. The media oftentimes doesn't understand that. I think sometimes they don't quite understand, you know, that's our place to get away. When they come to the ballpark, they stand around our office. With the beat writers—the guys that are there every day—you almost have to make them part of the team because they're always hanging out there.

I have to deal with it, yeah. I'm fine. The media is one of the biggest reasons why we get paid the money we get paid. Their ability to make what we do interesting is sweet in this game, and I recognize that. I know that. It's just how it is.

Scouting reports? Yeah, each team pitches me differently. I might face the Giants and they might throw everything away this series, and then all of a sudden I come back, and—who do we play next? We play the Nationals next. The Nationals can throw everything inside, you know. Then, say, I go face the Marlins. They might throw everything off-speed, and I go back and face, you know, the Cubs, and they throw me all fast-balls. It's a constant chess game. It's a game of cat and mouse. I mean, as soon as you adjust to them, they readjust to you; it's a constant readjust-ment. Every move that you make is watched. Every at-bat that you have is scouted.

It's a scrap when you get to the top. It's tough, but it's the nature of the business, especially once you start making money in this game, you know. Some teams don't deem you worthy enough to make that amount of money; don't deem your production worthy enough. In my case that was the deal with Baltimore. Baltimore didn't think that I was worth the price tag that I was going to have, so they released me. That's fine. I don't blame them for that, you know. Everyone is always trying to get younger and cheaper. As a guy who has been around for a little bit now, I think that my job is to show them, "Look, this is something you can't pass up on. This is something I'm going to bring to the table; something that is going to help your team."

Really, that's what it is all about: making a team better. That's one thing I can do. I don't know how I am going to do it, but each day I come to the ballpark and try to do a couple of things to help our team win. If I can do that, I'll have done my job. This is the type of thing that will stick in a man-ager's mind, the general-manager's mind, an owner's mind, and that will make them want to bring me back, say for next year, and if not, I'll move on and find a job elsewhere.

I care and, like I said, I put a lot of emotion into it. At the same time, when the day is done, you get into the locker room, chat with the guys, maybe go out and grab some dinner, grab a drink. Just chill out. It's a new day tomorrow.

As long as I play this game still, I love it. And I love what it is. But when it's done, it's going to be done, and I think it's going to be nice too. It's move on and get after some other things that I want to do in my life. But for now, it's a great job, and you can't beat the money. You can't beat the working environment. Like I said, I am just going to enjoy the ride while it's still going.

Byrnes was re-signed by the Diamondbacks in 2007 to a thirty-million-dollar, three-year contract.

*　*　*　*　*

FIELDIN CULBRETH

Umpire, Major League Baseball

Courtesy of Rich Pilling, MLB Photos via Getty Images Sport

"It'd be nice if the only thing you had to do is sit there say it was a strike or a ball. But I'm just like everyone else. I've got three kids at home, and I might have Randy Johnson and Roger Clemens pitching tonight, and right before I get ready to go to the park, my wife calls and says, 'I'm stuck on the side of the road and the tire is blown out.' That just adds another little kink. I've got these two pitchers getting ready to pitch, and I've got troubles at home, and they are 3,000 miles away right now. So there are a whole lot of things that go on that I don't think people realize. I'm just the man that people yell at.

I am absolutely amazed at just how tough it is. I think people think, 'Well, hell, it's just a strike or a ball, what can be so tough about that?' You're talking about the best players in the world. Johnson isn't just throwing that thing over the plate just to be throwing it over the plate. He's trying to make it do different things and doing it at 95 to 100 miles per hour, and I'm supposed to tell you if it's a ball or a strike in this imaginary box out in space with this thing that's lying on the ground. And there's somebody in front of me and somebody to the side of me. It's a whole lot more complex than it seems."

Only sixty-eight men have his job. He spoke about it in his hotel room.

*　　*　　*　　*　　*

I've been a major-league umpire now for ten full seasons. I played baseball my whole life. Just like every other red-blooded young man, I dreamed of playing baseball, and was fortunate to be a decent enough player to earn a scholarship and play baseball in college. I went to the University of North Carolina, Charlotte. To be honest with you, I thought there was a chance of a future just like I had planned. However, my senior season, I went to pitch the ball—the ball basically went two or three feet up in the air and landed two or three feet in front of me. I knew something was wrong. I came to find out I had a rotator problem and an impingement syndrome, which is I guess some kind of nerve pressing on the bone, or something like that. This was back in 1985, and back then, they didn't have surgeries like now where they cut a couple of holes in you, and two weeks later you're back on the field. That ended my playing career.

It just so happened that my coach was an ex–minor league umpire. He always talked about umpiring. I was finished with baseball and thought, you know, what am I going to do now with my life? I hate to say it: I went to college get an education, but I was going to be a baseball player. My coach didn't just allow me to sit around and do nothing. He made me wear a sling on my arm and umpire. That was how my umpiring career started. I went down to umpire school and a few years later my dreams of being in the big leagues came true.

I was working in the Pacific Coast League in Tacoma, Washington, in 1992. It must've been six o'clock in the morning. One of the supervisors for the American League called me and said, "Fieldin, I've got some good news for you." I thought at six o'clock in the morning there's not a damn thing you can tell me that was good. He said, "You're going to the big leagues. You're not going far; you're only going to Seattle." For a guy that started off in Inman, South Carolina, a place with about 2,000 people, to show up one night, and there's about 40,000 people in the stadium, life got big. It got bright in a hurry. I went up there for about three games, worked the plate, the whole deal. It was everything that you would think it would be. It was exciting, it was scary, it was the big leagues, and it was all those years put together preparing for that one night. It was beautiful.

It's unbelievable how I played baseball my whole life, and I thought there was nothing about baseball I didn't know. Through umpiring I came to find out there was very little of the game that I actually understood. There are people out here making big-money decisions on these fields as far as who plays and GMs are making trades, but I guarantee you very few people actually know the rules. There are some that are tough enough where it would take four umpires together to make a decision. Let's take interference for instance. In the rulebook, it says, "No runner shall advance or score on interference." It's plain and simple. There it is. Four pages later, there's a situation where there's interference and a guy can score. Well, wait a minute; you told me no one could ever score on inter- ference on page ten, but on page twenty-two a man can.

During the regular season, we'll umpire anywhere from 125 to 130 games, and another 15–30 games during spring training, and then what- ever might come during the postseason. During the regular season, we get four one-week vacations that are spread out throughout the season. The "we" are my crewmates. Tim McClellan is the crew chief—he's the senior guy on the crew—myself, Marty Foster, and Bill Welkie. Every crew chief puts in for two or three people he'd like on his crew, but he only gets one of them. Then Major League Baseball assigns the other two. They try to go stagger by seniority to make sure all crews are pretty much set up the same way as far as time, experience, things like that. It actually works out well. We'll stay together the whole season. We're basically married to each other. You get to know all the things they do out on the field. Whenever you run down that third-base line and wonder if your back is going to be covered at home plate, you know it's going to happen because you know he's going to be there.

I've been with McClellan before, but I haven't been with this particular crew. It's rare for a whole crew to stay together a couple years in a row. We rotate every night. Like, if I work home plate tonight, tomorrow night I work third. It goes clockwise. The next day second, the next day first, and it goes like that at the whole year. I'll be first base tomorrow.

We typically get to the ballpark an hour to an hour and a half before the game would start. So with a seven-o-five start, we'll get at the ballpark anywhere between five thirty and six o'clock. We have our locker room and we have an umpire room attendant. We call them "clubbies," just like the players have clubbies. We have a guy that'll have our equipment washed, dried, and hung up in our locker room just like the players do.

We don't want for much, and I don't mean to say that to sound snobbish. It's just the way you think it would be in the big leagues. Some people might say that does sound snobbish, but I don't think many people travel and stay gone for six months either. It's those little things that help you get by. I remember in the minor leagues, you had to go wash your equipment and had to go wash your uniform. Lord, between driving up and down the road and umpiring those games and all those other little things, you were dead by the time you got to the park to actually do the job. So these little things makes life easier to where you can concentrate on what you've got to do, which is umpire the baseball game, as opposed to worrying about how all these other things at the park are being taken care of.

Technically, three of the four guys just have on a pair of issued slacks, shirt, and a hat that are all Major League Baseball logo'd, and that's typical wear for the three guys on the bases. The umpire on home plate will have body armor from head to toe. He will have on steel-toed shoes and a pair of shin guards that are underneath the pants. That's the thing: to look at him, he doesn't look any different than the other three guys other than a face mask but he has a pair of hard shin guards underneath his pants to protect his shins and his knees, a chest protector, and a facemask to keep him from getting any uglier.

Everything is set up for you, it's all ready to go, and it's in my trunk. Everybody has his own stuff. You can look at our equipment and you can get over there near it, but don't put it on. It's weird. I don't understand how you get a bunch of grown men to act so damn childish sometimes but we can get that way. I don't know if it's just sports in general or if it's just sports people, but God, we're awful. When you find something that works for you, you're just scared to do anything different, 'cause it works. So don't mess with success.

I think anybody that tells you they don't have superstitions is looking you in the face and lying. I don't have anything that I've just got to have happen; but I notice when I've got the plate, I'll start getting dressed at a certain time before the game, and doing little procedures, and everything goes on the same way every time. So, yeah, there's little things you do until years later you realize, "I'm one of those, too. I'm superstitious, and I don't want to be."

This was the first year I went to a new set of shin guards. I had used the same ones since my first day in professional baseball and when rats finally started jumping out of 'em I realized it was time to change them and try something new. Baseballs can hit you in the knees—it shouldn't hurt as much as it had for the previous six years.

It's tough to change. I've got the ball bag that I carry my baseballs in and I can't throw it away. I've had it since day one. It looks terrible—it's ripped and it's been patched. I stitch it up myself when it ripped so it's got pink thread in it, blue thread, purple thread. But it still holds the baseballs, so I just can't get rid of it; I don't know why that is. I know it's got nothing to do with me getting that pitch right. Hell, if it's worked, why in the world would I tempt fate? The bottom line is there's no fear when I walk out there. It's not anything I'm scared of. Nobody is going to shoot me, and they can't eat me; it's against the law. Nothing like that's going to happen. But at the same time, the pressure of wanting to do well—this is the big leagues; it's played on TV; the whole world is watching. I've got kids. I don't want them to go to school the next day and someone says, "Hey, I saw your dad make a clown out of himself again."

A player goes out there, and if he does well, he's cheered, and everything is great. They get their thrills hitting it out of the park and getting that extra base hit, or an extra base trying to turn a single into a double. If he does bad, there's still going to be a certain number of people who are going to say, "Hey, keep your head up, you're all right." Hell, if I do 100 percent right, 50 percent of the people there are going to be upset. So if I do great, they're going to say nothing. If I do bad in their eyes, then the whole world comes down on me. So you're signing on for a job that's never going to have a pat on the back. It takes a nut to sign up. But that's also where you get your thrills. There's nothing like having this close play and there's 40,000 people just coming down on you like you can't imagine, and you're the only person walking away going, "40,001 people are here. All of you got it wrong, and I'm the only that who knows who was right." You get your thrills that way. There's nothing like walking away knowing you're right when nobody is.

The thing about working the plate is that no matter how you look at, it you're going to have 200 to 300 decisions to make. There will only be fifty that are close; I mean, really close. But you never know when that pitch is coming, so you have to treat every pitch like it's the golden egg. By the time when you're done working the plate, you're mentally exhausted; you've had all you can take. A lot of the stress is self-induced. There's this thought that people have at times, "Oh, they're just umpires; they don't care; they just make the call and go on about their business." I mean, that couldn't be further from the truth. You know that any mistake is going to be on *SportsCenter* 101 times. The bottom line is no player, no manager, no fan can ever be as hard on me as I'll be on myself. It'll beat me up a whole hell of a lot longer and harder than what anybody can ever imagine. We miss some; we're human too. Thank goodness you don't come up wrong too much 'cause, like I said, it just absolutely eats you up.

We're trained for what to look for and what to listen for. It's not a guess. Everybody says, "God, how did you get those things right?" They think, "Well, you start off with a 50–50 chance." When it happens, we make the call. Every now and then, you don't get the sound that you normally get, or you don't get the sight that you normally get, and it puts a little doubt in your mind. But still you think you're right. The ultimate is when you go back in the locker room and look at the video. If we've had a close play or a sticky situation we'll go back and we'll fire up the video. In every major-league umpire's locker room we have the DVD set up. We'll evaluate what happened. I think people think we show up, umpire, and go home. There's no home to go home to. This hotel room is home. How do you like it? Why would we rush to get back here?

There's only been a few times where I actually walked away going, "You're wrong; you're just wrong." One of the times, I hate to say it, but it was in the minor leagues. For some reason, I saw it, and in my mind he was out. My arms flew out "safe" before I could bring 'em back in. It was just a regular play at first base. I saw him out, but my arms came out safe. That kind of thing only happened once.

I can't even describe the things we're talking about now to my wife, because I've always told her she can't understand what it's like being on that field any more than I'd understand what it was like giving birth. I've watched her do it. I saw the beauty of it. She can come to a ballgame and watch me do it, but she's just watching. She's just a witness.

I think since I've been in the big leagues I've only had three or four games that were not televised at all somewhere. Every single game is televised somewhere, whether it is locally or nationally. So, now with the technology that they have, they're checking our work right away. If this ball bounces and we said it was caught in a situation where we can get together and possibly change it, and another guy on the field says, "I saw it," then why wouldn't we get it right? It's tough for men, women, anybody to take on a job like we have and say that I'm willing to do this in front of people and then have to admit you made a mistake. But if there's a chance we can get together and change it and know that we're getting it correct, that's the right thing to do.

A lot of people say, "Well, they should've changed that call." You can't change if you're not sure you're changing it to the right call. If somebody—when those four guys are getting together—if somebody in that group can't say, "I know this is going to be the correct call," well, then you can't change it because if I'm saying, "He didn't catch it," and the other guys says, "I just couldn't get a good enough look to overrule you," and the other guy says, "I just couldn't get enough," you can't say, "Well, the way the crowd is reacting, let's change it." You can't do that; that's our job; we get paid to say he did or didn't.

I loved listening to the announcers after I ejected Randy Johnson last year. To be honest with you, I guess a lot was made of it at the time. It was just a typical situation. He was doing his job pitching, and I was doing mine umpiring. He disagreed with a couple calls I'd made. I told him to knock it off, and he disagreed with a couple later and started back up, so he was ejected. I got a call from one of my friends saying they had said something on *SportsCenter* about me. I never watch *SportsCenter* because I just choose not to. But he said I needed to watch it, so I did. I went back and watched it, and one of the guys, I won't say who, said, "Culbreth is a little bit of a hothead. He's had a few ejections this year." I had *two* ejections last year, including Randy—the most people I've ejected in any season in the last five or six years. That's out of 130 nights. That's not a lot of people. People think there are tons of ejections, but there aren't any more ejections than there were fifty years ago. It's just every one of them are played now cause they're on ESPN now from 6 a.m. to 11 p. m., and they just keep recycling and recycling.

Usually if somebody gets personal with you, they get ejected. If they say, "*That* call is terrible," that's one thing. If they say, "*You're* terrible," that's personal. If they put "you" or "you're" in front of it, everyone understands where the line of demarcation is. There's no surprises out there.

It's not always personal. As a matter of fact, I would say 99 percent of the time it's not personal. When Randy Johnson did what he did, five minutes later it's over as far as I was concerned. It was *him* doing what he thought he needed to do at the time; and it was *me* doing what I thought I needed to do at the time. It was just two grown men that disagreed on how we were going to get there. That was it. If I would've seen him three minutes later back in the runway, I'd said, "Randy, how are you doing?" And I'm sure he would've said that same thing. I hate to blow holes in everybody's great myths, but there's a whole lot more coexistence going on down there than everybody realizes. They think we've got switchblades in our pockets, and they've got Uzis underneath their shirts, and at first disagreement we're going to come out and go at it. That's just not the way it is.

I think everybody has their different ways of getting ready for the game. I personally don't do a whole lot, and I'll tell you why. I don't care if it's Greg Maddux, who's been pitching for what, twenty years, or if it's Joe Blow who's pitching his first inning 'cause it's this box out here that the ball has to travel through. It doesn't make any difference how it gets there. It doesn't know if Joe Niekro threw it or Joe Blow threw it. It either goes through that thing or it doesn't go through that thing. So I don't understand why I would do any more preparing for Greg Maddux than Joe Blow.

By the rulebook, [the strike zone] is within the boundaries of home plate that are in the hollow of the knee and the area between the armpits and the chest. Anything that falls within that is supposed to be a strike, and anything that falls out of it should be a ball. I try to tell people, that sounds really nice on paper, but it's more difficult than that 'cause that thing has four corners and height, and the baseball is traveling 98 to 100 miles per hour. It'd be nice to say, "Oh, that thing just nipped that corner every time," but we're talking about humans throwing it, and humans deciding it.

We have checks and balances now: the QuesTec system. QuesTec is a system that's set up to tell you whether the pitch was actually a ball or a strike. So, when I got finished working the plate the other night in Oakland, the next day I walk in and for every call, I have a disk that shows whether I called it wrong or right. It's a lot of pressure. It's causing hair to fall out. It might sound sick to some, but there's a certain thrill in that, too. We're not like most people. We don't wake up and go, "Well, let's go get yelled at today." Most people wouldn't walk out that door if they thought somebody's going to yell at them. We don't walk out that door; we run out of it and we invite 40,000 people to come do it.

Day in and day out, every umpire in this league goes through the same thing. I can tell you, as a group, we're unbelievable. There are two things about umpiring that amaze me. First is just how difficult it is. And the second thing is—and I say this proudly—I'm amazed and astonished at how good we are. I know some of the numbers that we put up. They're not make-believe; they're true numbers. You can rest assured that every time you see a play out on that field that you think we missed, you better check yourself, because the odds are you just messed up—not that guy that you are yelling at. We have supervisors in a lot of cities. They're evaluating 50 to 60 percent of our games. Any time we have a close play, it's written down. They go back to check the video, and fill out reports. The numbers would knock you off your feet at how many plays were witnessed as being close. We're not talking about plays my mother could call; we're talking about plays that they hire us to do. Of the thousands of calls made, 99.7 [percent are correct]. The number would be staggering to most people, and I am just proud to be a part of it because I think if people knew more about that, they would realize those men down there playing that game are the absolute best in the world at playing that game. God knows. I look at it and go, "How in the world do they do that?" But I can also assure people that the people down there umpiring that thing are just as good at what they do.

There's no such a thing as a tie goes to a runner. As a matter of fact, I defy someone to find me where it states in a rulebook what an out or a safe actually is. An out, for me, is when the baseball is in the first baseman's glove, on a play at first base, when that baseball is in that glove before the runner's foot touches first base. I would have to have the rule-book in front of me right now, but the only thing I can tell you is that it sure doesn't say, "This is an out, and this is safe." Nowhere in the rulebook does it say that. It just says something like, "The player shall be safe if he reaches first base before the ball." Okay, well, what happens if it is a tie? It happens a whole lot more than you can imagine. You always hear the saying that the umpire is blind at first base, or something like that. Well, if the truth be known, you could umpire first base with your eyes closed because more than the sight, you go off of sound. I could actually close my eyes and tell you if he's out or safe at first base. That's the reason we're so accurate. Me blinking doesn't make any difference. First of all, you're not going to blink on that, but if you did, it wouldn't matter. There are two distinct sounds. One of them's the foot of a guy's foot hitting a base. The other is the sound of the baseball hitting the mitt. You just got to decide which made the sound before the other one.

Every now and then, you get your tie. I call him safe because I think personally that they didn't do what they were supposed to do: that ball was not in the glove before he touched first base; it's in the glove while he's touching first base. At the same time, I could also say, "I think he's out," because he has that baseball in his glove and that's all it takes for him to be out. He got there at the same time. So how are you going to argue with me one way or the other? But I call him safe.

And, there's no such thing as ["the phantom play"]. If you don't believe it, I want you to try to go back and see replays. That shortstop and that second baseman, they touch that base. They're quick. I mean look, they're not going to hang out on that thing. They've got a grown man barreling down on 'em trying to take them out, so they're not going to hang around for everybody. They touch the base; that's the only thing I can tell you. There's times when if you look as the guys throwing the ball, he's five feet from it, but you look at where he was when he caught that baseball you'll see something different.

I think at the end of the day most people understand that everybody out there has a job to do. It's obvious nobody has an easy job, or every-body would be lined up around the street to do it. If hitting a ball were easy, there'd be a line of people from here to the park down there waiting to take someone's job. It's not easy. God knows. I tell you about the pressure I feel, but I can't imagine what it's like trying to hit that 3–2 pitch on the corner, and then trying to do it over and over so you don't end up back down in Albuquerque. Everybody's got pressure and as much as we do have battles from time to time, I think everybody understands nobody has a job that's easy. The key to surviving in the big leagues is you can't wear every emotion on your shoulder. I can't let an umpiring decision bother me, or this is going to be a long, tough career. That's how I look at it. Missing a call just kills me, and nobody will be tougher on me than I will be on myself. At the same time, I have to find a way to put that to bed.

I've umpired everything but a World Series. I've had divisionals and the league championships series. I had the All-Star game this year. I was honored to be picked. They had the home-run derby contest the night before. I took my wife and my son, who is my oldest child; the other two are too young to go. So I went to the home-run derby, and I actually sat in the stands, which was the first time I sat in the stands of a major league ballpark. I've always been on the field. It was unbelievable. One, to share it with my family, and two, just to sit down and, believe it or not, I actually had a beer. And I had some peanuts. I watched some of the guys that I'm normally umpiring do their home-run contest. For me, it was a real thrill just to sit there like everybody else and take in the sights of the park and the sounds and everything.

I've told you that most people wouldn't walk out that door if they thought they were going to get booed. I told you I wouldn't walk out of it; I'd run out of it. If I'm going to do it, I want to do it on the grandest stage. I want to walk out there to where it all counts; to where there is not a tomorrow. Somebody is going to win it and somebody is going to lose it. And after that, there isn't going to be a game for a while. That's what the players play for; that's what we umpire for—to one day do it in the ultimate game: the World Series. Hopefully one day that will happen for me.

We can talk about all these great stories and anecdotes but the bottom line is that if there was one thing I wish people could understand about umpiring is that every third day I'm getting on a plane going somewhere else, and it's not to go home and see my kids. That's tough on them. It's tough on us, but I signed up for it. It's how I make my living more than anything else. It's how I pay the bills just like anyone else. At the same time, I'd be lying if I didn't say you become a fan of the game. I can't imagine my life without baseball. Since I was five years old, I've been involved in baseball. It's what I woke up in the morning thinking about. It was one hell of a turn to think I was going to end up wearing an umpire's uniform. But that's how it turned out, and, god, I couldn't be happier. I'm proud of it, and it's something I think I earned. I went out and worked for it. Nobody handed it to me; that's for certain.

Fieldin Culbreth? It's a name that sticks out. We were talking about that the other night in the locker room. I'm the third, and just named my child the fourth. One of the guys said, "How'd you come up with a name like that?" I'm ashamed to say as different as it is, I've never done one ounce of background check on it. I should because my father is getting older, and if anyone knows, he would. As a matter of fact, one of the Braves' announcers says, "It's good Fieldin Culbreth," like I'm a good fielder. I guess Bob Uecker has some little skit that he puts together whenever I'm umpiring. He loves my name. He says, "If that's not a Southern boy's name . . ."

*   *   *   *   *

OMAR VIZQUEL

Shortstop, San Francisco Giants

In 2007, eleven-time Gold Glove winner Omar Vizquel participated in the 1,591st double play of his career, setting the major-league record for the most double plays turned by a short-stop.

He and I didn't have a scheduled interview. I was looking for Giants broad-caster Mike Krukow when I saw Vizquel sitting in front of his clubhouse locker examining his glove. We talked while most of the media huddled around Barry Bonds a few feet away.

Courtesy of Terence Wong

*   *   *   *   *

I'm a professional ballplayer. In my experience, everything starts when you leave your house. You know, you get in touch with the people that are coming with you to the ballpark. As soon as you turn into the parking lot, there is guy that will valet park your car. There's people that work in the gate that you say "good afternoon" to. There's people that work along the hall. They have their offices; you don't even know what they do, but you recognize them by looking at them every day, and you say "hi" to them. Then everybody else that works inside the clubhouse—the clubbies—the guys that clean the shoes, wash your clothes. You have the chef that made your breakfast when you come in or make a sandwich if you are hungry.

There's reporters that are trying to look for information. There's a lot of people that we deal with every day.

I loved baseball since I was eight years old. My dad took me to a baseball field to practice, and then I belonged to a team until I was sixteen years old and I signed my first professional baseball contract. Ever since, my life has changed because everything was revolving around baseball. Everything. If you have a vacation planned, you have to plan it around baseball. If you have a wedding to attend—if you have a party—all these have to be when the season is not going on. There are some things that you can't have control over, like your son's graduation because it's right when the season is. Sometime you don't have time to share with them that moment that is not going to come very often.

But I think baseball players are spoiled in a way. Every time you need something, and every time that you want to do something, there's a lot of people around that open the doors. You don't have to look too far to attend to that particular event. If it's a rock concert, or if it is like a theater—a play—you've got agents, and you've got people that have connections. They find you the tickets. You don't have to stay in line. All these things happen because of the position that we are in. I think, because of the amount of money that people are earning these days, you meet so many people, like your agent and all these people that I just mentioned. They say, "You pay me money, we might as well do something else for you in return." So you have those kind of connections.

What I love about my job is that I have to come, every day, prepared mentally and physically for a challenge. You have to be able to entertain sometime 40,000 people. You have to be ready for that challenge. I love my job because of that. I've still got passion to play baseball, and sometimes we have the chance to change people's lives just by signing an autograph, or just by sitting five minutes with them to talk about baseball. You don't realize how big of an impact a player can have outside the field just by signing that autograph. There are people out there that drive three hours to come to a ballgame and try to get just one little autograph from one of their favorite players. If you can make that person happy that day, they will be talking about it for a long time.

My main tool is my glove. When you play shortstop, you cannot forget your glove. You are always really picky about the place that you put it in your bag; about how you treat that particular tool. I'm still here in the big league because of my glove. I've been playing with a Rawlings glove my whole career, but this year I changed to SSK. It's a Japanese glove. I fell in love with the glove, and I've been using it.

You know, it's kind of silly. I wanted to do something different. I guess sometimes you get a little bored by routines, you know, just wearing the same glove all the time. I got bored of it. I guess I needed a little more challenge to be out on the field with a different glove, and try to concentrate; try to make every play as well with a different glove that I did with the old glove. The shape, the measurements, and everything else is kind of similar, but it's a mind thing. It feels different. By having a different glove in your hand, you have to try to concentrate a little more. I think that's one of the reasons why I decided to change my glove.

The bat is another one of my tools. I have been using the same weight and model bat for about seven years now—an F123; 34-32. The brand is a Route 66 Klubs, which is a company I own along with two of my friends. My two friends used to work in the company, and they decided to leave the company but they have all the ideas and how all the machines work. They got together with me and we came out with the idea of having our own company—you know, the old Route 66 from the West Coast.

Ten minutes ago, before you came here, my infield instructor came to me with a sheet and told me how we're going to defense the other team. You know, how we're going to move in different situations. That's the way you prepare in the first game of every series. Once you do that, you know you are ready to take on the other team.

Shortstop is one of the most demanding position on the field because you are involved almost every play out there. You have to know who's playing left, who's playing right. You know who's around you, and all that. And you also have to know your enemy—how you are going to defend the lineup. You have to know the little things like that in order for you to be successful on the field.

The other thing is you have to be able to have fun. If you don't have fun playing shortstop, it's going to be hard for you to play in the big league. You have to be able to communicate with your teammates in the field. You have to be able to think right before the play. How can you call that? You have to anticipate. Anticipation is really important when you play shortstop. Think about all the situations that can go through your mind. At the moment you get the ball, you already know what you have to do with it. You have to know the count; know if you are going to move somewhere. I mean, every pitch is entirely different. Guys change, and adjust to every pitch during each at-bat.

I have a lot of interests outside of baseball. I always have been involved in art. Every time I have an opportunity to visit a museum, I go. Like last time I was here in Pittsburgh, last year, we went to visit the Andy Warhol Museum. It was amazing, the kind of different techniques and collages and different things.

Lately, I have been hooked up with photography. I'm interested in taking a lot of black-and-white photography. It looks like photography from the sixties, you know, those great photographers like Ansel Adams that take a lot of pictures of landscapes in black and white. And guys like Henri Cartier-Bresson. It's just awesome what they can do with light and contrast.

I also paint. I've been painting for eight years; developing my technique of watercolors. At this time, I am doing oils, and I like to find figurative bodies—to paint bodies with different colors.

I'm a big fan of sculpting too. Last year, I was a sculpting a big piece of stone that is like seven feet by five feet wide. It's a piece of stone that came from Italy—a white carrera marble. It is one of the most beautiful stones to work on because it's white. Then when you polish it, it's got all this tremendous light that come out of it, so the light makes the stone come alive. I hooked up with a guy from Cleveland that's an Italian. I was visiting one of his galleries, and his son came out and started talking to me about art. He gave me an opportunity to see what he does in his studio; to kind of like teach me some techniques and stuff. Right after that, I picked up sculpting; started doing sculpting in clays, and then move on to stone. The piece of stone is two figures: one is emerging from the ground, and the other one is kind of pulling him down back to the hole. Kind of like resembling the give and take of life—how somebody can really be successful and come out of a hole, and the other people trying to drag you down into the same hole. There is a tension between being successful and being down in the hole. We find that in every aspect of life. No matter what you do—if you are a reporter, if you are an architect, if you are a guy that is picking up garbage—I mean, there's some people that want your job. They want to take it, and some people also envy you because you have that kind of job. You know, it's always in baseball. You see it a lot. A lot of guys, of course, they are going after your job. There are a lot of guys—Triple-A, Double-A, Single-A—that want to be in the big leagues at the same position that I am in right now. That's why it's such a challenge to be in the big leagues every day. You've got to be able to stay strong and to perform every day to keep your job.

A lot of people are aware that they are here in the big leagues, and they realize how big of a responsibility it is for you to be an every day player, or just to belong on a major league team. There are some other guys that get in so easy that they don't realize the kind of example you can set for the other people around you. They confuse their job. They think, because they are here, they already made it, and they don't work as hard because they already have a spot here. I think you have to work twice as hard to maintain that position and not to go back down to the minor leagues.

In the off-season, I'm doing a lot of extra work. I'm working harder now than I did five or seven or eight years ago because I'm already declining as a player. I'm thirty-nine years old. Things are getting tougher for me; to wake early in the morning and try to play a one o'clock game; to go through 162 games and stay healthy through the whole year. I really have to maintain my focus and my abilities to play at the same level than I did five years ago. You have to push your body to try to stay healthy and to try to do the same things. So my work has been intensified a little more than before.

There are a lot of exciting moments in baseball. You can't ask for anything else than for that competitive moment. We get those moments at least twice a week, so it's pretty cool. It gets twice as exciting when you are in the eighth or in the ninth inning, and the game is on the line; where you are in that spotlight. You have the chance to turn the game around for your team. It's awesome.

This job means everything in my life because I wanted to be a professional ballplayer since I was nine years old, and everybody says how hard it is to make to the big leagues. I mean, it's almost impossible, especially coming from a third-world country like Venezuela. I overcame all of those challenges, and all of those people that were talking all that crap about me. I really pushed myself to try to become a major-league ballplayer. There's very few people in life that do what they really want to do, and I am one of them. I wanted to be a ballplayer. I am a ballplayer. Still a ballplayer. I fulfilled my life because of that. Not many are able to do that. I stayed focused on that. That's still what I'm doing. I am probably going to be dead by the time that I leave the game.

*   *   *   *   *

DOUG MIRABELLI

Catcher, Boston Red Sox

"We are with these guys more than we are with our families during the year. We're here so much, and we're on the road so much together, that you know these guys almost as well as their families know them. So that's a special bond that you have. It's strong. I've been here for five years now. Some of the best friends that I have in the whole world are in this clubhouse."

Mirabelli wasn't in the starting lineup this night for the Red Sox game against the New York Mets because Sox thrower Curt Schilling was taking the mound against Mets ace Tom Glavine. Mirabelli primarily plays only in games when knuckleball specialist Tim Wakefield pitches. He uses a fast-pitch softball catcher's mitt instead of a more traditional style.

* * * * *

There are lots of kids out there who want to be major-league baseball players. Obviously not all of them are going to make it, but you go through the course. I mean, you have to go through Little League. You play in junior high school and high school. For me, it just started out like that just like everybody else. I just started. I got better and better at it, and the next thing I knew I was playing in college, realizing that maybe I have a chance to play at the next level. When that happens, then you realize that this is something you can use as a profession and make a living at it.

I grew up in Las Vegas, Nevada. My brother was two years older than me, so he started playing Little League before I did. I got to go out there and watch him, and then I followed in suit, and started playing. I didn't become a catcher until I was about nine years old. I was playing in older leagues, so I couldn't catch if they were throwing too hard for me. You've got to love catching. It's not for everybody. In Las Vegas in the summer, it's a 110, 115 degrees outside. You get all the gear on. You've got to catch batting practice. You got to do a lot of stuff that if you don't really like the position, you are not going to stick with it.

I think it's like any position that you are good at. I mean, you are not going to sit there and work if you are terrible at it. I wanted to play shortstop. In my head, that seemed like the best position, but I wasn't good enough to play shortstop. I wasn't fast enough. Catching was the next best option for me. I think there was an identity that I was a good catcher. Even in Little League, you start getting that feel that, "Hey, you are one of the best catchers," you know what I mean?

I've been a catcher since I started catching. Once I started, I never wanted to leave it. You have to really love to play there. If you are not having fun doing something, you are not really going to succeed in this game. I mean, baseball is supposed to be fun. Just by playing, you are going to get better. You work on blocking the ball and throwing the ball and stuff like that. It didn't get until like high school when I really got into honing my skills—blocking the ball, working on timing, throwing to second base, and stuff like that. That's when I really realized that there was more to catching than just, you know, throwing on the mask and gear, putting the glove on, and going back there.

I was drafted by the Giants after I got out of college so, you know, it's just a progression. You go into the minor leagues in A-ball. I spent two years in San Jose. And then you go to Double-A. I spent parts of four different seasons in Shreveport; parts of three seasons in Triple-A. I was up and down.

I was traded to the Padres this off-season, in January, and then traded back here in May. What happened was there was a police escort to get here because it was so close to game time. They had my uniform in there. I decided to dress in the police car. It was a night game—seven-o-five game, and I got here at like seven o-three.

Wakefield is the only one I catch. He throws probably at least 80 percent, if not 85 percent knuckleballs, and then he throws a fastball and curveball. You've still got the normal signs as everybody else. He has the knuckleball instead of a changeup. The knuckleball, in general, is just a wild pitch. I mean, it's doing all kind of wacky things. That's what makes it so special, because you can throw it 60 to 70 miles an hour and still get people out with it. Nobody else in baseball can throw a ball that slow consistently and get away with it. Nobody knows where it is going to go. Yeah, he has an idea. He has a circular area of the strike zone that he is throwing it into. He doesn't know exactly where it will strike, though. I think he aims at my facemask. I don't really give him a target that much. He throws it in the general area. It is moving so much it doesn't matter. He just needs a starting point to where he can throw it.

Wakefield has been throwing it for so long. It's such a tough pitch. If you come up through the minor leagues and live and die on a knuckleball, it's tough because there is not a lot of room for error if you don't have a real big one. Wakie's knuckleball is so exceptional that he can do it. He had the ability to throw a knuckleball coming up in the minor leagues. He was a first baseman, and they were going to release him because he wasn't hitting very well, or something like that, and so they were just going to release him. They saw him throw a knuckleball and so his pitching coach was like, "Let's give him a chance throwing knuckleballs." He had no other choice because he knew that's why he was there, to throw knuckleballs.

We weren't a real good team the year that I started catching him so when I messed up, it wasn't as magnified as it would be now. I could go through growing pains by having passed balls, you know what I mean? The team wasn't very good anyway. There were a lot of other things that were higher priority than catching him, per say. And then we had new ownership—a new GM, and we got a new manager. The manager said, "You did pretty well the year before, so why don't you just continue to catch him, and we will let [Jason] Varitek have a day off." So that's how it started, and that's how it is right now. It's a specialty.

We go over every hitter with the pitching staff before each series. As a catcher, my job's a little bit easier because he is going to throw knuckleballs anyway so the thought process going over how he will pitch certain guys isn't like it would be if Curt Schilling was pitching, or somebody who had to mix up their pitches more.

Garret Anderson used to hit them pretty well. [Jimmy] Rollins, with the Phillies, hits them very well. But they don't do it all the time. It's streaky. That's the fame of the knuckleball. It's moving so much, so they have to really stay with the pitch a long, long time because it moves so much at the end. It can be just unhittable, or he can give up—I think he gave up six home runs to the Tigers in one game once. So it's hit or miss, but it's not very often that he totally misses. He still has the ability to get outs with it.

We have we pick our spots to throw the fastball because it's only 76 miles an hour, so you can't really go into unpredictable situations. Sometimes you are just trying to break momentum. Maybe he's throwing a lot of balls in a row, or maybe they will get some hits in a row. A lot of this game is about momentum, and a team senses a guy's in trouble. They want to get up there and keep a rally going as much as possible. They don't want to slow down the tempo, so it's my job is to slow it down for him. He wants to get out on the mound throwing it, throwing it, throwing it. I've got to slow him down sometimes.

They always say winning hides a lot of things, so it's a good thing to be on a team that wins. That's a huge part of being happy, and being successful because when you are winning ballgames, it hides a lot of deficiencies that guys are having. Maybe they are in a slump or whatever, but you win ballgames. You figure out how to win together.

You've got to understand we have had a history of "Here it goes again." In 2003, we had a great team. We end up losing against the Yankees, but you know, you're down three to nothing, and three games to nothing [in 2004], and then it's the bottom of the ninth, and you got one out already, and you just know it's over. You know what I mean? Like you just have a sense of, "We just got swept." Basically you've got [Mariano] Rivera on the mound and there is really not a whole lot of hope. And then the next thing you know—it happened so fast—Dave Roberts stole second, and the next pitch was a base hit, and he scored, and all of a sudden you have energy again. It just takes a spark like that. That wasn't really a spark; that was more of a brushfire. [David] Ortiz hits a walk-off homer to win that game. It was a quiet confidence: "All right, we've won one, and we got two pretty good pitchers coming up the next two days in Pedro and Schilling." You are like, "We can win those games." If we win those games that's three to three, and in game seven we're going to have Derek Lowe, and they're going to have Kevin Brown. It was, "If we can get to game seven, we will definitely win it." We win it because of the psychological letdown that they have to have after being up three games to none, and being two outs away from going to the World Series. Now they are looking at a game seven. You can argue that no game has the bearing on the next game as far as you still go out and play the game the same way, but psychologically if one thing goes bad for 'em in that game, they're saying to themselves, "Oh my god, here we go."

* * * * *

PHILIP MERKORD

Ballboy, Texas Rangers

"I'm twenty-three. If somebody asks me, I just tell them I work in the Texas Rangers' clubhouse. I usually don't say, 'I'm a ballboy.' It has certain connotations. People think: it's kids; teenagers do it; which isn't completely true. The guy on the visiting side, I know that he is twenty. Our guy down the line is twenty-four, and the guy that I sit with down here by home plate, he's about to turn twenty, so we're really not kids, but people think that. I just don't like to say, 'ballboy, batboy.' I just say I work in the clubhouse."

*   *   *   *   *

I am a clubhouse attendant; work in the clubhouse. I am also a ballboy-slash-batboy. Basically, I come in about one thirty, two o'clock every day for a night game. About five hours before game time, no matter what time the game starts.

I do all kinds of things: bring towels down, set them up right here along the bench; put coolers down in the dugout and the bullpen; stash waters and Powerade, sunflower seeds, candy, bubble gum; and bring the base-balls down that they're going to use for batting practice. Just get all that stuff ready for the home team. There is another guy that does it for the vis-iting side.

In between setting up everything there's always laundry to pick up constantly, and just a bunch of little things like that. That takes us up to about three thirty. At three thirty, some of the players come out and take early batting practice, and that lasts for about thirty to forty-five minutes, and then they finish up, go back inside.

I stock refrigerators constantly. We have one in the kitchen, a big gigantic one, and then we have one in the trainer's room, and the coaches' room, and the video room. Those are always being emptied, especially in the Texas heat. Guys are thirsty coming of the field all the time. Constantly have to refill those refrigerators. We have every soft drink you could think of. Every kind of juice. Water. We have four to five different flavors of Powerade. Anything a player might want, it's pretty much there already. Michelob Ultra. Coors Light. No one drinks it before the game. After the game, yeah, guys drink some of it.

During the early batting practice—since the rest of the team doesn't come out—I go out there and chat. It's part of the job. Some of the coaches will come out just so we have enough people to pick up baseballs. Early batting practice ends at about four fifteen.

The team comes out at four twenty-five; stretches for fifteen minutes. Batting practice for the entire team starts at four forty, and that lasts till about five thirty. The whole team's out here at this point. We set a screen up right behind second base, in shallow centerfield, and we put a bucket out there. I usually stand there with Dustin, my partner. The players that are in the outfield will just throw them back into the bucket where I'm standing. I put them in the bucket, and when the bucket gets full, I run them up to the batting practice pitcher, and take it back. When that's over, Dustin and I will bring the balls off the field. We'll pack them back up and take them back upstairs, and I'll start setting up the dugout for the game. I'll get all the helmets out and put them in the helmet rack. I get all the pine-tar rags and the rosin bags, and all the batting accessories.

By the time BP's over, we have about an hour and a half till game time. I just basically make sure everything is set and ready to go for the game; make sure there're plenty of towels out—you know, cups and everything. I get the catcher's gear out of their bags, and we hang it up in there so the catchers can grab it when they come down. And then we go inside and stock the refrigerators again because they get emptied out after BP. I'll make a bucket of ammonia water. Some of the players like to dip their heads in it. I'm not real sure what it does. I think it maybe hydrates you better. I put two towels in there, and they can kind of soak their head with the towels. It smells great—kind of minty. I've never dipped my head in there. It smells really good, though.

I come down about half an hour before game time, 'cause as players start to make their way down to the dugout I just want to make myself available in case anybody needs anything—you know, another bat, a pair of batting gloves maybe; anything little like that.

Then, about twenty minutes before game time, we go down to the umpires' room. We bag the game balls. I think we fill it up with about seven dozen baseballs to start the game. Usually we get low in about the seventh or eighth inning, and we have to go get another dozen or so. Rub the balls down with mud? I don't do it. There's a gentleman who runs the umpires' room. He does it. Rubs them down real nicely. Mud from the Delaware River. Pretty much it's ready for the game to start.

That's my chair. It's just a little stool—probably about a foot and a half off the ground. It's got a Texas Rangers logo on the cushion. We set it up right against the padding on the wall. The wall is almost like a backrest. It's comfortable; not too bad.

We have our own little duties during the game. Dustin typically handles the bats. When the Rangers are hitting—after a guy has an at-bat—he runs up, picks it up, brings it back. Every player has to have two bats. We have one in the on deck circle in case a guy breaks a bat during an at-bat. We have to have one close by; it's a major-league rule. That's what he does.

I handle the balls. I'm the guy who restocks the umpire's balls. Every third ball that goes out of play, I take them three more. I like doing balls, only because I'm on the field pretty much the entire time. It's right next to the owner's box—right by the Rangers' on deck circle.

We go through probably seven to eight dozen for a normal game. The bag is right next to me, and when a ball goes out of play, I take one out. When the second ball goes out of play, I grab two more balls. That way, I have the third one out, and as soon as that third ball goes out of play, I run up real fast and restock the umpire. It isn't that hard. I just have to pay attention. It's pretty simple.

Nothing unusual has happened. I thought we would have more plays in our area than we've had. When I started out, that was something I was worried about. You can count the number of pop-ups we've had right directly above us on one hand. We just pick up our stool and kind of try to get out of the way without distracting the catcher who's running over there.

I've had two close calls: line-drive baseballs off of a hitter's bat. Foul balls. One was, I think, in the second game of the season. Since it was my second game ever, I was like, "Oh, this is going to happen to me all the time!" The other one was probably about mid-point of the season. I don't remember who was up to bat that time. He hit a line drive; it probably went about six feet directly over my head. It makes you keep your eyes open. We sit so close to the plate. You don't miss a pitch. You don't have time to react. It's just amazing I haven't been hit this year.

The other night—I forget the player—but he lost his bat; slipped out of his hands, and it went in the front row over by the visiting team's dugout. Dustin needed to go get it because the batter still wanted to use that bat, because it's the one he had pine tar on. It was his game bat. Dustin ran over there to get it from the fan. He asked him nicely, "Hey, can I just have the bat back?" He got booed a lot. The fans don't understand. They think we're taking things from them. The player did go deliver the fan another bat. Yes, the fan got another bat to replace the one that was taken from him. Every now and then if a bat breaks, fans will ask, "Can I have it?" It's kind of up to the player, you know, what happens to it. We don't want to make those decisions for the players, so we usually just say we can't do that.

We keep a bucket right beside us. We keep all the rosin bags and pine tar and stuff in there, and we throw the used baseballs in there that the umpire throws out of play. They are scuffed up. I usually give away five to ten baseballs a game, to fans. Kids come down there and ask. Some kids are nicer than others. I try to give to the ones who are asking real nicely for a ball with "please." That'd be a polite kid. Some kids demand a baseball:

"Give me a baseball, ballboy!" That's not going to fly with me. I try to ignore it because I don't want him to think that he's getting underneath my skin, which he's not.

Dustin and I joke around that we're like the umpires: nobody likes us because people only want balls. All they want us for is to get a free baseball. People get on us, especially towards the end of the game. Maybe the team is losing; it's not a very good game. People, every now and then, can get pretty mean about it. They call you names, but it's all fun, I guess. I just laugh it off.

Some people will bring down their babies, like that's going to make me give them a baseball. People do that every night. *Every night.* They think I'm going to find it cute. You know, if you want a baseball, just ask me for a baseball. I'll give you a baseball. It's not a big deal. You don't have to try and almost bribe me. I usually don't give them away till at least the seventh inning, just because if we start giving them away early, kids see that, and we'll have lines up and down the aisles. They get in the way. That's a distraction to the fans sitting down there. The ushers tell kids, "Don't come down here right now; maybe at the end of the game."

Some umps are real talkative. We run water out to the umpires every three innings. I'll stop at first, and then I will drop one off at the second-base umpire, and then I will go on to third base. I stand there with the third-base umpire while he drinks it, and then I'll make my way back around to pick the bottles up. Usually I'm there talking to the third-base umpire for about thirty seconds. Some guys are real talkative, a real laid-back sense of humor. And some guys are quiet, you know, real focused. Most of the guys that have been around for a while seem to be some of the quieter guys. I say the older guys are quieter. I don't think they're more serious, they are just quieter usually—not all of them, but I'd say most of them. They're just regular guys. I usually talk to them about what series they just did, where they're going next, you know, just anything. Sometimes a trivia question's on the scoreboard, and we'll talk about what we think the right answer is. Stuff like that.

As soon as the game's over, Dustin and I come inside the dugout and we clean everything up. We'll pick up all the towels, dump the coolers out, get the bats and helmets back inside. We get every piece of equipment cleared out of the dugout—usually takes ten to fifteen minutes. Then as soon as we're done with that, we go upstairs to the clubhouse and start cleaning shoes. I say "upstairs" because it's up the ramp.

Sunday afternoon it rained pretty much the entire game, for two and a half straight hours. When it rains, it usually takes us forty-five minutes to clean shoes. Cleaning shoes is always the worst job we have all day. And then when it rains, it's even worse. We have to scrape all the dirt and mud until really there is nothing left, and then we make them look as new as we can. Usually somebody will brush them off, and the other guy will wipe. We'll just kind of like wipe off the stains, dirt, and mud, and make them look as white and as glossy as possible. On a day where it doesn't rain, it takes us about half an hour.

As soon as that's done, we pick up whatever remaining laundry is left out. By the time we finish that, most of the players have left already. Some of the coaches are still around. We want to get the laundry picked up as quickly as possible. The quicker it's in the washing machine, the quicker we can put it in the dryer. The quicker we can get it out and hang it back up, the quicker we get out of here. Every piece of clothing has a player's number on it. There is so much laundry; that's why it takes so long to get out of here. And then we get a batch of towels and we fold those. That's usually the very last thing we do. Once the towels come out and are folded, it's time to go.

I didn't mention that after a game, we go in and eat—usually about eleven o'clock for dinner. It's catered from various local restaurants. Free meals. Can't beat that. That's one of the perks you have to take into account. Maybe we don't get paid very much money, but we get free food all day long.

On an average night, if the game starts at seven and ends at ten o'clock, we usually get out of here at one. That means we usually have about three hours of work once the game ends. It's tedious, but the team's gone by then so it's just us, and we joke around. We have fun.

When they come back from a road trip, we come in when their flight gets in. If they play a night game on the East Coast or West Coast—it doesn't really matter—they're going to arrive in the wee hours of morning. The team arrives at the ballpark, and we start unpacking all of their bags, and we take all of the equipment off the truck. It takes about three to four hours to do all that. It's part of the job, but it's no fun coming in at midnight or one o'clock in the morning and starting to work. You've been up all day, and then there is a game later that day. So we are back, in like six or seven hours for a full twelve-hour shift. Those are the worst.

We make $81.50 a game. It's about twelve hours a day. We also get paid if we come in when they come back from road trip. We get paid for that day, too, even though we might only be here for a couple of hours. It doesn't seem like much, but players tip you at the end of the season. Since this is my first year, I haven't seen what those are going to be. It's hard to say. It depends how many rookies a team has. Rookies are probably not going to tip as much just because they haven't been around as long as the others. And when guys get traded, like we acquire a guy midseason—he hasn't been here all year, maybe he doesn't think he needs to tip us for a whole year—you know, stuff like that. I'm looking forward to seeing what that's like.

You know, it's not a lot of money. All of us, except maybe two guys, that work here are college grads. It may not seem like much, and some people might think we are kind of crazy, but you're around the game. I mean, you're around *a major-league team* for an entire season.

This is my first season. I just graduated from the University of Oklahoma, back in December. I got a degree in English, and I wasn't sure what I wanted to do. I want to work in baseball. I've always known that. I love baseball; love the game; always been around it.

I didn't know until right as I was graduating that I would maybe do this. Like two days before I actually graduated, I called the guy here who runs the clubhouse, and asked what they offered. I didn't know anything about it really. I just knew that there were guys that do work in there. Basically I said, "Do you have any openings in the clubhouse?" And he said, "I think I'm going to have one at the start of the new year." This was about December 15 when I called him. He took my name. Right after the new year, I came in and interviewed with him; two different times. Then he told me it was down to me and another guy for that one spot. He kind of preferred the other guy just because he had worked with a college football team and he had experience working with equipment and with a team in a locker-room atmosphere. But then he called back and said, "I have an on-field spot, a ballboy-batboy spot. Some guy is not coming back." He asked me if I'd be interested. I said, "Yeah." So he hired me.

Home games only. April third was the season opener against the Boston Red Sox, so that made it all the more special. It was something else: walking on the field; not a cloud in the sky; about 80 degrees; Charlie Pride singing the national anthem; 50,000 people in the stands; not an empty seat in the house; the planes flying over; and the Red Sox. It was just gorgeous. Ah, it was something else, you know. That was neat. It was really neat.

I'm here for the year. So I probably have just five more games. I need to move on to something else, you know, something more permanent. I'm not sure. I honestly have no idea. I don't think this is for me. I'm moving forward. It's been a great experience being on the field for major-league baseball games. The kid in you really comes out. How can you not enjoy this if you're a baseball fan at all? You're in the dugout. You hear their conversations about the game. You hear them talking to the batting coach about pitchers and how they're pitching them during the at-bat. You get to hear a lot of stuff. You're around it. You see how a major-league team operates. It's a great thing. I've enjoyed every game. I look forward to coming out here every day.

*   *   *   *   *

GARY MATTHEWS, JR.

Outfielder, Los Angeles Angels of Anaheim

Courtesy of Ben Liebenberg

Matthews went 3 for 5, including a leadoff homer, the night we talked. At the time, he was batting a solid .319.

*   *   *   *   *

My father played, you know, so my early childhood memories with this game involved riding to Candlestick Park with my dad. I was really young at the time. I would hang out for a few minutes, and then my mom would take me back home. Or we would go to the game and I would hang out with my dad after the game.

I was born at Stanford. We lived in Foster City. When I got a little bit older I collected baseball cards. My brother and I had a huge collection. Baseball cards were all over. Ron Cey spent time at the house; Rick Sutcliffe. We had everybody at the house from Pete Rose to Dusty Baker.

All these people that are still in the game I've known since I was, gosh, probably four years old at the time. It's really interesting to see them now still involved in the game in one way or the other, you know, like the roles are sort of reversed; like they are watching me play now. Some are in coaching. Some of them are in broadcasting. It's really odd to see the cycle. When I was a kid, I used to watch them play.

I'd like to say that I had other plans, but the truth is that this was my dream growing up. This was really what I wanted to do. I wanted to be a professional baseball player. I used to tell my parents, when I was five years old, that this is what I was going to do for a living. I think any child who has a parent who is in a certain field, you know, is going to be influenced by that parent, whether they're a police officer, a doctor, or a lawyer. That field is going to be a strong influence in your life, and probably a field of interest for that child. My father happened to be a baseball player. He was going to have a tremendous amount of influence on me whether I wanted to play the game or not.

It was normal to me. People say it was tough. I've heard kids comment about, you know, it being tough with their dad not around, and stuff like that. I understand sometimes it is hard, but in my family when I was growing up everybody had a role, and there were no excuses. Even as kids, we had certain things that we had to do; we were expected to go to school and do well, and to obey the rules whether my dad was there or not. My parents always encouraged us to be individuals, and let us express ourselves. At the house, you had to watch what you said, but we were definitely encouraged to have our own personalities.

I'm thirty-two. I was nineteen when I was signed. I have three younger brothers and two sisters. I'm the oldest, so I had a really big responsibility in sort of taking care of things while my dad was gone. Even though I was young at the time, I think my dad was giving me responsibility; preparing me for manhood, so to speak. I sort of thought I was the man of the house, and that it was my job to take care of everybody while he was gone. But I've heard kids complaining about how hard it was on their family and everything. It was difficult, but we were still expected to go out and do what we were told to do, and so we were fine.

I've always expected that I was going to be successful. Sometimes as a kid, you think about what you want to do, or how it's going to be, but no matter what it was I always expected to be successful. It really was a source of pride for me, and a source of confidence. So it's not something that was hard for me to come to grips with. It was sort of expected; expected not only from my parents and family, but something I expected from myself. It just seemed normal.

I was talking to my girlfriend last night about how I really try to separate my job from my personal life because I don't want to become accustomed to the attention. All the things that happen—they're real—but in a sense they are not real. This is my work life; doing interviews with people, and fans wanting your autograph, and wanting to talk to you and meet you; people looking up to you. It's probably part of the game that I'm not really crazy about because people don't see you as like a real person. It's almost like it's not real. So I try and make it a point that when I leave the stadium, I go back to being a normal person—a brother, a father, a son. Those are the things that I really work on just as hard at as I do with my job because at the end of the day, your family is the most important thing. So I really try to take the time to have a normal life away from this because I spend so much time here. It becomes like a gray area where the work person blends into the real person away from the stadium.

My mother really doesn't care about 50,000 fans sitting in the stands, or that I make $3 million a year. She doesn't care about any of that. She has no problem telling me when she feels like I haven't spent enough time with the family or when I haven't called enough. I think every player needs family who will keep them grounded; let them know when they are not pulling their weight, so to speak. It's important because a lot of people are afraid to be honest with you because they don't want to rub you the wrong way, or feel like they're going to lose your favor, or something like that. My family really doesn't care about any of that. Still to this day, as adults we're expected to pull our weight.

I really like being considered a player who is multidimensional: able to help my team win in different ways, whether it's with the bat, with the glove, or a base-running play. I take pride in being able to do all those things. It's a constant battle to try to perfect all those things because some days you fall short in certain areas. It's all about figuring out how I can bring a complete game every day. Trying to perfect, that is what I enjoy most about the game.

I'm always careful about showing guys up. I feel like it's a fine line between being confident and trying to embarrass other players. It's something that I learned from my dad: that you don't show players up. People remember it. This game is hard enough. There is going to be success, and there is going to be a lot of failure. That being said, players do have a certain presence. It's sort of like a mental edge. I would be lying if you don't want to let certain people know that during a certain time of the game. People can sense when you are scared. They can see it. So it's important to carry yourself a certain way. Sometimes, in the batter's box, I like to have that confidence in me. You see it at crucial points in the game—ninth inning, man on second base, two outs; when a pitcher steps off the mound to take a deep breath and the batter steps out of the box—at the same time. And there is nowhere to look except at each other. Sometimes it's a little bit of a stare down—a look. You see if they're ready, see what they've got for you. I like to step out of the box, and sort of take it all in and enjoy it, because there is really no place that I'd rather be at that time. It's really something that I love. Sometimes you succeed, and sometimes you fail. But I step out of the box at times just to enjoy it, you know, to take in the sounds and the feel of it.

There's never a time when I don't want it, and that is the absolute truth. I dreamed of situations like that when I was a kid. I truly fell in love with this game in '84. My dad went to the playoffs. He was playing for the Cubs. They were playing against San Diego, in San Diego. I was living in LA, so my dad let me skip school and come out to San Diego for the series. I remember the first game of that series, seeing 60,000 people packed in at Jack Murphy Stadium. Screaming fans. It was the largest crowd that I had ever seen at a baseball game. I saw what they saw; at field level. Right then I knew what I wanted to do with the rest of my life: I wanted to be in a situation like that. So now, when I am in that situation I thoroughly enjoy it, and you understand that sometimes you are going to come through, and sometimes you are not going to come through. But either way, I still take it in and enjoy it. That's something that I just love about the game.

After the 2006 season, Matthews signed a reported five year, fifty-million-dollar contract extension with the Los Angeles Angels of Anaheim.

*   *   *   *   *

NICK JOHNSON

First Baseman, Washington Nationals

Nick Johnson usually is among the first Nationals player to arrive at the ballpark on game day. He was watching video of the opposing team's starting pitcher when I arrived for the interview six hours before the first pitch.

"We're on the road a lot. I'll be on the road for ten days. Getting done with this game, getting on a plane, playing the next day, and you've got to get it done. It ain't just about showing up. You've still got to produce. They don't care that we got in at four thirty or five in the morning. I wake up about ten thirty or eleven; watch a little *Price is Right*. I don't like going to the malls and that sort of thing. I go out to eat. Hang out. Go to the park. That's it."

*   *   *   *   *

I can remember pictures from when I could first walk. I always had a bat and ball in my hand. That's all I did. That's all I have done. My uncle played, so I was always around it. I mean, not too much with him, but when he would come to San Francisco we would always go down there. When I got older, he would bring me on the field and put me around that environment: take BP at Candlestick, take outfield, the clubhouse, and the guys. I was in awe. When I started getting older he used to tell me to do one thing for baseball, every day. Just do one thing a day for it. Maybe it's just hit off the tee, or just do something that would make me better for the game.

This is my fifth year playing. They didn't rush when I was signed. I had turned eighteen. I went up one level each year. I got hurt in 2000, so I missed that whole year. Check swing in spring training, and popped my wrist. They never found out what it was. I went to every hand specialist. They put a cast on it for six weeks.

Me and my roommate were watching a Yankees game, and they took Tino [Martinez] out in the eighth inning or so with like a hamstring or something. So we're looking at each other like, "No, this is not going to happen." So we go to bed, and the next morning the farm director calls. I'm sleeping. I wake up and I see it's an 813 phone number I didn't know. So I screened the call. He calls back. Same number. I screened it again because I'm not going to answer it too early because I wasn't a big weightlifting guy. If you weren't lifting weights, they would call you in and fine you. I wasn't lifting, so I thought maybe that's what they are calling for. So I called him back, and he told me.

Then I called my mom and said, "Mom, I just got called up to the big leagues!" I think it was five in the morning. She said, "Nick, don't be fucking with me right now; it's too early in the morning." August twenty-first—Columbus to Texas, and I played that night. I was nervous. Started. Went two for four. We lost.

Defensively, I think I was all right. Offensively, I don't think I hit even two hundred for the first month and a half. I wasn't really aggressive at the plate. In the minor leagues I got away with it, I guess. Up here, they just pound the strike zone. Before you know, you're 0 and 2. They put you away. I'd always take, and get behind. I'd always be hitting from behind the in the count. It's just trust. Just let it go. I remember one guy on the bench said, "Nick, no matter where his pitch is at, just swing. Just let it go. Just trust what you've got." It feels good sometimes just to let it go. Go out there and just swing and miss. Get it going. That's the thing.

But sometimes that's the problem. There's a fine line between being patient and being too aggressive. If they start throwing them in there then I can get too aggressive early in the count, and then I'm not comfortable.

Because I am patient, I think people know that I like to see a lot of pitches; that I want to sit on a heater. So I am trying to get as comfortable early in the count as I am late in the count, because I don't mind hitting with two strikes.

We talk all the time about staying back. You don't want to slide forward. I slide a little bit forward. It's so hard, you know. The ball's coming. I want to go get the ball. Everybody does. I get too jumpy. But when I see the pitch, I start getting into it. I just see it and hit it.

I had a toe tap, and I still do it. I used to go back and forth. In '96, when I got drafted, I didn't have a load. I just stayed there and then fell forward. So the hitting coach that winter tried to get some weight on my backside, before going forward. Try to figure out the load, you know. You could do a leg kick, whatever. Went home. Watched the World Series. Saw the Yankees playing the Braves, and I watched Chipper Jones doing a toe tap. So in the family room, I started doing that. It's like, "That works. Feels pretty good."

So I go to spring training with it. Nobody knew about it. Last time they saw me was with a leg kick. Now I'm just trying to tinker with it a little bit. I'm just trying to pick it up, and put it down. Just trying to inch back, so it's less movement for me to go forward.

How do you get out of a slump? For me, it's thinking too much. Everything starts popping in your head. When you're going good, nothing's in there—you see it, you hit it. Swing. Try to clear your head, and just let it go.

I've had the same mitt for a while. Rawlings. I haven't picked it too good this year. Maybe taking my eyes off the ball at the last minute and it just cuts or does something. I try to play real relaxed. Maybe just taking for granted that the ball is going . . . you know, and at the last minute you just take your eyes off of it. Maybe I need to focus a little bit more. Just do my work, and go out and have fun on the field. But prepare.

I'm supposed to be here, I'd say, at three forty-five. If I got here at two thirty or three o'clock, I'd feel rushed the whole day. If I come in here at one o'clock I can eat lunch, get a massage, hangout, relax. I can read the paper. Watch video of the starting pitcher. I want to know what kind of action his ball's doing. I would like to know the speed of the pitch. Sometimes it's hard because the guns are off. I like to know how hard the guy is throwing and if he doubles up—if he throws a heater and another one right behind it. During the course of the game—I mean when I'm sitting on the bench—I watch if a pitcher will throw their curveballs, changeups, and the fastball. Will they go fastball, fastball?

*   *   *   *   *

CHAPTER FOUR

IN THE BULLPEN

RHEAL CORMIER

Relief Pitcher, Cincinnati Reds

Cormier and I talked twice about his job. At the time of the first interview he was with the Philadelphia Phillies, and his 1.59 earned run average was the lowest among all National League pitchers who had a minimum of twenty-five game appearances. The left-handed thrower had just finished his pre-game running routine along the outfield warning track when we found a spot in the Phillies dugout to talk about being a major-league reliever. Four days later, he was traded to the Cincinnati Reds. The second interview occurred on a road trip with his new team, again in a dugout after his daily run.

*   *   *   *   *

I'm a professional baseball player. I play major league baseball at the highest level. I'm a left-handed pitcher, in the bullpen, which means I come in late in the game when chaos is on the bases. My job is to face left-handed hitters and try to get people out. What you see on TV, that's what I do for a job.

I'm from Canada from a small town called Cap-Pelé, New Brunswick. The main language is French. When I went to the city, I learned English and then moved on to college where I really started speaking English.

Hockey's always been the sport in that town. Baseball was a sport that kids just picked up in the summer. We were not a wealthy family, but baseball was always one of those things my mom and dad could afford. A baseball glove and a pair of spikes could last you a few years.

I have three brothers and a sister. I'm the youngest of five. My dad was a truck driver for a local company that hauled lobster. My mom worked at the factory that my dad used to work at. She used to bag lobster in cold storage. My older brother is a truck driver supplying hydrogen for the hospitals. And my sister and one of my brothers work for a local newspaper selling advertisements. My other brother still lives at home with my parents. He works at a local bakery.

We only had three channels on the TV when we were growing up: two French channels and an English channel. On Saturday night, hockey was always on. And we used to watch the Expos and the Blue Jays because they had just gotten into the league. But Boston was actually closer to where we lived than Montreal. So, I got hooked on baseball in about in '76 when my dad took us to a Red Sox game because he used to haul lobster to Boston. My brother and I decided to go. My dad said, "We'll just buy tickets." I still remember sitting in Fenway. I'm thinking, "Man, we're going to get good seats." So we get to Fenway. I'm sitting behind first base, but I'm behind a beam. I'm doing like this all game—side to side—you know. But it was cool. They were playing the Yankees. I remember [Dave] Winfield hitting bombs over that Green Monster. I'm like, "Wow, this is really cool." From then on, it was baseball year round. Like, we played catch in the winter in snow banks. I remember people would drive by on this dirt street we used to live on and make fun of us in the winter or early spring. Like what are these kids doing? But you know what? We were kids, man, just being kids. We played it all the time.

As a kid, I threw a little harder than everybody else, and the coaches at the time put me on the mound. I never really hit that much; didn't really play a position. So growing up, I always pitched. I worked at the same factory as my parents did when I turned like sixteen. I had a summer job there butchering crabs, but baseball was always in the back of my mind, like, "I'm playing tonight." Never missed games. Always practiced. And that's the one thing that my parents always pushed—that we never missed practice.

Then I went to college. My first year, no scout even recruited me. I was 7–0 in junior college, and I'm kind of like mad; I can't believe nobody's looking at me. So I went back a second year, and I was 14–1, or whatever it was. Then the scouts started coming. I got drafted by the St. Louis Cardinals—a fifth-round pick. I didn't play my rookie year. Decided to give up my first year of professional ball to go play for Canada in the Olympics in Seoul. Ah, that was great walking into that opening ceremony with like hundreds of thousands of people. We ended up winning one game and lost two, but the game we won was against Team USA. I pitched that game against Jim Abbott. Went like seven innings. Team USA ended up winning the Olympics, and that's the only loss they got in the tournament.

After the Olympics, I knew I had to start my professional career so they made me go to a winter instructional league in St. Petersburg, Florida. That's where the Cardinals have their camp. At the time, I was more like a thrower; more like a guy with just one pitch. I probably threw like 90 [miles per hour]. I threw a curveball that was very inconsistent. The changeup was good. I threw a split-finger fastball. Four pitches.

Then I pitched in A-ball in '89. I went to Double-A in '90 in Little Rock, Arkansas. I didn't have a good year. I really struggled. From A-ball to Double-A ball is the biggest jump. From Double-A to the big leagues, there's not a very big difference. I struggled badly, but they still moved me to Triple-A at the end of that year. Did good in Triple-A.

I went to big league camp in '91, pitched well, and then later on that year Kenny Hill, who pitched for the Cardinals, got hurt and I ended up being called up August thirteenth of '91. I ended up pitching—this is really weird—I pitched on August fifteenth: Acadian Day. It's a big holiday for French-speaking people in Canada. So it's like it was meant to be, you know?

So I got called up. I was at the stadium in Louisville. The manager called me in. "Listen," he says, "Kenny Hill got hurt and you're going to the big leagues." And at the time I was saying, "No, this is not real."

Well, my girlfriend at the time—ended up being my wife—I told her after the game and I called my parents. They're all excited. So we did the five-hour drive from Louisville to St. Louis. Had no air conditioning in my car. It was so hot. We drove. We made it. I get to the Marriott right next door to Busch Stadium. Some friends from college sent me all kinds of stuff. They had figured out where I was staying. Somebody sent me seventy-two Coronas, like I'm going to drink seventy-two Coronas before I'm going to pitch.

The next day, I walked over. Joe Torre was a manager. He told me, "We're going to pitch you two days from now." So the next night I charted the game, and then on the fifteenth ended up pitching against the Mets and beating them in my first game.

I still remember my first play of the game. Keith Miller, the second baseman, was the leadoff hitter for the Mets, and he hit a dribbler off the bat right down the first-base line. Pedro Guerrero was playing first base. He goes behind the bag, and I'm running over there. I say, "Throw it to me.

Throw it to me." He throws it and I totally lose sight of where the bag is, so I just fall on my butt. And I don't know if I'm on the bag or not, but I grabbed the ball and went behind me, not even looking at the runner. I just faked like I tagged him. I raised the glove up, and the umpire called him out—my first play in the big leagues. Oh, I got some serious love on that one there. I think I pitched like six and a third or something like that and ended up winning, 4–1.

I really wasn't nervous. I thought I was going to be. I hear guys all the time talk about how nervous they are in their first game. I don't know if it was because of the preparation of a couple years before when I played on the national team for Canada. It was definitely a huge moment for me to take the mound and pitch at the big league level.

My very next start I pitched against the Mets again. My first hit was off of Sid Fernandez on a breaking ball, right over the second baseman. I was like, "He threw a curveball. Woo!" His curveball used to be really big. And his mechanics were very deceiving. He was hiding the ball very well, and he actually still threw pretty hard. When that ball started on my head, I said, "Well, that's a breaking ball; at least it's not going to hit me in the head." I flared one over second base for a base hit. It's in my trophy case at home. Our clubhouse guy wrote FIRST MAJOR LEAGUE HIT so it was cool.

Going to spring training '95, I got traded to Boston with Mark Whiten for Scott Cooper, the third baseman for the Red Sox and some other guy [Cory Bailey] that was a left-handed pitcher from the minor leagues. I played in Boston for one year. I was platooned from the rotation, kind of like covering when guys were hurt and pitching out of the bullpen. I had like twelve starts and like thirty-six relief appearances.

I got traded after the '95 season to Montreal for Wil Cordero. I speak French Canadian, and it was great to be able to go to Montreal because I used to watch them on TV all the time. It was cool going there, being able to speak to the press in French.

In '97, I went to spring training, and the first game of the year, I threw a curveball in warm-up and ended up blowing out my elbow. I only pitched like an inning and a third. So I had "Tommy John" surgery, which is a ligament transfer. I thought I was done.

I started rehabbing during that winter. Came back in '98 and signed a minor league contract with the Cleveland Indians. My velocity was like 80 miles an hour. I was getting hit hard. My arm was still bothering me. I thought I had ripped a ligament again. I pitched until July, and then I shut it down. I was pitching a game against the Yankees' Double-A team, and I was like in the second inning. I called time. Eric Wedge, the manager, came out and I told him, "I'm done. I'm not gonna pitch any more. My arm's killing me. I don't know what's wrong." I decided not to throw again that year.

At the end of '98, I called Joe Kerrigan, the pitching coach of the Red Sox, and said, "I want to make a comeback. I want to go to big league camp." So the Red Sox ended up signing me on a minor-league deal with a lot of incentives. I went to big-league camp in '99 with the Red Sox. I was out there one day throwing and felt something pop in my elbow, and thought it was my ligament. I'm like, "Uh, that hurts." So he took me out of the game.

I was a week away from quitting. I called my wife, told her "I'm going to pitch with the pain. If it blows out, it blows out." That way, I can actually have a sense of relief. My family is not in the chaos of moving. It was scary at the time because I was thirty-three years old. I probably would have gone back to the same factory I worked butchering crab.

I came to find out later that tendonitis was built on the nerve, and that's what's causing the pain the whole time. The scar tissue broke, and then I started pitching again. My fastball started going from like 80 to 83, 85, 90. The pain was gone. I felt good.

So I finished camp and I was pitching good. Well, the day that the team was breaking camp, I show up. The bus leaves at 10:30 a.m. And I don't know if I'm going to Boston or coming home. Like I told them, I'm going home if I don't make the team. Now, all of a sudden, it became a decision to make between me and John Watson. They thought he had no options left. They went back and looked. For an option to be wiped out, there's a twenty-day period where if you get called before twenty days, that option does not get wiped out. He had been called up like at nineteen days. He had an option left. So they sent him out to Triple-A and I ended up making the team. Sometimes it becomes a numbers game, and Kerrigan wanted me. That's why I'm still here today.

So, in '99, that's when I actually became a full-time reliever. Nobody gave me a shot to start again. I was a starter my whole time, you know. I went to the bullpen, and I ended up pitching sixty games that year. It felt good. They never abused me because Kerrigan was good at treating guys the right way, especially when they come back from surgery. I had a good year. We made the playoffs. I pitched well in the playoffs.

I was in Boston again in 2000. Had a decent year. At the end of that year, I ended up signing with Philadelphia as a free agent. I've been a reliever for the last seven and a half years. I'm a free agent at the end of this year, but they have an option for me for next year, with a buyout. An option would mean I have a contract for next year, but the front office has the priority to take it or decline it. You have a certain amount of money that's guaranteed from that contract that if they don't sign it, they give it to you next year.

We call ourselves pieces of real estate. This time of year, everybody's available. There's teams that protect some of their players. Like here in Philadelphia, they will not trade Chase Utley. They will not trade Ryan Howard. But they could trade guys like Pat Burrell or Bobby Abreu. If the team is in it, you buy players. You get players to improve your team or you become sellers, which if you're not going to compete or you're trying to rebuild your team for next year, then you try selling the bigger pieces of your team, which is the guy with the highest contract and try to free up some money to try to sign guys over the winter. In my case, my name has been mentioned because I'm in the last year of my contract, and most guys that get traded are guys who are in the last year of their contracts. That way, the general manager, Pat Gillick, if he's going to move you, he's going to try to get as much as he can. I'm classified as an older player because I'm thirty-nine years old. On this team, I am the oldest guy, so they could move me or they could say, "We want to keep him for a piece of our puzzle for next year." There's a chance that you might get dealt, but I really don't pay a lot of attention to that because there's a lot of names that get thrown out there, and it never happens. So why lose sleep over it?

I think as a player you can only take it a day at a time. You cannot worry about stuff like that. If it happens, you deal with it when it does happen. I can't see myself playing for another team. But, at the same time, we know we're just pieces of real estate. It's a job, and we know that. And sometimes there is a move that needs to be made.

I usually arrive [at the ballpark] around 2 p.m. I have the same routine everyday. Every day, I come out and run ten foul poles at a regular jogging rate. Then, I do five eighty-yard sprints and then I'll do about 200 sit-ups. After that, I have a rubber-tubing program that I do for my shoulder. It has about thirty exercises. I do those everyday, once. On the days I pitch, I'll do it twice, before and after. I'll do it right after I pitch because I feel the blood flow in my shoulder makes me recuperate faster. That might just be a mind thing, but to me it works. Every other day, I do an upper-body workout, which is lifting weights in the regular gym we have behind the clubhouse. I go in there for about thirty minutes.

Every three days, a new team comes in. Preparation comes from looking at videos of the hitters you're going to face. I kind of know which hitters I'm going to face. Most of them are left-handed hitters. I can go back and look at every single pitch I've thrown to every single hitter to kind of break it down.

When I get to the ballpark, I don't stress about the game itself. Trainers work on us because we're older, so it takes a little longer to get us loose. I get to the bullpen in about the third inning. I have a stretching routine I do every day in the pen almost always in the fourth inning. I try to finish by the fifth inning. Then I watch the game. I watch every pitch that's thrown. When the phone rings from the dugout, they get guys to warm up. When they call my name, I have a certain routine I do to get loose. I throw four fastballs inside to a righty, four fastballs on the other side of the plate, and I'll throw a few changeups, a few sliders, and a couple of split-finger fastballs. I'll finish it with a fastball.

When you get to the mound, you get eight more pitches before you pitch to hitters. I throw the same eight pitches all the time: two fastballs away on the inside part to a righty, two away; I throw a changeup; I throw a slider; I throw a split; and I finish it with a fastball. Then I go behind the mound, I do my cross sign, you know, I thank God for where I'm at and for being with me during the good times and the bad times. When I come back on the mound, it's time to concentrate on the hitter. I feel I can come in, as a reliever, and pitch a whole inning, and I really don't care who I'm facing. I've done it like thirty times this year.

I have habits. Like the way I tie my shoes. I always tie my right shoe first, and I'll tie it where the laces will come through the tongue. Then I'll double-knot it. Then I'll go to the left shoe, and I'll put the tongue under-neath, so only one lace shows. And when I go to the bullpen in the third inning, I try to keep everything the same. It's a rhythm. That's why I run every day the same, because your body gets used to it. Like when I'm driving from the house to the park, I always listen to rock 'n' roll. That kind of pumps me up, puts me in the mood. I know where I'm going. I'm going to work.

Cormier was traded from the Phillies to the Cincinnati Reds on July 31, 2006—the trading deadline—and talked about it a month later while on the road with his new team.

I had to break in brand new shoes [after the trade]. I wear the same shoes all year, and I had to go to a different color. So I had to wear a whole new pair of shoes. Now my big toenail is cracked in half. My nail is falling off. What a disaster.

The day before the deadline there was a trade that almost happened. The Phillies approached me because I had a no-trade clause. You have the right to decline the trade so they have to approach you and tell you what team is interested, and then you have to accept or not. Pat Gillick and his assistant, Ruben Amaro, approached me. They said, "We have a deal on the table with the St. Louis Cardinals, and we want to know if it's one of the teams you want to go to." I said, "Yes." I said I would waive my no-trade. So I thought the deal was done. They had to work out the terms, and then they said, "We'll call you back in after the game." So they actually called me after the game. They said, "We'll let you know tomorrow morning."

So the night goes on. The Phillies' minor-league coordinator had the deal on the table, but he supposedly forgot to call them back to confirm the deal with somebody in St. Louis. The deal was probably myself for a minor-league player. So the next day I come in, and Ruben told me the deal was off.

Sunday was a doubleheader. I did not pitch in the first game. After the first game, Ruben comes in. He says, "The Cincinnati Reds are interested." So I said, "I would think about it." Before the second game, I told him that I called my agent. My agent called Ruben, talked about it. I ended up not pitching in the second game either. That night, the deal was finalized like at 1:30 a.m.—the last day of the deadline. So I'm in Cincinnati. And now we're in the pennant race.

Before they approached me, the team had traded Bobby Abreu and Corey Lidle; David Bell got traded to Milwaukee. Within a couple of days, we had three of our starters get traded. Obviously, they're sending a sign that they were going to rebuild. At the time, I really thought we were still in it. We weren't playing that well, but at the same time we were only five or six games out of the wild card, which is still very reachable with two months to go.

Other teams were interested, but it was a matter of which one. When Cincinnati came in, we decided to negotiate to try to get another year to the contract. They ended up adding an option for 2008. Adding a year was big because when I first started playing professionally, I felt if I ever got there, I wanted to play till I was forty. Next year is going to be forty, so I'm signed up.

I had never been traded during the season in my whole career. I've been traded in the winter where you go to spring training, you get to know the guys, hang out the first six weeks. You work out together. Here, I came into a situation where the team is first place in the wild card. They're in it, which is great. But at the same time, when you've been with a team for five and a half years in Philadelphia and you get traded to a team and you really don't know anybody, you've got to try to fit in.

I've been here over three weeks now. It's been tough not having pitched as well as I was pitching in Philadelphia. Maybe it's because of the transition. I don't know. I'm really quite laid-back, quiet. I feel like I need to get acquainted better with my new teammates. Most of the guys I know from playing on the other side, but it's still tough.

Obviously, I had to agree to get traded. I thought it was going to be easier than it ended up being. I just felt like I was in limbo for like a week. There's times when I felt lost at the beginning. I don't know what it was. I was always on teams where we stretched together; we hit together. There's pitching meetings. Well, I came to a new team where you stretch on your own. There's no pitching meetings. You can shag, but you don't have to. It was a big difference. But it's getting better.

Since I got traded, I tweaked my hip. I pulled a hamstring. I've been trying to pitch through that. Today's actually the first day in probably ten days I've been able to run. So I was looking forward to coming to the park today because my body is feeling normal again and I can start doing the same routine. All year in Philadelphia, I wasn't hurt, and I think, "You know, I think it might've reflected the way I performed on the field since I've been here." So all those things I'm trying to figure out. At the same time, I can't worry about yesterday. I just gotta worry about today. You can't worry about tomorrow. It's just today.

I found an apartment in Cincinnati for a couple of months. I'm going to sell our place in Philadelphia. We have a home in Florida. We'll go there in the winter and we'll rent, and then we'll see what happens next year.

Cormier was released by the Reds in early 2007 after pitching in three innings over six games. He then played with Atlanta's Triple-A team for a month before deciding to take off the rest of the season, hoping to sign with another major-league team in 2008.

*   *   *   *   *

LUIS ISSAC

Bullpen Coach, Cleveland Indians

"This job is my life, you know. I never made a dime outside of baseball. I raised my family with baseball, and I'm still in baseball, and I thank God every day because I'm here. Baseball is baseball no matter where you are. I like the bullpen that I'm in on any given day."

We met in the weight room located across the hall from the clubhouse at Jacobs Field.

Courtesy of M. Reynard

* * * * *

I'm the bullpen coach for the Cleveland Indians, and my job is to work with the manager and the pitching coach. To be the eyes in the bullpen.

I worked with pitchers all my life because I was a catcher in the minor leagues, and have been around for so long that they thought I was the right guy to do that job. Catchers, they know pitchers. I know pitching. The catcher, he runs the game. He calls the game for the pitchers, and he's the one that watches everything in front of him. Catchers learn from watching. Squatting down, they watch everything. The third baseman, he can't see the rightfielder or the leftfielder, but the catcher, he can see everybody. The pitcher is always looking at the catcher and the hitter. He doesn't see what's going on behind him. But the catcher, he can see everybody on the field. That's why they become really smart. They watch everything.

I played baseball when I was a kid, and I signed a professional contract in '62 when I was fifteen years old. Roberto Clemente, he was the guy that helped me to sign with the Pirates. I always played catcher. When I was a little kid, the first thing I saw on TV was a catcher with catcher's gear. I said I would like to do that. Then I started catching and I was good. I was playing in Puerto Rico. Those years, I was supposed to be the best young catcher in Puerto Rico. The Pirates, they had a tryout. Clemente brought me there. Clemente, he likes me, and pulled for signing me. His scouts saw me working. So I signed. I signed for ten thousand dollars. In 1962, that was a lot of money in Puerto Rico. My father was really happy.

I played rookie ball in '62 and '63. I played for different teams. I played in North Carolina. Moved to New York. They sent me to California. I was traded to one of the strongest leagues at that time. And after that, believe me or not, I got released by the Pirates when I was sixteen years old. I still don't understand why they released me when I was still so young.

I kept trying. Boston gave me a tryout. They signed me in '64, and they gave me eight thousand dollars. I played in Waterloo, Iowa. Then Cleveland drafted me in '65 on Rule 5, or some kind of draft. They sent me to Double-A. I was a player until 1979; then I managed one year; then I became a pitching coach; then I was a third-base coach; then I was like a guy that was helping in different capacities; then in '87 they brought me to the big leagues. I've been in the big leagues with Cleveland since '87. I've always been a bullpen coach in the big leagues.

Most of the time I come real early to the ballpark; always about noon. I do some exercises, get in the whirlpool, and then I wait till everybody gets ready. I just sit and wait. It's not that I have to be here, but that's my routine. I keep my routine. Always the same stuff.

When the players and the other coaches arrive, I'm ready to go do whatever they ask me to do. Most of the time, at like three o'clock, one of the pitchers in the rotation needs to throw in between his starts. I go with the pitching coach. I'm watching what he does with the pitches, and stuff like that. I might give him my input. It's up to him to think whatever I tell him is good.

Then when we are in batting practice, and I hit fungoes to the guys. After I hit fungoes, I just watch BP and what's going on, you know. Once in a while I throw batting practice. As a coach, if somebody asks me a question, I can give them the answer. If they ask me for a suggestion, I give my suggestion, and it's up to the pitching coach or the other coaches to take it. If I see something I think that will have to be addressed I might address it, but most of the time the coaches know what they are doing. Sometimes they see the same stuff that I see. I don't mean I'm right all the time, but it's up to them to take it or not take it. Once in a while I'll work with the catching instructor, and because I was a catcher I'll give him some suggestions. It's up to him to use them or not.

I was a bad hitter. I was really bad. I've been in this game for forty-five years. My mother, before she died, she said, "The devil, he knows more because he is old, not because he is the devil." I got an idea what's going on. I've seen so many good hitters and bad hitters. I know when this guy is doing good, and I can see the mistakes that they make.

Then I come in here. It's a waiting period; like one hour.

Then I go to the bullpen and I get everything set up there: baseballs, rosin bags, heaters, sunflower seeds, bubblegum, and stuff like that. We've always got water, coffee, and tea. I do tobacco. I chew. When the pitching coach comes with the pitchers, they've got everything set. The [starting] pitcher throws his plan, and then he leaves for the game, and I just sit there watching the game. Waiting for the call.

Our home is nice because there are no hecklers. When you go on the road, there are hecklers. I always tell my guys to forget about it. You show the hecklers emotion, they keep pounding on you. If you don't say a word, they get tired and they don't say anything. Everywhere it's about the same. Most of the places there are always one or two guys, they get out of hand, but that's why they've got security. Security takes care of that.

If something is going bad with the starter and they think we should start making a move, they call me and tell me who they want to be throwing. When the guy who is throwing is ready, I tell them that the guy is ready. It's up to them to make a change or leave the pitcher in, depending on the situation.

I know when they are ready because they've got all their pitches in. I've have been with pitchers all my life. I should know that. If I didn't know that, I don't think that I would be working here. Human beings, they are different. Some guys, they get ready with less pitches, and some guys, they take a little longer. That's part of my job: to tell the pitching coach and the manager who takes longer and who does it really quick. Most of the guys are about all the same—fifteen to seventeen pitches and they are ready. And sometimes the situation dictates if they are going to get ready quicker because everything is going fast. When everything is going slow, they take a little time. Then I ask, "Are you ready?" Most of the time they go, "Yeah, I'm ready."

We are always watching what is going on in the game. Everything can go really nice, but from one second to another everything can change. If the other team is getting a lot of runs then it gets busy. Last night was really nice. I never had a call; that doesn't happen too often. I've seen that only four times since I have been in the big leagues—2,700 games—only four times in eighteen years. We were spectators. We didn't have to do anything. We just clapped after C. C. Sabathia got the third out. He pitched the whole game.

I'm like a father figure, you know, because I have been around so long. I have seen so many superstars. They come for advice because I'm like a psychologist to them. I have an idea. Sometimes when they are too frustrated, they come to me. I know frustration. And I talk to them: "You've got to take your time," I tell them. "Remember it's 162 games. Everybody goes through tough times. Don't panic. You've got to stay positive."

The most important thing when the players ask you a question about something: give them the right answer. If you don't know the answer, say you don't know because if you start lying to them, they are going to know. I never lied to a guy. Every time they asked me about something, if I know the answer, I give the answer. If I don't have the answer, I say I don't know. It's bad for the player when you don't know the answer and then you start talking and talking, and they don't know where you are going. You never lie in this game. When I'm gonna say a lie, you know what I'm going to say? I don't say a word. When you don't say a word, did you say a lie? No. It's as simple as that.

The biggest frustration that I ever had in baseball? I had two big frustrations: One was in 1995. One was in 1997. We went to the World Series, and we lost both. In '95, we lost to Atlanta, and in '97, we lost to the Marlins. That was a frustration for me. Just those two days. Other days, the frustration is at the end of the season when we don't make the playoffs. If we don't make the playoffs, but we were improved from the beginning [of the season], there will be no frustration because that means the team really did a hell of a job.

A good day for me is every day. Every day, I give my best to the team, to the organization, to the players, to myself, to my family. I'm always looking forward to when I get up in the morning; to come to the ballpark. This is my life. I have been in this game so long, you know.

A *real* good day is when we win the game. Like last night, we were clapping. That's awesome. The payoff was being at the ballpark and seeing a guy pitch a game like Sabathia did.

Sometimes it's tough because you're away from your family for long periods of time, but I've been lucky that my family understands that all the stuff that they have is coming out of baseball. And for me to get all that stuff, I've got to be away. I had a meeting with them and I told them, "Hey listen, we have all this stuff—this nice house, the cars, you can go to nice restaurants, and stuff like that. If I'm always *here*, we're going to starve to death because I don't know nothing else to do." They understand.

I will be sixty in a month. When they get rid of me, well, it's time to quit. But right now, if they keep me, I'm going to be here doing the same stuff. I love my job. The ride for forty-five years has been great, and I hope that I can be around for forty-five more. I won't live that long, but I'm hoping.

Everything that I told you is the truth. I told you, never lie.

*   *   *   *   *

WOODY WILLIAMS

Starting Pitcher, Houston Astros

"Well, I can't speak on being released. I've never been released. But as far as being traded, the first one is the hardest. It happened in the winter of '98. I had a decent season. Second year as a starter, and then got traded here to San Diego. It was for Joey Hamilton. You know, after a while in Toronto I was kind of getting sick and tired of being an eleventh guy on a ten-man staff. No matter what I did it was never good enough for them. Once I got traded, it was kind of a sigh of relief. A lot of guys hate trade deadlines. I think it's an exciting time because basically, if you get traded, you're going to go to a team that wants you—a team that usually is contending. To me, it's a fun time."

Williams talked in the Padres' dugout at PETCO Park during his team's batting practice. At the time, he was on the disabled list with a torn calf muscle.

*   *   *   *   *

Hopefully next Saturday, I'll be ready to pitch here against the Giants. You really don't have to prepare as much for a team like that because you've faced them so much, and they know what you try to do and you know what they try to do. With an older team, everything you throw, they know. It's just a matter of execution. If I execute, I win. If I don't, I get pounded. I mean, there's no iffy.

I was born and raised in Houston. I started playing when I was six; pretty much every position, with pitching being secondary. All I thought about was playing baseball. And it's still that way today. I'm going to be forty in August, and I still get a thrill coming out to the ballpark, just knowing I'll get a chance to go out there and perform and compete.

I always played in the neighborhood with the kids, my brother, my dad. My dad would always take time out after work to get out there and catch. Pretty much do whatever we could before dark. That is something I'll never forget.

I love the day I get to pitch. The days in between, I turn into basically a glorified cheerleader just trying to keep my teammates positive and work on their morale. The day I go out there I know I have to be prepared, and I know they're counting on me. The fans are counting on me. The organization's counting on me.

Every team now pretty much has a video room, a video coordinator, as well as guys that log all the pitches for every other game that's going on. You can pretty much see every game, so it's a big advantage because it makes you more aware of what's going on around the league. In 1993, with Toronto there was very little video, and if they did have some, everything was on VCR. And then it went to the Hi-8s, or the smaller tapes. Then it went to the disk, and now everything's digital. It's amazing everything they have now. Basically at the touch of a button, you can see whatever you want. You don't have to rewind or fast-forward. It's just boom, there it is.

The day after I pitch, I start watching film and studying; figuring out who I'm going to be facing, and making sure I'm mentally prepared as much as I can be in knowing the hitters. Mostly I'm looking at the video of the opposing team against right-handed pitching; those comparable to me. It doesn't have to be how I did. I know how I did against them. But I may be able to get a tip or something from somebody else—the way they're having success against a certain hitter that I may struggle with. I mainly see what the other hitters' strengths are—not as much as their weaknesses—but what pitches they hit and at what counts, and if I can throw my curveball to them, or I can throw a cutter, or what off-speed pitch is the best speed to pitch to them. When I get out there, all I have to do is execute. And if I can stay away from their strengths—see it doesn't have to be their weakness—it gives me a better chance of getting them out.

I throw a fastball, curveball, cutter, and changeup—basically four pitches. And most of the time I have at least two of those working where I can throw them for strikes. And the days I have four, obviously, those are the days that work out a little bit better for me. You find out really quick, as far as feel. It's not so much the hitter's hitting them, but it's the feel—to be able to locate; the mechanics are right; I'm able to repeat my deliveries.

I think it's all preparation. It's a full-time job getting prepared to pitch the next game making sure I keep my shoulders loose. I believe if I work hard the four days in between my starts, no matter what happens out there it's the best I could possibly do.

Early in my career I got in a bad habit of shaking my head "yes" too much. The catchers didn't know me as well as I knew myself and what my strengths were. I found myself pitching to hitter's weaknesses, instead of staying with my strengths: my strength to the hitter's strength. When I'm out there, basically I'm in control of what I'm doing. When I walk off the field, I want to know I did everything I could to give my team the chance to win that day. It doesn't matter if it's good or bad. If I walk off second-guessing the pitch I threw because I didn't want to throw it, then that's the worst thing that could possibly happen.

I don't really have a big routine. When I get to the ballpark, I like to study the hitters once I get the lineup and then make sure I'm on the same page as the catcher. Let him know what I want to try to do, and then get prepared with the trainers. The trainers do a great job here in San Diego as far as the maintenance program they have for pitchers.

Right now I'm just trying to come back from an injury. I tore my calf muscle, just running between second and third at Wrigley. No reason or explanation. It just blew up and tore. Six weeks into it. Have one more rehab start. Doing maintenance work. Stretching and strengthening with weights. Hopefully I'll be back July first. I'm hoping to rebound.

After being in the league awhile, you kind of get a sense of what's a strike and what's not. As far as a definition, I don't know if there is a league rule. I believe it's more consistent the way umpires approach it now. Just like everything else, everybody has different personalities and different ideas. There are some umpires who are tighter than others. Depending on who the umpire is, you know if you fall behind the thought process is: You can't fall behind because then you have to throw too good of a pitch. And there's others that are a little bit more loose and give you a little bit. If the corner is a little bit wider some days, you're able to have a little bit of leeway and you have a little bit better chance at winning when behind in those counts. The umpires are just normal people that go about their job. But at the same time, you're still trying to make quality pitches.

I think many athletes are too proud and think they're something they're not, and forget that they're just people like everybody else. I don't think that guys sign enough autographs or give the fans enough. But at the same time, there've been times when fans have gotten out of control. They have no idea that you just signed for an hour outside the stadium or inside the stadium, and then they want to run their mouths. So it's a touch and feel situation.

You've have players that are jerks. You've have media that are jerks. There are media people going to make you out to be as bad as you can possibly be. And you've got players that, you know, don't give anybody the time of day, don't treat people with respect, and don't treat people the way they want to be treated. And then all of a sudden it's a big deal. But it's basically all part of the job. I mean, you've got to make yourself available. If people have the right attitude, everybody gets along and everybody's happy.

I was never really taught pitching until I got over to St. Louis in 2001. That's when it really started hitting me. That's when I think I finally got it. It just clicked. All the things that you've done for so many years, and all of a sudden, you figure out how *I* can do it, not how *you* can do it. It's always: How can I get the hitter out? You learn how to be consistent with that, and then put it all together. I was always taught how to throw pitches, but I never really knew how to pitch. I mean, you know when you feel good and when you don't. Young kids struggle with the thought process, and letting one game turn into two games, two games into four, and it snowballs before they know it. Then they end up back in the minor leagues. That's one of the hardest things about this league: being able to approach it mentally. To me it doesn't matter how hard you throw. I think the baseball world gets too caught in guys that throw hard.

I'm always looking to improve. Rhythm is everything to me. Rhythm is crucial. Everything is learning what works the best way. As far as the way I pitch, I've learned to throw the ball lower in the strike zone, and work the outside corner a little more than I did when I first started.

Anything I can do to help myself I'm gonna do it, whether it be bunt, or hit and run, or drive the guy in. Whatever I can do to score one run, the other team has to score two. Way back when, pitchers weren't welcome in the batting cage and didn't take batting practice all the time. But now, it's a big deal. Pitchers take a lot of offensive practice.

Every manager I've pitched for knows I want to stay in. I always want to stay in. The only time I ever come out of the game is when I don't think I can go out there and do better than the guy that's going to come in for me. It may be five innings. It may be eight innings. It all depends on how long the innings were and the situation of the game. Usually, when he comes out, you're not doing very well, or it may be a crucial situation. They basically come out there and give you words of encouragement and words of advice. He's the manager; I'm going to listen to him. If I'm in a groove, he's not going to be out there. He won't come out there if everything's good. If I'm struggling, you're taken out the game most of the time.

When the catcher comes out early in the game, they may come out just try to figure out what you want to do with a hitter in a certain situation, because once you go out between the lines everything can change. It doesn't matter how much you're prepared. You have to make that pitch at that time, and that's what it's all about. When a reliever's warming up, the catcher might as well not come out because he has nothing to say. He's just wasting time for the manager. He usually says something stupid: "You got to get the ball . . ." You know you're coming out of the game, so beat it.

Williams finished the season with a 12–5 win-loss record and a 3.65 ERA. He signed a two-year contract the next season with the Houston Astros.

*　　*　　*　　*　　*

DERRICK TURNBOW

Relief Pitcher, Milwaukee Brewers

Turnbow and I talked next to his locker in the visitors' clubhouse at RFK Stadium in Washington, D.C. He had pitched in relief the prior two games. He warmed up during the eighth and ninth innings in this night's loss to the Nationals, but did not get in.

"You know, the music starts playing and the crowd is up cheering. It's part of the whole closer's role. It's special. There is no question it gets you ready to go. That's part of the stress and pressure of being a closer."

*   *   *   *   *

I throw a fastball, a curveball, and a changeup. Early in the year [my fastball] would be 99 [miles per hour]. Now later in the year, it would be 95 to 97. My curveball is usually 81, 83—something in that range.

I started playing sports like every other kid. It's a gift to be able to be really good at it from a young age. I was able to throw harder than a lot of kids. Just fortunately born with the talent to be able to do it. I had dreams of playing professional sports, probably like a lot of kids do.

I was born in this place called Union City, which is in west Tennessee. Moved to Nashville after my fifth-grade year and we lived in Nashville from that time until I got drafted out of high school by the Philadelphia

Phillies in the '97 draft. In middle school I played football and basketball, and then in high school I played basketball for one year, but I played baseball for the most part. I played rightfield and pitcher. They didn't want me to use my arm too much at shortstop every day. When I got drafted—second pick in the fifth round—I was strictly pitching. Came up as a starter. Most guys start out as a starter.

I was just hoping to get drafted. I knew that with the kind of season I had, I had a chance of going maybe in the top ten rounds. In high school I had a pretty good year. I don't remember the specific numbers, but I had a really good year. That's when I started coming to my own as far as throwing it harder and hitting in the low nineties consistently. That kind of elevated me on the chart a little bit.

I went to rookie ball in Martinsville, Virginia, for like the last six weeks of the rookie ball season, and then went to the Instructional League. The next year I went back to rookie ball, and then the next year I went to Instructional League again; went to the South Atlantic League, and then I got called up to the Florida State League in 1999, but I never got to pitch. Then I got Rule 5'd by Anaheim. Got to spend a year in the big leagues. I pitched thirty-five innings that year. Didn't pitch a whole lot, but I got to experience being in the big leagues, and I learned a lot.

I was home in Tennessee and I didn't even know I was going to be eligible for the Rule 5 draft. It was my third year with the Phillies, and they have to protect a guy on the forty-man roster and they decided not to. Thought maybe I'd slide through, I guess. Anaheim picked me up and gave me a chance to be with them the whole year. It was good. I just got one start, against the Rangers. The rest of them were relief appearances.

So I finished the 2000 season in Anaheim, and in 2001 I went back to Double-A Arkansas to be a starter again. I came from A-ball to the big leagues. I wasn't ready for the big leagues yet, so I went back to Double-A. In my third start of the season I broke my elbow. They said it was stress. My arm couldn't handle it anymore. I think it was mostly just mechanics. I used to throw across my body a lot when I was young, and I think over the years it just got to be too much and gave away. I was twenty-three. Now my delivery is more over the top. I don't step across my body as much. My mechanics are a lot better; more solid. You kind of get better over the years as you learn more and more. It wasn't an overnight thing by any means. It took a while.

Oh man, when I had my first surgery, I had two pins and a wire put in. I had three surgeries in nine months. They took the two pins and the wires out about six months later, and then about two or three months after that I had another permanent pin put in there. Rehab took almost two years. Going into my third surgery, I started to get worried. I had my college paid for by the Phillies so I'd probably have just gone to college [if I couldn't make it back]. I don't know what I would have done. Get my degree and get a regular job, I guess. Fortunately the doctors did a great job to get me back.

I was out the rest of 2001. I was out for most of 2002, and then in 2003, I went Double-A, big leagues, Triple-A, big leagues. And then in 2004, Triple-A, big leagues, and then I came here in 2005. They picked me up off waivers from Anaheim. You know, it's weird—a lot of times guys don't know they are put on waivers. I was put on waivers, and the first phone call I got was from the general manager from the Angels, and he said that I had been picked up by the Brewers. I never really knew that I was on waivers. I thought it was a great opportunity. Get to start all over, kind of. So it was a good thing.

Bullpen guys have to be ready every single day. It's more closely related to a position player because a position player gets to play every day. You've got to be ready to play. It's a different lifestyle. When I started, I had four days off [between starts] and kind of relaxed. I mean, starters get to stick to their workout routines more consistently, and they get to come in here and watch TV and chart games. And they get to sit in the dugout, but you also got to go there and throw 200 innings a year. It kind of evens out.

Early in the game I just have a good time. It's kind of hard to stay focused all the time because you're so far away. You really don't watch the whole game. You goof around out there, cut up, and you get your mind off the game a little bit. Each guy knows what their role is. About the sixth inning you start your stretching and you start to get ready. You kind of quit talking, start to get your mind ready, and watch the game. Basically get your focus where it needs to be. Every guy has their own thing that they do. Some guys will stretch. Some guys will sit there the whole game and then get up and start throwing.

I'll stay in [the clubhouse], and then go out and watch the top of the fifth inning. And then about the sixth inning, I'll start stretching and moving around—trying to get a sweat going and kind of get loose. Just kind of focus on the game and get ready to go.

As a visiting team, in a lot of the ballparks you can hear the fans pretty good. Some places are worse than others. Philly is one of those places, especially when you get late in the game. They've been drinking for a while or whatever, and if the game is close it's even worse, but you expect it going in there. So it's not a full shock to you. If you're a closer, they're telling you not to blow the game. They will try to get into your head a little bit, but we get used to it after a while. I mean, you hear it everywhere you go.

Everybody is a Cy Young winner warming up in the bullpen. When a hitter steps in the box, it's different. As a pitcher, it's always your game. Sometimes you've got to shake the catcher off, but most of the time if you're a closer the game plan is pretty simple. You're not trying to trick anybody. You're just trying to make your two best pitches. I think what makes guys like [Trevor] Hoffman so great is that every time out, he has the fastball-change, and some guys like myself may have a fastball-change one day, and the fastball-curve another day. That's the goal: Get your two best pitches.

If I'm feeling really good, feeling comfortable, maybe it will take me twelve or fifteen pitches [to get ready]. If I haven't thrown in two, three days I may need a little more work—maybe between twenty or twenty-five. Every guy is different. Basically I usually throw four nice and easy ones and try and get the arm going. Get it loose. Throw about three fastballs each side. Then I will throw a couple of breaking balls, a couple of changeups, and go back with the fastball. That's pretty much it. Always end up on a changeup. Right before I'm about to go in the game, I'll throw one last pitch and then will head out.

I made the All-Star team this year. Had twenty-three saves. Yeah it was great. That's one of those things that you always hear, "It's gonna be the time of your life and a great experience." It's every bit of that. It's amazing. I couldn't believe I was there. You just walk into the locker room and there are all these great players. You can't believe you're part of that. There's stuff going on, and people everywhere; interviews, and then the home-run derby. So much chaos.

I got to be with Trevor Hoffman and Tom Gordon. I also got in to the game and pitched a scoreless inning. Faced Paul Konerko, Troy Glaus, and

Michael Young. It didn't feel any different for me than when I come in for a save situation, you know. The adrenaline is already so high that you really can't go much higher. Everything is already going at 100 percent. I gave 'em a hit; then I got a groundball double play and got out of there.

It's been tough, you know. I went through a slump. Started off like twelve for twelve. Picked up where I left last year, and then around like June thirtieth I just went into a slump. It just happens. I think the big thing for me is that when I was going through my slump, I would come in and give up a run, or two runs, and blow a save. I was giving up multiple runs and I just couldn't control the damage. I was getting killed. My ERA went up from a 3.0 up to 6.4. Yeah, it feels different. When you struggle, you start doubting your ability. You question things. You lose confidence. I think the hardest thing you've got to do in this game is maintain confidence. Once you lose that, it doesn't matter what you do; nothing goes your way. It's hard to get back.

It mostly had to do with mechanics. Everything kind of escalates from there. Whenever you go out there and you blow one save, it's okay whatever happens. You move on. When you blow two in a row, okay. Three—you start getting worried. I blew like five in a row. That's when it gets tough. If a hitter goes two for thirty, it's not as much. A closer blowing four saves, it's more escalated. You're in the spotlight. Fortunately at home, everyone has been real supportive. Milwaukee fans have been great. You know I was going to hear a little bit from the media—that's just part of the game. I can't complain how a few people react. The organization was supportive and behind me. They told me they would give me a break, and give me a chance to kind of gather myself again. And they traded for [Francisco] Cordero, who early in the season went through the same thing and lost his job. He got back on track and he stepped in for me. He's done great, so he has been closing.

I wish I never went through it. I talked to Billy Wagner. He went through it at one point in time. I think I've been pitching better for the past three weeks, and I can say I am back on track now.

I don't get too down; don't get too crazy. You will know when I am excited, but I don't get too overboard or anything. I'm pretty quiet and reserved. I think everybody is different. Frankie Rodriguez is animated when he gets a save. To Mariano Rivera, it's just another day at the office. I'm kind of right in the middle.

Yeah, some guys will tip pitches. It's not done on purpose. Maybe they will get the grip on their fastball one way, and then they will do something different when they throw a changeup. Hitters are smart, man. They pick up on that. Coaches pick up on that. Me? No. I always try to keep my glove open and keep everything moving the same on every pitch. I don't care if I give anything away. Some pitchers know they are doing it, but they just keep throwing and try and make a good pitch.

Overall I don't pay a whole lot of attention as far as scouting reports go. What I worry about is if the guy has a certain thing, like if he swings at the first pitch 50 percent of the time or he's not a good breaking-ball hitter. Just a little something like that could save you. I don't try to memorize. I just pick out the key things about certain guys. That's it.

Video is good to watch sometimes. I watch my game after I finish to see where the pitches were. You know, you think it's going one way but when you watch a video it's a different way. It's always the foundation for me for changing speeds, pitching down, throwing in. I think you can watch a video of yourself pitching and you can see things that you normally don't feel. Sometimes you've got to be careful watching videos, though. You can be too critical and it can actually mess you up.

My move's bad. Horrible. Being a closer, you don't really have to worry about picking off too many runners. But I did pitch over once this year, and the ball got away. It cost me. If it didn't happen, a groundball double play would have gotten me out of the inning, so it cost me the game. Most of the time with the closer is being there, the teams are not going to run. They don't want to take a chance on getting the guy thrown out. All your focus is on the hitter. You just don't worry about what the other guy is doing. Now if that run can beat you, you will pay a little more attention, but most guys don't worry about it. I think as a closer you don't work on it [as much as you should].

Yeah, I collected tons of baseball cards. I liked a lot of guys: Nolan Ryan, Roger Clemens, Ken Griffey, Jr., Barry Bonds. You forget sometimes that you're playing against guys you grew up watching on TV, and you still can't believe it. It is the enemy, and you want to get them out honestly, but you know who you are facing; makes it more fun and more exciting.

The book on Bonds? Try to make your pitches, keep it down, and hopefully it goes in your favor. A lot of times with that guy it doesn't matter what you do, he's going to find a way to get you.

*   *   *   *   *

CHAPTER FIVE

IN THE STANDS AND ON THE STREET

CHRIS HANSON A.K.A. BERNIE BREWER

Mascot, Milwaukee Brewers

Courtesy of Michael McNulty

"This is my thirteenth year of mascoting. I originally worked for the Wisconsin State Fair, in the PR department there, and we had a couple of characters: Violet the Cow and Willy B. Bacon. I had done this pig and cow, so it gave it me some mascoting experience.

It's weird I've been doing it for that long. I really enjoy doing it. I really do. I enjoy the camaraderie. I enjoy coming to the ballpark and seeing all the people. You know, it's like the opposite of all day when I am teaching at Our Lady of Good Hope. I'm always with kids. It's nice to also have a job where you are dealing with adults, even though I'm wearing a goofy outfit. You know it's kind of comfy out here. Nobody can see your face, and you dance around like a goofball. I'm one of those guys like when I was in second grade who thought I was too old to dress up for Halloween."

*　　*　　*　　*　　*

At County Stadium, Bernie Brewer had this beer mug that he would slide into. I thought how cool that would be: sliding into a jumbo mug of beer. So, like in '94, I applied. I didn't get the job, and I was really disappointed. Then midseason, I got a call from Chuck Ward, who worked for the Brewers at the time, and he was like, "Would you like to come in for an interview?" It turns out the Bernie Brewer they had hired before me got in trouble for being excessively friendly with females. They got a lot of complaints from girls, so I got the job. He told me that it was just a trial basis–type of thing, and I looked at it like that. I didn't think I'd go into this thing like, "I'm a major league mascot," or anything like that. I looked at it like, "Well, this is a fun summer job. Whatever." Thirteen years later, I'm still doing it because I love coming to the ballpark. I don't know how I could not. Even when my knee gives out, or whatever, I want to get a job being an usher, or something.

I think the Brewers have gotten a bit more fan-friendly at Miller Park than they were at County Stadium. I'll tell you, as far as me coming to the ballpark, it's a huge difference because underneath County Stadium—the bowels of County Stadium where it was a dungeon—I literally had rats running between my legs. But County Stadium was a good time. It was an old ballpark—the place where I went to ball games when I was a kid. I was sad to see it go, but I'm not complaining about Miller Park at all.

People loved it when Bernie would slide into the beer mug [at County Stadium]. It was a cool contraption. There was a trap door that I would lift up. It was connected to this tube that was filled with balloons. When I hit a button, it would start a fan going. And when I pulled open the trap door all the balloons would be blown out by the fan. So it was kind of like the suds of a beer coming out. When we came to Miller Park, I don't know if we were trying to do a little, you know, "Hey kids, don't slide into beer."

In Miller Park, we slide into a home-plate thing. Instead of people watching the guy run around the bases, every eye is like watching Bernie go down the slide. It's pretty cool. The slide's like ten times better than the County Stadium slide. I have a flag up there that I wave, and we have fireworks that go off. There is a button up there that I press, and that sets off air cannons. Originally we were going to go with some confetti cannons, but that got all over the field depending on how the wind was blowing. It was a real mistake. We had to get rid of those.

Bernie slides if the Brewers hit a home run. It's really hard to see up there because I get a lot of glare with the costume, so I'll usually depend on how the crowd reacts. This year, we've got this new ribbon board and it will say "home run" on it, so I will wait for that. Milwaukee is a big bowling town, so I usually will do a bowling kick down the slide. You ever watch bowling? It's like your follow-through in your bowling approach; like the end of your kick. I am a Catholic school PE teacher, too, and there's a couple of Brew Crew members that I've taught. It kind of started because we had a bowling unit. We were laughing about answering the phone, and doing this kick. So that's kind of how Bernie started doing the kick.

No, Bernie doesn't talk. He swears sometimes when it gets really hot, or somebody hits him. I'm just kidding. He doesn't do that. I don't think mascots should talk. I've known some that do, and it is kind of like my pet peeve. I don't like it when they are talking. The lips don't move, so they can't really be talking.

Bernie's got universal appeal. People think he's a male. I haven't been felt up too often or anything. I think pretty much they know he's a guy. Kids love me. They want a hug. A lot of people like Bernie Brewer. "Can we get a picture, Bernie? Bernie, can we have your autograph?" The chicks dig the mustache. Older folks like him as well.

Bernie is pretty easy compared to a lot of the other costumes I've seen around the league. I can machine wash most of it at home. I'll usually soap up the inside of the head because the head gets gamey. I would say it needs to be done right now; every two home stands, maybe. When it stinks, I can't take it any longer. I notice it. I think *everybody* notices it. There's a guy who'll sit with me in my hut, and I feel bad for him because it's a small, closed-in area. He puts up "K's" for strikeouts when the other team's up, and then he is just kind of like a personal assistant, which means he gets to fetch Bernie Brewer a hotdog. Bernie loves a hot dog at the ballgame, and a Mountain Dew with no ice.

As far as the costume, Bernie wore lederhosen [at County Stadium] because he was a German character and had a big Rollie Fingers–type mustache. He looked kind of like a chipmunk. It was pretty cool. Then we came to Miller Park, and Bernie got a makeover—a baseball get-up–type thing. I used to wear batting gloves. Now, Bernie's a character that's got beautiful green eyes, yellow hair, a large head—like myself—a jumbo yellow mustache, four fingers, size sixteen blue shoes, shoulder pads. He's a big dude so he looks kind of muscular, but he needs to lose a few pounds. I should weigh it some time. It's heavy, especially in midsummer when you're sweating. That thing will be drenched. I have to get some water up there today because I'll really sweat.

I come in, talk to the Brew Crew members. See how they are doing, and then we usually go through the parking lot. Tailgating's a big deal in Milwaukee. I'll go out, meet and greet the fans, and stuff. Then about fifteen minutes or so before the game, I'll go through the 300 Club, which is a pretty nice restaurant in Miller Park. I go through there, and climb up the stairs to get into Bernie's Dugout.

Bernie has a "Bernie Opener" where they play a bunch of highlights of home runs, good hits, and great plays. I'll wait until there's one scene. When that scene comes up, I hit the button, go down the slide and wave the flag. It's in the first inning when the Brewers are up at-bat.

I'm up there most of the time. I'm always up there for every inning that the Brewers are at-bat. Sometimes I'll be asked to do suite appearances on the club level. Suite appearances are set up so that when it's someone's birthday, I'll give them a bag filled with a Bernie Brewer bobblehead, or a baseball and a hat. It's always kind of nerve-racking when I do these suite appearances because we couldn't have Bernie miss a home run. So there's times we have another Bernie—Bernie II; the evil Bernie—that will go around and, you know, shake hands and kiss babies. I'll just go in my little hut and watch the game.

I've made every single home run, which is pretty good, but I've had a couple of ground-rule doubles, including opening day of last year, where it was really foggy because we had fireworks and the roof was closed. I lost it. I think it was Damian Miller who had hit a ground rule double. Maybe it was Lyle Overbay. Anyway, I thought it was home run, so all of a sudden these cannons go off. I'm sliding. That's bad.

We were playing the White Sox at Country Stadium once. I believe it was John Jaha who had hit a home run—well I thought it was a home run. It ended being a ground rule double. So all these Sox fans—because just like with the Cubs' fans—they always come up here, and we get invaded. These guys were totally taunting me. Laughing at me. Next guy up was

Greg Vaughn. I think he hits a home run, so I got to go down the slide again. Now it's a legitimate two-run home run. So I go back up, and I am waving at the guys, you know, kind of taunting the Sox fans that were taunting me. They ended up mooning me, so I called security and got them thrown out. Those guys were showing their butts off. So that's two times I've gone down the slide for ground-rule doubles. Not bad for thirteen years.

Because I'm up there in the terrace level, I'll get some drunk guys that will get on my case. It's really cheap seats, so I swear some guys get loaded and come in just to razz me: "Bernie, Bernie. Bernie sucks." I kind of laugh. Sometimes I wave at them, you know, give them thumbs up, or whatever. That gets them more angry.

The Cubs' fans are brutal. Some really like me, but others are downright nasty. We're so close to Chicago that they just invade Miller Park. There's so many of them. I've seen some signs that say WRIGLEY FIELD NORTH. It just seems to be worse when the Cubs are here.

All the mascots around the league know each other, by the way. It's like a big fraternity. I call Wally the Green Monster, from Boston, all the time. I call the San Diego Friar. Us three are kind of like best mascot friends. We give each other crap. We just mess with each other. I recently called Wally the Green Monster and asked him if he saw *SportsCenter* because I knew I made the show. You know, stuff like that.

I was talking to the Friar one time, and he's laughing. He tells me "Watch behind home plate. I'm going to have two bananas." He's a human mascot. He was going to take two bananas, like Bernie Brewer's mustache, and stick them underneath his nose. He was going to do that when his team was up, but it was getting late. So he did it when his pitcher was pitching, and Geoff Jenkins was up. So he goes down there and he is doing this—he seriously goes down there, puts the bananas by his nose—I don't know if he felt like he distracted the pitcher, but anyway, Jenkins hits a huge home run. I mean, it's like you can see the Friar run off. Like he caused the home run. That was pretty great.

So yeah, we do goofy stuff like that. You know, you got to be a little sophomoric to be a mascot. You've got to have a sense of humor.

I've been doing this a long time, and I really, really want the team to get better. I've been through some really rough years as a Brewers fan, and they're finally looking like they are kind of turning it around. I'm afraid that maybe it's not going to happen. I mean, we were .500 last year and I'm hoping for better things this year. I've been doing this for thirteen years, and we haven't sniffed the playoffs once. On the other hand you have this mascot—this girl—who gets a job for the White Sox. She does it one year and gets a ring. One year! If the powers that be are reading this, I sure would like a ring, too.

It's a fun job though. Hey, I'm not going to lie. It's great. That's why I've been doing it for so long. I can't give it up. I'm pretty good at making every game. I've only missed a couple. One in particular I was just dreadfully sick and couldn't move; just one of those nonfunctional sick days. I rarely get so sick that I can't do it. I'm pretty good at not getting ill, but that time was really bad. I haven't been seriously injured, either. I hurt my arm once, but that wasn't while I was in costume. That was just a result of some front yard wrestling, which was just goofy. Messing around with friends at a party. I couldn't move my arm above my head. It was terrible.

Advice to new mascots? Ah, I would say, "Don't do it. Get out of it while you can. You are going to waste your youth away; become crazy; get heat exhaustion. Make sure you're really funny. And don't stink—wear deodorant." Yeah, I wear a deodorant. Old Spice. Sometimes Arm & Hammer. I go on the cheap side of deodorant.

*   *   *   *   *

JOHN GUILFOY

Sausage Vendor, Fenway Park

"We've all got our catch phrases. I like: 'Sausages, five dollars. Give your wife the night off.' The women appreciate that one."

While selling sausages and sodas to customers on the street, Guilfoy talked to me about his job against the background sounds of a baseball game coming from across the street at Fenway Park.

Courtesy of Brian Bourke

*　　*　　*　　*　　*

I'm general manager of The Sausage Guy. I work on Lansdowne Street, at Fenway Park, directly behind the Green Monster—the famous left field wall.

We sell all of our sausages for five dollars. We're the cheapest on the street. The rest of them around the ballpark sell it for about six or seven. We keep it real for the fans, you know. Five dollars since the day we started nine years ago. We have ketchup, mustard, hot sauce, and barbecue sauce. Mustard is the big one. We sell Coke, Diet Coke, water, and Sprite. Those are two dollars.

We start prepping for the day at the home base at about noon—cutting onions, mixing peppers and onions, filling ketchups, loading the van. I usually get out here at about two o'clock. It depends on the hype around the game.

I've got about eight guys that work for me. I always have another guy out here collecting money. It's kind of being like being a runner—replenishing bread; putting ice on the soda; we keep a lot of stuff in the van—plus being a money collector. We take turns cooking sometimes. You have to have two guys out here for health-code reasons—you can't handle food and money. So you have to do one or the other.

Tonight's game I'm going to cook I'd say 360 of 'em to be exact. That's how many sausages I brought and I plan on selling all of them. So far I'd say I've sold about 200 or so. Hopefully I'll sell the other 160 on the way out of the game. The ins are usually better than the outs. The "ins" meaning before four and seven [o'clock], and the "outs" between the eighth inning and an hour after the game. I'm here till pretty much the street clears out and no one wants to eat any more sausage.

What kind of onions do we use? I don't know. Just regular brown onions. How many? Well, jeez, we'll use about forty onions tonight, and about—I don't know—probably sixteen cans of peppers. They're just sweet red and green peppers, and our famous sweet Italian sausages with fennel seeds. It's pork. That's the only way. We call it, "About nine inches of pleasure." We put 'em on rolls made straight up the street in a local bakery. We pick them up daily. The freshest rolls on the street.

I can cook sixty sausages on the grill at a time. I've got a big supply in that hot black box. Right now, there are probably about fifty sausages in there, so we got a back up. If they are selling slow, I cook slow. When you have a line, and you're just like flying through 'em, you are putting sausages on buns like probably every three seconds. You're just like flying through 'em. Yeah, we're pretty quick.

Yeah, I'll eat a couple of sausages a day. I switch it up once in a while. Sometimes I'll bring some chicken and cook it on the grill, but I typically eat a sausage. I actually eat mine with peppers and onions, and ketchup, mustard, and hot sauce. I eat my sausages quickly.

We're actually on private property, which is strange because we are pretty much right on the street. We've got a business relationship with the garage owner. There is a little inlet right here that we built specifically for this cart. I think we are about eight by nine feet. Next year, we are looking to extend out over here and make the area a little bigger. I'm thinking I want to get some speakers and a disco ball. You think I'm kidding? Extend it out to probably about fifteen by six. Maybe put a bigger grill in. Make it pleasing to the eye, you know what I'm saying?

What we try to do is—I mean as opposed to the other sausage guys—we try to have fun with everybody. We crack jokes and play the radio before the game. Our bumper-sticker logo: It's like a Bettie Page riding a rocket sausage. Open to interpretation. People love them. We constantly run out.

We get a kick out of everybody. I do all sorts of different stuff. I do: Sausage Guy. "Sausage and a card trick. Five dollars." Some nights I bring my cards and do card tricks.

You know what I do sometimes? Because we're behind the Green Monster, we're out here during batting practice and sometimes it's just craziness. People like running around everywhere for balls. They're chasing anything. People see napkins blowing. They think it's a ball. Anyway, sometimes I bring my own baseballs and I sign them, "You won a free sausage at The Sausage Guy." I roll them down the street and watch people chase them. They think it's a home run ball. I mean, you see them walking away and they are like, "Yes!" And then read it, and they are looking around like, "Who is The Sausage Guy?" Then they come back for their free sausage. We try to give a little different spin on it. We don't want to be some sausage vendor out here with, you know, a cigarette hanging out of our mouth.

I just had a customer who told me all he had was five dollars, and he wanted a sausage *and* a drink. I knew he was lying. We get it all the time. People come up to the cart, especially late night. We do the nightclubs after the games, and then you really get the drunk young kids, and they always come by the cart and they will say, "Give me a free sausage. Give me a free sausage." And I'm like "Man, what do you do for a living?" And he's like, "Oh, I sell paper." I'm like, "Well, you come back with some free paper, and then I will give you a free sausage."

It's like last week, this guy—he sells lumber—I said, "Well, bring me a couple of two-by-fours, and I will give you a free sausage. Maybe get out of the lumber business if you can't make five dollars to afford a sausage." Why do I want to give it away just 'cause we're out here having fun, you know? This is what I do for a living. I feel bad for those people. They work in jobs they obviously don't enjoy.

I'd say, tonight, we're probably going to make about fifty to sixty dollars in tips, on top of what we get paid. It depends. I mean, because we work with five-dollar bills there's not a lot of ones being changed over, so you don't get as many tips as you would if sausages were like six bucks.

We're not really here to make the tips. It's like of kind of a little bonus. What it really is, is money for beers after the game, when the night's over.

We get a lot of trades. A guy just gave me a box of golf balls—maybe like ten minutes ago. A lot of people always come up asking for trades— like T-shirts; food. Other vendors will come up and trade for sausages. A local beer company will come up and trade us a case of beers for a couple of sausages. Oh yeah, absolutely.

We've got an agreement with Gold's Gym down the street. We give them sausages, they let us use the bathroom. I probably run up there about three times a night, and they probably eat about six sausages. This might be a good deal for them, but they are nice guys and they let us work out in there. So we pretty much give them whatever they want. They give us whatever we want. It's a great business relationship. I think I got a free lifetime membership over there and all it cost me is a couple of sausages a game, so it's okay.

I was born and raised in Mansfield, Massachusetts. About a half hour south of Boston. A nice little suburban town. I liked going to Red Sox games.

The '86 World Series team was here last night. In 1986 I was ten years old and my brother was nine. The little bastard was a Mets fan. I don't know what happened. My parents must have made a little mistake some- where along the way. *And* he was jumping around the room giving himself high fives [after the Mets won the World Series over the Red Sox]. I was just sitting in the corner crying. I was devastated. I mean, I think he did it just to piss off his older brother because I used to kick the shit out of him all the time. But he's a Red Sox fan now. He got married last year, and I was the best man at the wedding. I gave a speech. It was an ode to a Mets fan. I wrote a big poem; pretty much just made fun of the Mets the whole time.

I was an accountant for a while, and I was a broker for a while. I was sit- ting in cubicles and just looking outside all day, and one day I was like, "I've got to get the hell out of here. This is just no good. I'm getting fat at my keyboard."

I've been in the food and restaurant business for, jeez, about twelve years now. I've done everything: dishwasher, busboy, bartender, man- ager, general manager, cook. Everything.

The Sausage Guy? He actually started his business at Foxboro Stadium, where the Patriots play. He used to sell buffalo wings, and at the end of the games people would always come out and be like, "Dude, where is my sausage?" And the Sausage Guy after a while, he switched from buffalo wings to sausages. People started calling, "What's up, Sausage Guy?" So that's how he got the name. I think it was about fifteen years ago. He's got three kids now so he can't get outdoors as much as he wants, but he is out here. He works hard. He owns this company and a couple of Mexican restaurants, one in South Boston and one at Bingham, which is how I actually met him. I was bartending at his restaurant. I've been out here about two years now.

This is fun. I get to sit outside everyday. This is—I swear to God—the best job in the world. It's like when I was a little kid, I always wanted to be a professional baseball player. I'm thirty and I still say I want to be professional baseball player when I grow up. I know I can't, but I get to be here and be part of the scene. It kind of, you know, eases some of the pain.

There are a lot of long days. On a regular home stand, I will work from maybe, jeez, eleven in the morning till twelve thirty at night every day. When the team's on the road, I do a lot of office work. I concentrate on marketing; developing sales. We do lots of catering. Right now we're working with a couple of radio stations. We do promotions with them. We do free giveaways in the morning. We do some sampling at different free concerts in the city, and we're trying to also sell our sausages all over the country. Yeah, you can buy our sausages on the Internet at SausageGuy.com. Once the order comes in, I pack them in like a Styrofoam cooler, throw some ice on 'em, and ship them to wherever.

When I first took the job I was like, "How the hell do you send sausages across the country?" It's fine. It gets there in three days, and they are nice and fresh.

After we pack up all the stuff, we take the cart home, and we drive the van back to our home base and unload. Do the inventory. Do the count—what we sold—count the money. Hopefully it adds up, or else the accountant will yell at me in the morning. Then we get ready for the next day.

Job hazards? Besides eating too much sausage and getting fat? Get some grease on your arm. Catching a hot onion. I've never been robbed. No one here has ever been robbed. Last year I was sitting down right in front of the cart, on my chair reading a paper, and like in the fourth inning—because it's kind of slow and I wasn't paying attention—[a ball] came right over the Monster and smashed me in the shoulder.

You know what the biggest job hazard is? It's late at night with a drunk crowd. We operate till three in the morning on club nights. Club nights are Thursday, Friday, and Saturday nights. There are dance clubs down on the left. They're dance clubs—techno and pop. We've seen multiple fights out here in front of the cart. Couple of years ago, some guy was sitting up right here next to the cart, fell backwards into the pit, and cracked his head open. Come two o'clock, all the drunks—I shouldn't call them "drunks"—all the *kids* are let out of the clubs, and they're just wasted. A couple of weeks ago a girl was drunk, fell down on the sidewalk, and rolled under the Sausage Guy's van. So her friends are trying to pull her out, and they couldn't pick her up. We had to go and get her because her friends couldn't. Apparently they weren't strong enough. So me and another guy went underneath, and pulled her out. She was trying to bite us, but at that point we just had to get her out. We felt bad for her. Threw her in a cab. So you do see stuff.

One of the best perks of the game is you get to know a lot of the scalpers out here and some of the security guards. On a slow night, they'll come over and hook you up with tickets. So last week, maybe it was the second inning, a guy gave me a ticket and I went into the game. I leave one guy out here during the game because it's slow. Sometimes, you know, we take turns sneaking in. So the guy gives me the ticket, I go in and I sneak down like maybe three rows behind the dugout, and I'm having a beer. And one of the other guys who works here for the Sausage Guy calls me and he says, "Hey, are you at the game?" I say, "No." He says, "Yeah you are, you liar. I can see you on TV with The Sausage Guy shirt drinking a beer." I am like, "Oh, shit!" So apparently every time there was a left-handed batter up at the plate, I was on TV. When he was watching the game, he saw me. It's all in good fun. We all take turns doing it. Most everyone that works here is a huge Sox fan.

*　　*　　*　　*　　*

PETE QUIBELL

Usher, San Francisco Giants

Courtesy of an unknown Giants fan

"I got hired in '93, the same year Barry Bonds came here. I've always been a baseball fan. Followed the Giants my whole life. I probably used to come to twenty or thirty games a year. I saw a flier that they're hiring for the ballpark, so I thought I'd check it out. I have a regular job too. I applied, and they basically hired me on the spot. To me, it's not like working when I come here. It's like having fun. I would work for almost nothing. I know I'm not getting enough, but it's not bad for what you do. I would do it for less, but I don't want to tell them that. I'm going to take the money they want to give me."

Quibell is forty-seven years old. He also has a full-time job as a recreation program coordinator with a city south of San Francisco. "I run all the sports: softball leagues, baseball leagues, the umpires, basketball leagues, the swimming pool. My whole life is around sports."

*   *   *   *   *

I'm an usher. I'm in charge of the seating near home plate at AT&T Park, right in close there by the dugout. That's what I do.

Some of the seats there are removable, so if somebody comes in a wheelchair, I can take the seat out. The wheelchair then can wheel right in, and people don't have to get out of their wheelchair. There's only probably about thirty seats that are handicap accessible where I have to do special stuff. They use two or three at the most during a game, because people just don't come in a wheelchair very often. But if they do, I can take care of it.

I do a lot of directional stuff. I'll tell a guy "You want to go two doors that way to get to your seat." I usually see them coming down there in the tunnel or I'll see them coming down the stairs—that's where I will run into them because I'm in a spot where people get confused, because as you come into the park, you have to kind of loop underneath to get where you want to go. It's not just going straight to your seat. Sometimes you might have to move down, so you don't have to climb across everybody to get to where you want to go.

And I do a lot of checking tickets for people trying to find their way into the Field Club seats, that's where the higher-priced tickets are sold. It's kind of different every time. It's mostly people looking at their tickets kind of looking up and looking perplexed. I say, "Hey partner, can I help you? What are you looking for? Can I see your ticket?" All some people want to do is flash their ticket at you and go on their way: "I know where my seat is."

Sometimes there's a fine line. There's other people you can really tell are confused, so they'll come down and look to their left, and then they will look to the right, and then they'll be looking around. You can just tell they're not sure where they are supposed to be. I just go right up to them; I don't wait for them. "What you got there, partner? Can I help you? Section 110. Okay, you want to go up there four or five rows, and you will find it right there on your right," or whatever it might be.

The people that bought Field Club seats basically own the seat, so they are much more particular about their seats. There's an usher there stopping everybody to make sure they have a ticket to get into the right area. In the later innings if the people haven't got there, sometimes there will be people—say toward the back rows—that filter down a little closer. As long as they have a Field Club ticket, I don't necessarily bother them because they've paid that extra price. But we really do keep people out who bought way up in the upper deck [from] coming down into the Field Club, because those are our instructions. We're much more of a stickler with that now.

I have to come up and approach them and say, "Sorry, this is not where your seats are at. You need to go where your seat is." Where I'm at, all the seats are sold, so the people coming in here are going to be in the wrong place. A lot of seating is mistaken seating, so it's not necessarily that they are trying to pull something, but there are people that are trying to sneak down to the better seats. I think it's all actually kind of part of the game. We send them back nicely.

When we first opened this park seven years ago, they had everybody who came over from Candlestick work different areas of the park so we'd know where everything is. I worked in the bleachers a couple of days—a very different kind of crowd out there. We get the college crowd out in the bleachers. Those people are more out there to have fun and, you know, "Are we too far from the snack bar? Where we can get beer?" They are really more concerned with that than they are with watching the game. They want to have a good time.

In the bleachers, there tends to be a little bit more fisticuffs than anywhere else in the park, especially when the Dodgers are in town. I mean, it's always the case with the Dodgers. They like to ride each other. That's part of the game. The bleacher people are very unique in themselves because the Dodger guy knows he's wearing the Dodger stuff in the San Francisco ballpark. They will get on him with "Dodgers suck." They will yell at each other, and they will do some fisticuffs.

We try to warn them and get it broken up before anything happens, but it's impossible to be everywhere at once. We try to keep our eyes open for problems. The usher out there would have a radio and would probably tell their supervisor, "The guy in row K, whatever, seat 12, is a team player." That's what we call someone who basically has had too much to drink. And they will try to warn them, "You guys, that's enough swearing. I'm giving you a warning. If you keep it up, I'll have to call security." And then we might have to call the police to take them out of there once they start fighting.

Sometimes people get really mad and they'll swear at us a little bit. These things happen. We'll come across a situation where people have brought beer in cans into the park and you've already told them they can't have it, and you take it away.

"It's BS," they'll say. "You can't just take it away from me."

You know, people are always only concerned about themselves, for the most part. You don't take it personally. "Do you have any more? If you don't, it will all be good. You can stay and watch the rest of the game. But if I come back again and I find another can of beer, I already told you, I'm going to have to have security throw you out." I'll be just as plain as day with that kind of stuff. You have to deal with the situation on a case-by-case basis.

In the lower boxes, as you get down the lines, there's the crowd of the hardcore fans that really want to see the game. I think they like being near the bullpen. They would love to be in the premium seats but it's just probably too expensive for them. There are some hardcore fans in the Field Club, but it takes a lot of money. Typically they will be the ones who will have their Giants coat on and their Giants hat on. The ladies will have Giants earrings on. They'll have their scorebook, all their accoutrements on, and everything—the whole nine yards. They're unique. They're cool.

A typical day? I leave my home for my regular job at seven thirty, and I work eight to four with my regular job. I have very flexible hours, so as long as I work eight hours a day, they don't really care when I work those eight hours. When I get off, I get in the car and drive straight down here to the park. I have to report by four forty-five. The game will be at seven fifteen tonight. These days, the biggest concern is trying to get parking, There are places where you can park for free still. We don't spread that information around or else we wouldn't have any parking left. Otherwise, you can park in the lot and they charge six bucks for us as an employee. If I'm running late, sometimes I will have my wife drive me up and drop me right at the door.

We typically have a little briefing meeting with all the ushers. There are over two hundred, I guess. I've probably seen everybody, but I don't know everybody. I know most of the ushers all in my general area. We're pretty good friends.

We'll all congregate in an area of the ballpark, and the supervisor will tell us, "Okay, tonight, we're going to have some giveaways, so we are giving away baseball cards to the kids in this inning," or whatever it might be. It's usually different every day.

After the meeting, everybody breaks off to where their section is. I check the area to see if there might be anything broken. Sometimes there will be a seat that might be loose. I might have to tighten it down. And we clean the seats. Sometimes seagulls and pigeons leave their marks. You get something to clean it off. If it's something that you really can't take care of, then you call maintenance: "We need bird patrol over here. Bird poop on the seats." They're here all the time. They've learned that there's food when the game is over, so about the sixth or seventh inning you will see them start landing on the top of the stadium, just waiting to come down to get leftover hot dogs and buns and peanuts; whatever they can find.

Two hours before the game, the gates are open. As soon as they are let in, we'll typically see the autograph people running down the stairs. There's probably more adults than kids. Some of them are dealers, and some aren't. Some are real fans. I pretty much let them go as long as they have the right ticket. Sometimes you get the ones who get too anxious. They'll stand on the seats. "No, you can't stand on the seats. Keep your feet on the ground," I'll tell them. Obviously, if they start doing things like standing on the seats or doing something they're not supposed to be doing, I'll tell them, "If you want to stay here, don't stand on the seat or you are going to leave."

"But I got a ticket."

"Doesn't matter if you got a ticket. If you're not doing the right thing, you can't stay."

Usually one of the other guys will say, "Shut up and do what he says. Get off the seats." Or one of the other guys will give him the elbow. They actually almost monitor themselves. I've been doing it in the same spot for four or five years now, so they pretty much know what to expect. I let them get autographs all the way through batting practice, at least. Usually I let them stay almost till when the umpires come out. Once the umpires come out, I'll start clearing them out.

I feel like I'm an entertainer. I entertain the kids more than the adults. I have my top with me. I'll bring my puppet. I'll bring my stuffed ball. I'll joke with anybody pretty much. Actually, what I do is bring stuff in my pockets. We have a sign that we hold in between batters telling people not to walk up the stairs because you might get in somebody's way. It says PLEASE WAIT, BATTER IN BOX, I think that's what it says basically. The other side says PLEASE HAVE YOUR TICKET AVAILABLE UPON REQUEST. I kind of stick the sign out so they really can't go around it. I almost use it like a blockade. So, in between innings, especially like on a rain delay or a bad game, I will spin the top on it, flip it up and down. And I have little finger puppets that I will hold way up in the air and joke. Then I have a little stuffed baseball that looks like a real baseball. Every once in a while I'll toss it to somebody, "Hey, that was a foul ball." I think it's all fun, you know. It's really not too serious. It's all about having a good time.

I get to watch a lot of the baseball. On a normal night, I probably get to watch seven of the nine innings. I miss plays here and there, but most of the time I get to see most of the game. I love to talk baseball with people who are knowledgeable, and there's usually a lot of them. There are some people who aren't knowledgeable but want to become knowledgeable. They will say, "Oh Pete, what do you think about why they didn't take him out?" They have the dazed look on their face like, "Oh, I didn't know that. That makes sense." There's all levels of people who understand and don't understand the intricacies of the game.

When the game's over, a final announcement is made. If the Giants win, we'll hear Tony Bennett singing "I Left My Heart in San Francisco." We only play Tony Bennett when we win. When they lose, they just play some regular music. There's not a particular time, usually about fifteen or twenty minutes. I basically move towards where the front seats are to make sure nobody wants to jump on the field and do something. That's never something that comes up, but we still usually kind of wait a little while. Then, at a certain point, the music stops. Most people usually pack their stuff and filter toward the exits. I'm going, "All right folks, got to pack it up. Time to go. I need to go home and get some sleep."

I'll start getting people out. All the ushers line up and we get most of the people out. Then we will start big sweeping lines down the third-base side and the first-base side, looking to see if they've left stuff. People leave stuff all the time: cell phones, backpacks, coats, hats, shirts. Just about anything. I've found some interesting things over the years. Back at Candlestick, there was a guy from New York who was here, and I found his wallet. There was $1,200 in cash. He came back a few minutes later before we could even bring it up to lost and found. He said it wasn't safe to leave it in the safe at the hotel. That's what he said.

Well, after the sweep, then I usually go to another spot, which basically kind of stops people from wandering anymore in the ballpark. We direct them to the escalator to go out. There're still people up in the promenade buying souvenirs or in the bathrooms. You're still waiting for people that are slow. We just kind of make a human barrier. "Okay, folks, it's closed out that way. You need to go out this way."

They will go, "Oh, but my car is in lot C. I need to go that way."

"No, you need to go *that* way." Sometimes they argue. I'm going, "Go ahead, go that way. The gate's already locked, you will head right back." Ten minutes later, you'll see the same people walking right back to where we told them because the gate was locked, and they couldn't get out.

Typically, when the game's over, you are here about half an hour before you check out and go home. Depending on the length of the game, I usually get home around eleven.

Everybody just calls me Pete. Sometimes they call me "Pizza Pete." The other day they were having a pizza giveaway, and the guy coming around said, "Pete, you want a piece?" I took it. You could get into trouble for doing that. I probably shouldn't have done that, but I was just starving at the time. It was a Luigi's pepperoni pizza. Yeah, it's good pizza. So they call me Pizza Pete.

* * * * *

ARNIE "PEANUT DUDE" MURPHY

Peanut Vendor, Houston Astros

Courtesy of Sarah Owen

"I make most sales off of my throws. The fans like to see me throw. They enjoy all of the antics that I do: watching me throw behind my back, or make really long throws. Do you remember Meadowlark Lemon had the basketball that had a rubber band on it? I've got a bag that's got a rubber band on it. I stole that from him. I like to use it with the kids on Saturdays and Sundays. And I always kind of tell jokes; try to keep it light. I like to think of myself as an entertainer. You know, make contact with that fan that I do business with. I like to feel he walked away from it entertained, and not just with a bag of nuts."

*   *   *   *   *

I started doing this when Drayton [McLane] bought the ball club. He wanted everybody to come out to the ball yard and just have a ball. My friend was the concession manager for Aramark at the time, and he said that this new owner wants pizzazz out there; he wants something to happen; he wants fan-friendly service and fun in the seats. I kind of told him one day, "I used to throw peanuts to people before games when I was kid, back in Cleveland, Ohio." I was a basketball player in high school, and I could throw behind my back. I said, "Well, that sounds like something to do." So we went out there, and it just kind of worked for me.

Yeah, I was a high school basketball player in the Cleveland area, and I used to sell peanuts between '60 and '65. It's kind of an interesting story because it relates in a way. We went down to Fourth and Prospect at a place called Peterson Nut Company. You bought your peanuts and sold them outside Cleveland Stadium. You could sell them before and then you could wait and sell them after, when the people would leave. I wasn't working in the stadium. I was on the outside. I could sell four bags for a dollar—a quarter a bag. Now, they are four dollars a bag. I started throwing them behind my back, and all that kind of fancy stuff that I've done; just to make sales better. Most of the other guys would kind of go away from me because the people wanted to buy from that kid that throws them.

You know, getting to that story. When I started at the [Houston] Astrodome in '93, or whenever it was, peanuts were just like an afterthought in sales. Everybody wanted to sell beer, Coke, or whatever. Nobody really wanted to sell peanuts. The first day I went out to do it, I was a little nervous. I picked the bag up and it was kind of raggedy in my hands. I was deciding how nervous I was going to be about doing this, and I looked down at the bag. It said: Peterson Nut Company, Cleveland, Ohio.

I don't really go out to work until about ten or fifteen minutes before the game because I wait for there to be people in the seats. I think that most of the vendors come in quite a bit earlier than I do. My foremost thing is not the sale. I just do what I do: offering service to the fan. And then the sales come. I normally leave right around the seventh-inning stretch. That's when I check out and settle up my money with Aramark for the peanuts. Being the baseball fan that I am, most of time I kind of hang around and watch the end of game, or listen on the radio on the way home.

I basically define my own section at the ballpark. I've stayed over along the third base side because of the way the roof opens. The sun shines in when it's early in the game—first three or four innings. If I throw the peanuts, the people don't see them too well [along the first-base side].

The sun shines in their eyes, so I just have a lot better luck on the third base side. That's beside the fact that it's about 15 degrees cooler over there. It's a little better to work there, and there is only so many sections that I can work in a single night. And I usually go up to the club level because they kind of request me there.

Ordinarily, I don't pay that much attention to the game. I just work. But you can tell by the crowd when it's a rally and the bases are loaded, or there's a 3–2 count. The fans are going to be really into it when a moment is coming up like that. In quieter moments, when the other team's up, or whatever, for those few minutes I guess I'm pigheaded enough to think when I go down and start throwing, they are actually watching me. So I feel a responsibility to try to make it a good time.

I know well enough that if the bases are loaded, I'm doing myself a disservice if I go down there to that aisle to work because they are not going to look at me. They're into the game. They are into the moment. I just generally choose to stand at the top. That'll be the time when people say, "I haven't seen you all night." Well if I went down there when that was going on, obviously they didn't see me. So I wait.

I always say, "R-O-A-S-T-E-D peanuts!" That's my world famous peanut call. I let people know that I am the goober guy—some people in the South call peanuts "goobers." It's not so much what I say that makes the sale, as much as the throwing. Once they see me *firing* one, I'm firing over there.

My range? If I can see the money, I can make the throw. That's what my range is. I don't need to throw it any farther than that. I kind of hate to say it this way, but I hardly miss. If there's been an incident, usually the fan tries to make this swiping catch, or something like that, and he doesn't catch it. But who is going to get hurt with a bag of peanuts? It's just I have a very high concentration level. Without making it sound like it's too serious, it's almost Zen-like. I see the target and it's almost like I just let go, and they just go. I've always been able to do it behind my back. I wish I could do the same thing in my golf swing—see the target, and make the ball go there, but in golf you've got to think about everything, and it's tough. I even tried self-hypnosis where I'm imagining throwing a bag of peanuts at the hole. I'm a pretty good player, but never as good as I am throwing peanuts.

I think I'm about as good as you can be. I can't imagine anybody being it better as far as getting the peanuts there; and then adding personality to it, which is really more important than the skill level. I can underhand; overhand. There's times when I see an athletic-looking guy in a ball cap. I'm going to throw overhand over to him. Women, generally speaking, I throw underhanded because I get a lot more arch on an underhand, and it kind of comes down to them. Children, I always try to throw short to them so even if they have to reach out and miss them, that's better than having it be a little too long, and hit them in the face.

My benchmark? What I like to think is a really, really good night is a thousand dollars in gross sales—250 bags. As much as we love having the roof open, people don't buy quite as well when it's hot. And they don't buy quite as well in afternoon games. It's just been that way for so long. Who knows why? It's just the fact. I mean, when I used to sell cotton candy I always noticed the hot days were the worst days. Even kids can get so hot they don't want cotton candy. The night games are always much better. I'm always a little disappointed when it's a day game, but I am always here.

The biggest day that I've had? I really don't remember the number now, but I do know the biggest day was when we had the All-Star game here, in '04. The reason was just that I had a much larger window. The people were here all day, and I worked much longer. It was kind of funny that when we did the playoffs the last two years, sales were just awesome. But the World Series was a very strange animal to work. They kind of backed off a little bit. It was so intense. Oh boy, the adrenaline was running so high, and it was just very hard to work. It was surprisingly different.

There's kind of a sidebar story with what I do here. In '95, my wife got cancer and she died. She met some of these Sunshine Kids—they're kids with cancer. It's a real nice organization that does things for the kids. She had asked me to do something for the kids. "We need to do something for the kids. It's not fair," she said. I tried to get everybody to give a donation to the Sunshine Kids instead of flowers for the funeral. I kind of let it go with that. Didn't think much about it. But two years later, somebody from Aramark came up to me and asked me if I wanted to get involved with the Sunshine Kids. It was kind of spooky, if you think about it. It was almost like there was some plotting going on behind the scene, maybe from up above, or whatever. It turns out that we started this program—the Junior

Peanut Dude—where Aramark gives a portion of money to the Sunshine Kids from every bag that I sell. On Saturday and Sunday, we actually bring a Sunshine Kid and his family [to the park]. The Astros are great; they give them a seat. Aramark gives the kid a T-shirt. They give the family Aramark dollars to spend here, and they have a day at the ballpark. And then in the fifth or sixth inning, the kid's up on the big screen with me and they announce what's going on. Then the kid goes down to work, throwing peanuts, and I give the kid the money they're making while working. The kid I had last Saturday, he was eight years old, and he had little chubby cheeks and a bald head. He was just as sweet as he could be, and when I told him we were actually going to sell the peanuts, he just kind of looked at me, tilted his head, and said, "Are we going to split the profits?"

And the whole deal about being the Peanut Dude: I have done about five commercials here in town. I did a commercial for the dog track. I did Fox Sports, and I did a thing for the Houston Tourist Bureau. I've been on every local channel. I was on *Good Morning America*. I did a spot on the Food Channel. That was a biggie for me. Seems like opening day, World Series time, playoff time, there's a story. But the neat thing for me—other than the Sunshine Kids—is that I have found myself a place in my community. Everybody doesn't get to do that. I'm known in my community. I mean, I'm not bigheaded about it; it's just that I just enjoy when I get recognized. Sometimes I sign autographs; not a lot, but enough that it's fun, and not enough that it's annoying. People will say, "I know you. You're the Dude." I really enjoy that.

In 2000, the morning of the All-Star game, I made the front page of the *Wall Street Journal*. They did a story about me. They sent their reporter out about the fact that I was going to go the All-Star game, in Atlanta, and the little gal that followed me around did such a good job that they got it on the front page. My picture was above the Pope. Of course, I bought five copies for my mother. And I've been told that every day the *Wall Street Journal*'s computers look at the obituaries from all the local papers, all over the country. If they get a match with someone that they did a feature story on, they run that obituary in the *Wall Street Journal*. So my obituary is going to be in the *Wall Street Journal* one day. I got that going for me.

I'm fifty-eight years old. I guess you would say I am kind of semi-retired. I've been in the concession business my whole life. My wife and I had a cotton-candy concession at the Dome for a number of years and that's basically what I kind of retired from. I'm just going to keep doing this. I'm hoping maybe like four more years.

Last March, I had a heart attack and they put six stents in me. I was in the Astros' physician's office. I thought I had a cold. I went in the hope that maybe Dr. Muntz would give me something to get rid of that. He started giving me electric cardiograms and stuff. The next thing you know, I'm across the street getting stents put in there. Changed my diet quite a bit. I eat walnuts. They are really good for you. Peanuts? Yeah, I eat some.

*　　*　　*　　*　　*

JOHNNY "FROM CONNECTICUT"

Ticket Hustler, Fenway Park

Johnny "from Connecticut" was the only ticket hustler working along Brookline Avenue who would talk to me this night. The New York Mets were in town for a three-game interleague series against the Boston Red Sox, the first time the two teams had played in Boston since the 1986 World Series. He talked between the third and fifth innings of a 9–4 Red Sox victory.

Johnny had heard someone wanted to talk about ticket hustlers working the streets. "I check all the corners to see if other people have seats," the sixty-two-year-old said. "Check my cell phone to see if I got any calls. I'm going to get a ton of calls tomorrow, 'How much can you get me, John?' 'Let me check.' Check with a kid down the corner. He's got them at $150. 'Yeah, I got some reserves at $175, okay?' 'Okay, come on down. I got them.'" I make $25. We work together as a network, you know. They're all good people here. You won't see any thieves. Nobody sells counterfeit tickets."

Johnny asked that his last name not be mentioned.

*   *   *   *   *

Every weekend, if they're playing a good team, it's going to be a money-maker here. But it isn't like it is when they're winning, you know. I wouldn't go up here in the eighties because of the junkies and the heat—the cops. I've only been up here four years and they've had four terrific years, knock on wood.

People get tickets up here and they can make a decent living, but they also work very hard at it. There's a lot of a trickle-down effect of tickets coming out of this ballpark. Since I've been out here selling tickets, I've never seen a Green Monster ticket on the street or seen one go on sale to the public. The left field wall seats here are the most priced seats in the whole ballpark. Everybody in the world wants to sit there because they're new. It's a novelty; I think $90, or $50 for the standing room. Actually, I've seen two of them. I believe businessmen or some other large conglom-erate or some other Sox sponsor is paying huge amounts of money get-ting these tickets, and using them for what I call "corporate scalping." In other words, "Yeah, I can get you these, but make sure you do that 800 mil-lion dollar deal." And the Red Sox are giving them to sponsors for, you know, a terrific amount of sponsor money. I know this for a fact. They just don't go on sale to the public.

I think they occasionally put a couple of standing rooms on sale at that line over there around the corner. Between the standing room and reserves, there's 4,000 of them. But so far, none of the brokers in the industry have them. Someone should have them. Not one has ever hit the street. So I'm dying to find out whose hands those seats end up in, okay? That's just one of the interesting anecdotes to the outside of it, you know.

It's supply and demand. The ballpark holds 36,000, and it covers the largest geographical area in the Northeast corridor. Do the math. If they have a team with stars like Ortiz and young pitchers, and they're in first place, and it's a sunny Saturday, and there's 70,000 people trying to get in the ballpark, and there's only 36,000 tickets available, then you know what the ticket's worth. It's not the hustlers and the scalpers who create the demand. It's the ballpark itself that creates demand. Now between you and me, they could add seats here, 20,000 or 30,000 of them. They've already added a few, which they use for corporate purposes because they can make more money putting 2,000 Green Monsters in here than 20,000 seats out in centerfield. And that's why they'll never add a major amount of seats here, nor will they move to a spacious ballpark. Okay?

This is a hard place to get seats out of. It's gold. You know, on a weekend in nice weather, it's gold. If it rains, they're all over the place, you know. But then who wants them in the rain? Rain killed the ticket this summer. So nobody has made money. The past couple of summers it's been exorbi-tant, you know. The Internet is another factor. There's Internet geniuses that get into the program that the Red Sox have. They figure it out. They suck the tickets out of the machine before they become available to Joe Fan, who monitors the machine all night long. The Red Sox release maybe 1,500 seats a game. That's my estimate, in dribs and drabs at certain times. Now, for a big game like tomorrow night—the return of Pedro Martinez—they may have released only 500, but for most weekends they release 900 to 1000. Now, all of a sudden, the politicians call up and the seats are gone. On the Internet, these Silicon Valley people are writing their own programs. Yeah, the geniuses, you know what I mean? Far beyond my power to understand how they do it but they do it, okay? Because I get calls from Silicon Valley with people with twenty to thirty seats for a Red Sox game two days later. They've got them, and they want to Federal Express them to me and sell them to me. So this is what's happening.

I'm not on video, am I? There won't be direct repercussions?

The bad part is, it's such a small ballpark they could put the seats on sale in the box office and still sell it out. But by putting it on the Internet, they're valuable. If a guy hits ten bleacher seats at $20 each off the Internet, he can come out to the ballpark and get $120 each for that amount Saturday or Sunday. So if he pays somebody to sit next to a computer, and they have the code to get in to suck them out of the machine before Joe, they're going to come up here with eighty or a hundred seats, which people do, and walk away with $10,000 a game. And people have done it last summer.

There are amateurs doing this, too. Some of these people coming up here are not ticket hustlers. I hate to use the word "scalping." That term is denigrating to the American Indian, you know. Think about it. I was in court once in Connecticut getting yelled at by an attorney; about ready to have a civil fine against me. A rock promoter and attorney coming after me. The promoter wanted a total monopoly on the sale of tickets in Connecticut. They used the term "ticket scalping." When I said, "This is wrong. I see what you're doing here," they came after me. So I'm in court, and it was "Scalper-this, John-scalper that." I stood up and I said to the judge, "Listen, that term is a racist term. It doesn't belong in your courtroom. It's denigrating to the American Indian. It's like calling an Irishman a 'bogtrotter' or a Jewish person a 'kike' or a black person a 'nigger.'" I said that he shouldn't have that kind of a term in his vocabulary. It kind of turned his ass, you know what I mean? But, yeah, that's a terrible term.

Nobody comes along and takes a tomahawk, you know, and puts any kind of a ceiling on a ticket. It smacks of communism. They don't go after gas people. Gas is a serious thing. That could affect the national economy and imperil the national safety. That's a utility in my book. That should be regulated. But tickets are a luxury item. To put any kind of a ceiling on tickets is very dangerous. It's anti-American. What's going to be next? Is it going to be furs? Is it going to be jewelry? Whatever the market shall bear.

Last year was a terrific year because they had just won the World Series. They had Damon. They had gorgeous weather, and Damon was a media idol up here. He was more than a baseball player. Five thousand girls would come up here every night from the colleges with the Damon T-shirts on, paying $85 to $100 each to get in. It was a moneymaker if you had tickets. When it gets that big, though, you pick up three tickets a day and you get $90 each and go home with $270. You know, it isn't like you go home with $1,000. Then there's days when you lose money. I think if you really work hard out here and deliver ahead of time, you can make $50,000 a summer out here, but that's with a lot of work, not just standing there, you know, with thirty free tickets, which nobody gets. Ticket people lose money out here. People think we come out here and make $100,000 a year and make thousands every night. The past two months they've lost their shirt because of the rain, you know.

I'm independent, but I buy off certain season ticket holders. I'll take their stuff all year long. If I say, "I need *this* game," they'll make me pay them a little bit more, which I don't mind doing because of the demand. When it's a small ballpark like this and the ticket's that big, if you have four extra seats, are you going to go back to the Red Sox and say, "Here, sell them to a fan who cares"? Or are you going to call up John or Harry or Bill and say, "John, what are these worth?" Season ticket holders will call and they'll sell them to you. And, they're not selling them to you at cost either. They're good seats. They're going to charge you $100 for boxes. So you buy them ahead of time. They will cost $80, but they'll sell them to you for $100 to $125. They want to earn money, too. Everybody wants to earn money. For tomorrow's game, I just bought four seats for $175 each because Pedro is pitching. It's the biggest game ever. And I'll turn them over for $225.

I had some people who wanted four tickets, so I called up the season ticket holder. I said, "Look, I'll give you a buck seventy-five each. I got a guy paying two and a quarter." They said, "Fine." So I gave him the money. I'll go deliver them in the morning. And then he's happy. Then I'll come up here and try to grind out a few. Do you know what grinding is? You spend eight, nine hours on hot pavement walking around the streets as people walk by, "Anybody selling tickets, anybody selling?" And if you pick up three seats tomorrow, you know, at cost, you'll make two day's pay. A single seat tomorrow, if you bought it at $80, you could get $200 for it.

I'll keep talking, but I don't want to get in any trouble for this, okay?

A major-league team has a symbiotic relationship with the entire community. Look at these parking lots. Look at these bars. This whole thirty-block area, including the hotels, downtown, when the Red Sox are home; it's magic for them financially. It brings money and goodwill into the community. It's a major-league city if you have a major-league team.

If one of these other hustlers are with a customer, you don't barge in and say, "I have something better." You wait until they're finished. It's respect, you know, and that's why there's very little fighting. Everybody gets along; it's kind of a teamwork thing here because there's no fighting and bickering. If somebody's with a customer, they wait. If he doesn't want to buy the tickets and walks away, then you go to him. But otherwise you don't.

There used to be a real crackdown, okay, years ago. I'll give you the history of it. A [law passed] to make it illegal to re-sell a ticket in Massachusetts. It was a horrible, horrible law. They used to handcuff you onsite and then take your seats, and they'd sell them to the corrupt cops who'd take the seats and sell them to hustlers. Back in the eighties it was bad. About ten years ago, a dentist came up to the ballpark and said, "Hey, I got an extra ticket. The other couple couldn't go." They handcuffed his ass and took him. He was a rich dentist, too. Put him in the paddy wagon and brought him in. He'd never been arrested before, and it was a very traumatic experience for him. He took it to the highest court. And the judge ruled, "Listen, if you have two extra seats and you want to re-sell them at a nominal value over the price of the ticket . . ."—because he was selling them at half price—". . . you're allowed to do it. From now on, that's the law in Massachusetts." So he walked. You can re-sell at a reasonable surcharge. I guess "reasonable" hasn't been decided, but the judge did that, thank God, and it changed the whole complexion of things.

The heat was horrible up here. I almost got handcuffed one time because some hustlers would point out brokers from out of state. I took my father to "Yaz Day" and the guy wanted to handcuff him. Luckily, I had only two seats. I mean I was just walking into the game with him. "There he is." They were pointing each other out. A lot of junkies worked up here then. It's a clean group of kids up here now. Nice place.

You don't sell in front of the box office. It's their venue, you know. You have respect. You work down there a block away, two blocks there, three blocks over. You don't sell in front of cops. The cops don't want to come around and say, "Hey, how much did you sell that for?" They come out about twice a year and act heavy, you know.

I work anywhere from down near the—what's the name of that place down there? The pizza place. I work from there down toward the hospital, if I have to. On a day like tomorrow, it's so busy I'll go far away to try to get seats early because the closer they come to the ballpark, the more people are going to be selling them. If I try to buy a ticket here tomorrow night, by the time you finish selling it to me, there'll be eighty hustlers.

I did hospital food-service work. I went to a World Series game, '81. It was a beautiful balmy night like this. The Yankees were playing the Dodgers. I went with my cousin, and all the stars were out, you know. It was a huge night. It was big. It was beautiful. Fernando Valenzuela was pitching against the Yankee ace, [Dave Righetti]. Reggie Jackson was playing. It was just huge, okay. We didn't have any tickets. And I said to my cousin, "Let's go. Bring some extra money to buy tickets."

I get there at four p.m. I was kind of aware of scalpers. I said, "Anybody have any tickets?" And a guy says, "Yeah, I do." I said, "Where are they?" He says, "They're field boxes, right behind third base." I said, "What do you want for them?" He says, "Just regular price," which was like $50, $25 each, back in the early eighties. Today, they would be $110. The cost of living has gone up.

So I said to my cousin, "All right, we're in," and we're slapping each other five. Then all of a sudden a guy comes up and says, "Say, would you happen to have tickets?" It was a guy with a white trench coat and a pin-striped suit. And, I said, "Yeah, as a matter of fact, I do. I've got two beautiful field boxes." He says, "How much do you want for them?" I said, "$350 each," kidding around, okay, and he says to me, "Well, that's kinda steep." And my cousin says, "I don't want to sell them." So I kicked him in the leg because I sensed that this guy is interested. The guy says, "I won't pay you $325, but I'll give you $310." I must have been a natural or something, so I said, "Look, they are field boxes right behind third base." He said, "Very well, then. I need them for a client, and nobody's supplying Wall Street with tickets anymore." He peeled out $700 for me, and I handed him the two seats, and he left. I said to my cousin, "You fucking asshole. For $700, we can get a brass band, two bleachers, and ten people to lead us through!"

So now we're walking around the stadium again. I said, "We'll get two tickets cheap, and we'll have all this money to play with tonight." And I go up to another guy. The guy says, "I have two tickets. They're bleachers. I want $25 each." Well, he must have been a mini-scalper or something because I think the bleachers cost $8 each. But it was a huge game; it was sold out. So I said, "Fine." So now we're in. We're up $325 each. Then, another guy comes along. He says, "You got tickets?" I said, "Yeah, two bleachers, $100 each." He said, "Sure." Within an hour, we were up $600 each.

New York has a real problem, Yankee Stadium and Madison Square Garden. What's going on is—don't put this under me, because I go down there. I work New York, too, so I'll tell you—New York's mad. Another time, I'm walking around the stadium twice, and then when I get around the second time, the ticket taker says, "What are you guys doing?" I said, "What do you think we're doing? We're trying to get into the ballpark." He says, "I'll tell you what. If you grease my palm later,"—this is New York, everything goes. He says, "You're in." I said, "How much?" He said, "Twenties." I told him, "What if I space out some people?" He said, "That's fine." I said, "All right. I'll have them roll them. I'll give them bunches of tens and I'll give them a bunch of twenties. I'll have them hand you the twenty as I come through, and I charge them $40." It was a huge sellout. People were looking all over the place. I see six guys, "You want to get in? Come on. Come with me." They give me $40 each—$240. I put $120 in my pocket. I say, "Okay, here's your twenties. Come with me. Go in right here. Roll it up like a ticket."

We herded them in like cattle all night long. Some people came up and said, "There's five of us that've got to get in, and we only have three tickets." I said, "Come on. I'll get you all in." I went home with $2,300 and I said to myself, "That's five weeks in the hospital. I have a million headaches and only every other weekend off." I was a director of food service in a hospital in Connecticut. Took home $450 a week. I had a window view with fifty-two people working under me.

If I can do this in one fucking night, I can sleep for the rest of the month or do anything I want to do, you know. So I went in the following Monday and I just quit. I don't know why. I just quit. This is it. Didn't wait. Gave them my two weeks. I did the right thing, you know.

*　*　*　*　*

STEVEN CARLOVSKY

Beer Vendor, Milwaukee Brewers

Steve Carlovsky is an eighth-grade parochial teacher and principal at Salem Lutheran School by day, and he sells beer by night. He only had twenty-five minutes to talk before beginning his second job.

"When your back is to the plate, especially if I'm in the lower level, those line shots that go into the seats come at you quick. I've had a ball go over my shoulder and hit a seat in front of me. You hear the crack of the bat and you see the eyes of the people get big. I tell people, 'Just tell me if the ball is coming' because I'll bail out in a heartbeat, and I will. If the ball hits me, it'll hit me. But if I know it's coming I'm gonna get out of the way."

*   *   *   *   *

I'm a beer vendor. I've been vending beer for the last six years. I will be fifty-six next month.

When I first started working, I wanted to work every game. I started in 1989 by selling wine coolers. It wasn't the most popular item out there, but I got to work every game and I got to know all the vendors. Then after about three years, wine coolers tailed off and I went to Bacardi daiquiris. Those was really, really popular.

Once that started dying out then they had a Jack Daniels and strawberry product and stuff like that, which was, again, very popular. I was the only one selling it so I got to work every game. Then that wasn't very good, so after ten years I finally went to beer. The year that I did the best was the strike year, 1994. I had a fabulous year and then all of the sudden it was done at the beginning of August.

I usually work in the left field corner, second deck, all the way to behind home plate. On an average, if there's 25,000 to 30,000 people here, there will be the same eight to ten vendors every game. We can go anywhere we want in there. We get along; there's a lot of camaraderie. That's what's nice about it.

Last Saturday when we had the "Derrick Turnbow Bobblehead Night," the commissary I worked out of sold over 2,800 bottles of beer. If you do the math, times six dollars a beer, that's almost seventeen thousand dollars. But that was a sold-out crowd, and that's just the third base side. That's just vendors; the guys selling in the stands. That doesn't count all of the tap beers that come out of there too. Beer is very popular in Milwaukee.

Today, I'm gonna go to work over on the first base side on the second deck because with the smaller crowd, I can't work in the one that's my first choice so they move me to the first base side. Somebody from downstairs is coming up which means I get bumped over to another place, which I can live with because I am still working.

The more seniority, the closer to the field you can get. It goes by how many years you've worked here. There are only two of us left that started the year I started. The number one guy in seniority here in Miller Park started in 1954. I'm probably in the mid-thirties in seniority, out of probably in the nineties, if everybody came. I've probably moved one or two spots in the last six years. That tells you the people ahead of me probably aren't quitting. Eventually you're going to move up the seniority list, and eventually you're gonna get to levels that you want to be at. It's not going to happen overnight; it's not going to happen in two or three years. It may take six or seven years to get to the loge level here at Miller Park. But you have to be willing to stick it out. Hustle. Listen to people who have been around a while, and don't give up. Be willing to sell a product that nobody else wants to sell. Like now, they have margaritas. If you are willing to sell margaritas every game, you could work every game.

There are people I work with that could be at the field level but prefer to be where they're at because it's all volume. Sometimes we think there's more volume on the second deck than there is on the first deck—more groups; more party people come up there. The first level is a lot more season-ticket holders. When you have season ticket holders, the vendors who've been here much longer than I have, have their steady customers. They're gonna only go to this one vendor all the time. So you're not going to get their sales. On this level, you don't have very many I guess you could call regulars, even though there are some. But you have more chances I think to make money.

As you walk in, one of the things that we check is the bus parking lot. The more buses, the more groups; the more groups means people brought some money with them. They're probably going to spend money on food or beer or souvenirs or whatever. If you see fifteen to twenty-five buses, you know there's at least forty to forty-five people on a bus. Usually the groups are going to be on the level that I'm at, or possibly higher up. The buses mean a lot to us.

I work on the average probably sixty to seventy games out of eighty-one. I won't work if I have a function at my school that I have to be at or if I have a wedding. That's another nice thing about this job: if we want off, we get off. Like this weekend I have a wedding to go to. I just told my supervisor, "I can't be here." I'm the one who's losing money. They'll have one less vendor, but the guys will make up for that. It just gives them a chance to make more money.

I like to get here early. If it's a seven o'clock game, I try and get here at by quarter to six. Then, I check in downstairs so they know I'm here. Then, they tell us to go to our commissary, which is where we get our beer. In this stadium there are, I believe, seven commissaries: two in the first level, two in the second level, and three in the third level. You just can't pick up your product wherever you want.

Then at six-fifteen, we get our tickets. You get a ticket, which is basically a free load of beer, and at the end of the night you pay for that load of beer. If it's a big, big night like last Saturday night, we can bring money and buy extra tickets if we want, which means we don't have to stand in line to buy the tickets. We've already pre-purchased them.

If I only get one ticket, the next time I want to get a ticket I have to give the cashier $144, which is the price of a case of beer: twenty-four bottles at six dollars a bottle. I can multiply my sixes really well after working here. If I wanted to get four extra tickets, I then give that cashier $576. We make sixty-three cents a bottle.

I like the roof being open, but that doesn't guarantee that I'm going to be making more money that day. The only time I really see it having an effect is in summertime. If the roof is open in the summer, the heat gets too much for the people on the third base side where I work. They're gonna move someplace else, which means they're not going to be around for me to sell to them. In the long run, it ends up hurting me in the pocketbook because people just leave because it just gets too warm. What's nice about this retractable roof is, like today, it's a little chilly. You can close the roof and people are going to be comfortable.

I'm one of the few guys here that carries the beer on top of their head. It's a plastic container and in that goes twenty-four bottles of beer, plus I don't know how many pounds of ice we put in there, too. I would say it weighs ten to fifteen pounds. My head and neck are stronger than my arms. I'm not comfortable carrying it in front of me, especially where we have a metal railing down the middle of the aisles. The most beer I ever carried was last weekend: I carried fifty-two bottles of beer. That was heavy. That's two cases, plus the four beers I had left over. It was busy and I was walking farther away from where I got my beer, which means I could sell two cases of beer, come back quick and get another two cases of beer. The farther away you are when you finish, the farther you've gotta walk. And the farther you have to walk, that's money that you're losing.

One of those things about Miller Park is once you get down to the bottom of those twenty-two rows, you got to come back up those twenty-two rows. As you're coming back up people will wave at ya, so you just give them a nod to acknowledge that you're gonna be there. That's the easiest way to see them: look on both sides and they'll wave at ya or they'll say, "Beer here." You'll stop and kneel in front of them, ask how many beers they want and check IDs. If they're under thirty, we're going to check. They send the ID down to us and we check to see they're of age. Then we send the beers down, and you can tell them as the beers come down if they bought two beers, "It's twelve dollars." In general, we go through a lot of twenty-dollar bills.

If I were to get stiffed on purpose by a customer, our management has told us to find an usher and bring them down there. If worse comes to worst, I will go find a policeman, and tell my supervisor this is what the person did and the management will deal with them. Management won't have me lose my money. On a busy day they can scam you. If I lose a beer—if I give out one too many beers—it costs me the six dollars because I have to pay for all the beers I sell. If I make a mistake in how many beers I send down, I'm losing the money, not the customer.

They're all Miller products: Lite and Genuine Draft. The first year here we had Miller High Life, but they changed it the second year to Genuine Draft. We've had that for the last four years. Miller changed the way they're doing the plastic bottles for us now. We went from wide mouth tops to narrow tops just about two weeks ago. You couldn't squeeze the wide mouth bottles. The narrower Genuine Draft is sometimes a little bit more bubbly, so when you open it up there's a chance it's going to foam out. One of the things I've noticed about the plastic bottles is, it doesn't seem like as much plastic. Squeeze the narrow mouth bottles in the middle real hard, and you could lose three dollars worth of beer in a heartbeat 'cause it will come right out the top.

You've just gonna tell them it's "Cold beer; Miller Lite; Miller Draft." That's what you have to tell them. That's what they're looking for. We give them the bottle. We don't give them the cup. In Milwaukee, they like drinking out of that bottle. If they want a cup, we go find them a cup. But generally, they just drink it right out of the bottle—women, men—they all drink it out of the bottle. Pretty much you sell two Lites for every one Draft.

The bottom of the seventh inning becomes "last call" because we can't sell after the third out in the seventh inning. In other words, if it's three outs, and all of a sudden you look around and somebody says they want a beer, they can't have it. You have to watch it. Say I gave them the beer with two outs and they haven't given me the money yet, the beers are sold.

Then, you complete the transaction and that's it. Some people do get a little upset at the fact that we're not going to keep on selling, because they want beer. But that's the company policy, and I think it's a good policy.

I would like to do this until I am at least sixty-five or until my legs can't handle it anymore. My wife asks that every year, but she knows I like it. My legs are still good. This is very good exercise. In old County Stadium we used to wear navy uniforms; they didn't let us wear shorts until probably seven or eight years ago. One day I lost twelve pounds working, but it was all water. On a day like that, when you get home you can't drink enough fluids. The company now makes sure we have ice water when we're getting our beer and they say, "You gotta keep drinking. We don't want anybody to pass out."

I'll drink beer every once in a while, but it's not something I have to drink everyday. I just don't like the taste. When I was younger it wasn't bad, but now that I'm older it's not like I'm going to go home and have a beer. But I'll sell it. There are people who just like it.

I also am a parochial-school teacher and the principal of Salem Lutheran School. There are 102 students. Right now, I pretty much teach eighth grade. Some of my kids say, "Why do you do it?" It's a great job; I get to see baseball. I get to see cheering and stuff. Another reason people started working is because the Packers used to play at old County Stadium and that way you got to see the Packers games besides.

A lot of vendors are teachers. It's a great part-time job. After the season is done, when we come back for training in the springtime, it's great to see everybody again. It's like old friends are back together.

A bad day at work here is if you don't sell anything. You keep on walking and your legs get tired. If you go down a row and on the way up the row, you sell three quarters of a case of beer that's worth it. But, if you go down that row—don't sell any going down, don't sell any coming up, go down the next row, don't sell any—you walk three or four sections without selling any beer, it gets bad.

The best day I ever had was the last day at County Stadium. I think I sold more than twenty cases of beer, which was very good. In the new stadium, the best I've ever done was I made over $200 in commission. If you think about $200 in commission, in let's say two and a half to three hours, that's why the people who get the jobs here they don't quit because it's worth it. I've put my children through private high school. I've paid off my mortgage. That's why I do it. This is exercise. A mindless job for me. It's fun.

The worst night I've ever had is when I was selling, believe it or not, was with rum daiquiris in old County Stadium. It was 38 degrees out, and I'm selling an iced drink. I walked the whole game. I think I made seven dollars. That would have been nineteen daiquiris. That night I got to see a lot of baseball.

*　*　*　*　*

CHAPTER SIX

EYES AND EARS

HENRY SCHULMAN

Beat Writer, San Francisco Chronicle

Sitting in the press box in late July before a night game, Henry Schulman said, "I ask the questions the way I need to ask them. The players are usually very honest about what happened in the game. Some guys always talk in clichés. You just try not to interview those players when you want to get something relevant."

*   *   *   *   *

My job is to be the eyes and the ears of the fans inside the locker room and at the stadium. As a beat writer, it's my job to explain what's going on in the field, what's going on with the team behind the scenes; not so much give my opinion; that's really for a columnist to do. But give my assessment: analyze, describe, and basically ask the questions of the players that the fans back home would love to ask the players after a game—the guy sitting on the couch saying, "Jeez, why did he run from first to third on that pitch?" It's my job to go down to the clubhouse and say, "Hey, why did you run from first to third on that pitch?" so that I can explain what's going on.

Fifty years ago, the beat writer's job was mainly to just describe literally what happened on the field: "Player x singled to right; player y scored on a play." And this is what happened because if you weren't listening to the game on the radio or weren't watching it on TV—which most people didn't do in 1956—they pretty much got their total information from the afternoon paper. Most of the time people would come home from work, and there'd be a day of baseball, and the paper would be on their front stoop with the description of the game in it. Nowadays, it's really kind of pointless for me to just write, "Player x had a single and player y scored" because they either saw it on TV live, they listened to it on the radio, they saw it on the highlights on *SportsCenter* or on their local news, they were following the game on one of the Internet sites where you can get real-time action, or they read the basic description of the game either through MLB.com or SportsTicker. So that really has made my job evolve and probably forces me to provide more analysis of what I saw; maybe ask deeper questions of the players. You have to write with the assumption that the reader already knows everything that happened in the game, and ask the questions of journalism: who, what, when, where, why, and how. "Why" is the big question now for a baseball beat writer.

I didn't start out to be a sportswriter. I started out to be a political writer. Grew up in Los Angeles. I grew up a Dodger fan. My dream, as a kid, was to actually be the next Vin Scully. And I have a face for radio, too. That's what I'm told.

I was sixteen when Watergate broke. A lot of kids at that time who had any interest in the media wanted to be the next Woodward and Bernstein. So I kind of put aside the dream of being a baseball announcer and concentrated on journalism. Wrote for the school paper at Fairfax High in Los Angeles. Wrote for the *Daily Cal* covering the city of Berkeley. Graduated from Berkeley in political science.

I became a general-assignment reporter just so I could get a job and worked for a little 14,000-circulation weekly in a little town. I kind of started working my way up to bigger papers, and I ended up through an odd twist becoming a business writer. That evolved into a full-time business-writing job. I kind of enjoyed that, but after a few years I just realized I was sitting there in a suit and tie talking to people on the phone sitting there wearing suits and ties in offices, writing stories to be read by people sitting in suits and ties in offices. After a while, I said, "There's got to be a little bit more."

My first love was always sports. I was twenty-eight, working for the *Oakland Tribune*; already established as a journalist. I had already been there for three years. At that time—it's different now because now they're on the cheap and they just want to hire college kids—the *Tribune* had financial problems, and they offered buyouts to the older people to get rid of them. So I went to the sports editor and told him, "Look, I'd like to come to sports." I didn't say, "I want to be the Giants' beat reporter." I didn't think that I could just jump right in and get one of the highest profile beats in the paper. But he liked me, and he liked me better than anybody else on the staff to do the Giants. I went from business reporting straight to covering the Giants in 1988, and that's how it happened.

I started with [Giants manager] Roger Craig and went to Dusty Baker and Felipe Alou. As a writer, I mean, I was blessed because all three of them were personable. Craig is from North Carolina, and, you know, it was almost like talking to Sheriff Andy Taylor every night. He had a folksy way about him, and he was really old school baseball. Craig had come up at a time when the owners really did own the players, and things were done a certain way. His take on baseball was a lot different than Dusty Baker's, who was pretty much a player—his mentality was a player even when he was a manager.

Dusty was new school, about as new school as you can get. Most players retire reluctantly. They have to be dragged out of the game. Dusty was one of those guys. His body just gave up on him; and he actually became a stockbroker. Then the Giants hired him as a batting coach. When he became manager, he kind of saw himself as the twenty-sixth player on the team. He tried to be buddy-buddy with the players. There were two sides to Dusty. He was great dealing with us. I mean he was very articulate, very knowledgeable about the game. He was willing to share stuff with us. So he was a great manager in that regard. But the players on any team always have this thing: "We're a group. Always keep things within the circle." And he was a player at heart who felt there were just a lot of thing that the media didn't deserve to know. He would hide stuff from us. He would sometimes . . . I mean, he wouldn't lie; that's a strong term. I mean, he would stretch the truth a little bit sometimes and just felt that certain things had to be inside the clubhouse and certain things out-side the clubhouse. If he said it, you reported it. But you sometimes were a little more skeptical of what he said. If you heard something about what was going on with the team, you know, you might have to try and flush it out by talking to more players off the record.

Felipe is an old-school manager. In some regards, he also feels things should be kept in-house, but he's also a guy who's always been com-pletely honest in his life and doesn't seem to have the "distruthful gene" in his body. He tells us things all the time that are going on inside the club-house, to the dismay of the players. The players don't like the fact that he'll spill stuff. He'll volunteer stuff. The trainer doesn't like the fact that he, you know, will just out of the blue blurt out that a certain player has an injury, which they're trying to hide from the other team. He makes our job a lot easier.

There's two stories I write every day: There's the little notebook that goes inside with notes and quotes for the day. Then there's the game story. When we're on the West Coast I pretty much have to have the notebook finished and sent before the game is over, and I also have to write a game story before the game is over because of the deadlines. Our first edition goes to bed at about 10 p.m. And they want to try and get a game story, if possible, in that edition if the game is over. So at 9:45 p.m., I have to file what we call "running," which is everything that's happened in the game up to the point that I'm filing the story.

So on the West Coast, you try and get all the information you can before the game when you're talking to players—talking to the manager—so you can get a sense of what's going on that day; put that in the notebook. And then I pretty much just write a straight game story for the first editions: "This is what happened on the field." The writing is awful. As a reader, I really wouldn't want to read my running story. But my attitude is it only goes to about 60,000 people. I feel bad for those folks, but it's not my fault—make the paper change the deadlines.

After the game is over, I'll go down to the clubhouse and get quotes, come back up and really hump it. I'll usually have half an hour to rewrite my story, or if I don't have time, just plug quotes in. It's high stress. The stories are not as good. But that's just what you deal with in deadline pressure. Every writer deals with it.

On the East Coast, it's a completely different story. The games are starting at 4 p.m., California time. Deadline is not so much an issue. It could be 12:30 a.m. before I'm done with the story, depending on how much I want to agonize over it. I'm not really an agonizer. I get it done right off the top of my head; and anything that I write off the top of my head is usually better than anything I try and reword. It just works out that way. It's my feeling that any story that you write from paragraph one down is better than any story you write from paragraph thirty on up. When you're home on deadline, you're basically writing a story starting with paragraph thirty and then twenty-nine, twenty-eight, and then at the end, you write the last thing first. It's sort of the inverted pyramid instead of the regular pyramid. I just like to sit down, like an artist with a blank canvas. I get about 1,000 words a day. I never have trouble banging it out. It's always the opposite problem. I never have enough space.

One of the hard parts about writing on deadline is you don't get to watch baseball as much. I'm a baseball fan first of all. I love watching baseball. I don't want my head buried in a computer when the game is on if I can avoid it.

Yesterday, there was a kind of a twist. The Giants made a minor trade. They got Mike Stanton from the Washington Nationals. Ordinarily I might have just taken that—since it was a minor trade—and just made that my inside sidebar story, but I had a really good inside sidebar besides that. Solomon Torres, a pitcher who once pitched for the Giants—and is rumored to be going back to the Giants possibly in a trade—told me that he absolutely had a horrible time with the Giants. Barry Bonds was a bully to him. He had nightmares. He had night sweats. He doesn't like Felipe Alou because of an experience he had with him, and so, I mean, he's begging his team not to trade him to the Giants.

I taped my interview with Solomon Torres, and Barry Bonds did what we call a "gang bang"—that's when you have an interview with every reporter and his cousin. It's not a one-on-one interview or a two-on-one interview. It's an all-comers interview. So I did a one-on-one with Torres. We did a gang bang with Barry—which always happens the first night in Pittsburgh because he used to play here—and I came upstairs to transcribe my notes. I had barely put my tushy down on the seat when Blake Rhodes, the Giants' PR person, phoned and said, "Get back down here," because he wanted to tell us that the trade had been made. They announced the trade, so I came all the way up here to the press box, which is on the roof, went all the way back down. By this time it was twenty minutes before the game. I hadn't eaten yet, so I rushed into the food room, which is on the lower level behind the plate. I had just gotten my food, and I started to eat, and then my cell phone rings again. Rhodes says, "Get back to the clubhouse. We just got Mike Stanton on the phone. We're going to do a conference call with him." So I left my pasta and salad there—my pasta to get cold and my salad getting warm—ran back there. We did a short conference call with Stanton, and then I rushed back, gobbled up the food, came up here right about game time, and then started to do the transcription that I was hoping to do at about 6 p.m.

So that was my sidebar. It was such a good story that I couldn't hold that to the next day. I really wanted to get that in the paper. So what I did is what we call it a "weave job." And it has nothing to do with fake hair. A weave job is when you take two disparate notions and weave them into one story. In yesterday's case, I weaved the trade of Mike Stanton in with the fact that the Giants were shut out here in Pittsburgh, and they looked terrible. It's not the best way to write a story, but, you know, I think it worked. Some of the issues are related. The fact that the Giants would go out and acquire an old pitcher like that, even while they're losing, suggests that the management doesn't feel that the losing streak is really representative of how they're gonna play. So I kind of weaved both back and forth.

Typically, I usually get to the ballpark by 3 p.m. for a 7:05 p.m game. Go on the Internet. I mean, I'm just like anybody else. I go on the Internet to see what other people are saying; what rumors might be out there. The clubhouse opens three and a half hours before the game to the media. And that's when we spend our most quality time with the players—when we get to talk to them one-on-one—just ask them about issues going on with the team, issues going on with themselves.

We have a daily briefing with the manager every pre-game. The "we" would be any writer who wants to talk to the manager: any writer, any radio person, any TV reporter without the cameras because cameras are not allowed in the clubhouse before a game. There's usually a pretty good crowd inside the manager's office. The manager is mainly the spokesman for any team. Reporters get most of their important information with these fifteen to twenty minute daily pre-game chats.

Once we're done with the manager and the players, batting practice is going on. Each team has the option of keeping their clubhouse open, or closed, to the media during batting practice. Some players wander back in if they're not particularly doing anything on the field, or if they're injured; and you can go in there and chat with them. But with the Giants, what was happening when Barry Bonds was going through all of his legal troubles in 2004, ESPN decided to have Pedro Gomez, a full-time reporter, cover Bonds. And he had no interest in anything that had to do with the team itself. He was just there to cover Barry. So the Giants would keep the clubhouse open. There'd be no reporters in there except Pedro, and he'd just be there to, you know, wait for Barry so that he could talk to him, or if Barry did or said anything he could be there to record it. Barry didn't like it. The team didn't like it. So the Giants used their option under baseball rules to close the clubhouse during batting practice. And they kind of jokingly call it the "Pedro Gomez Rule." I'm not picking on Pedro; he's a friend of mine. That's just what the Giants kind of jokingly call it.

After batting practice is over, there's still about forty minutes. You can go back into the clubhouse before you're ushered out. Baseball rules require the clubhouse to be closed forty-five minutes before the first pitch. So there's still some more time. In some ways, it's made my job easier because that gives me time to maybe go upstairs [to the press box] and do a little bit of writing that I can just kind of get out of the way.

Postgame, you almost always stay in your own clubhouse. First thing you do is talk to the manager again. During the pre-game, you can talk to the manager about anything, ask him esoteric questions about baseball and life and history and all that. Postgame, you're pretty much supposed to just limit it to what happened in the game. It's like a five- to ten-minute courtesy interview.

Then you talk to the players; almost always talk to the starting pitcher, some of the key players of the game. And when you're at home on deadline for a night game, if you can talk to three players, you're pretty fortunate. The players don't stay in the clubhouse waiting for you. They're almost always in the training room. A lot of players do postgame workouts. Or they're in the food room, you know, getting their postgame meal provided by the club. Those rooms are off limits to the media.

So we walk ordinarily into an empty clubhouse. And we have to wait for the players to come in. The Giants lost their fifth in a row yesterday. I mean, they couldn't get a run against a pitcher who had an ERA close to a billion; just another hideous loss. And because they were shut out, we wanted to talk to some of the hitters, and there were no hitters in the room. I turned to one of my colleagues and said, "I pity the first position player who walks into the room because he's going to be descended on." And it was Steve Finley. Got a quote.

Fifty years ago, you could hear something in the clubhouse and not report it if you wanted to protect the players or the team and be a good guy. Now, there's nothing that is said that goes unpublished. Anything that's said gets on the Internet within an hour. So we don't have the luxury of protecting, you know, the players or the manager by not printing things.

One of the advantages you have as a beat reporter is you get to talk to the players every day and you get to know them. We travel to all the cities. We don't travel on the same plane. We don't stay at the same hotels. We used to, but we don't anymore. So you get to know the players. A lot of times they have things that they want to get out to the public and they don't necessarily want to be quoted on it. "Off the record" is a touchy subject for newspapers. A lot of times you will talk to the players and they will say, "Hey, off the record." And it's understood that you can print what they say, not necessarily quote them but you can paraphrase them or whatever. You just can't use their names. The players are smart. A lot of them have a message they want to get across. Or you, as a reporter, hear something and you want to confirm it, but you can't confirm it by getting a quote, which isn't really all that important. You just want to make sure the information is accurate.

Every PR department, in every sport, prints out every story written every day. It's called "clips." They go to the media mostly, but they wind up in the clubhouse. The running joke is how everybody says, "Well, I don't read the clips." Well, everybody reads the clips; and if they don't read the story and their names are mentioned, you know that someone will call them. I remember Dusty Baker one time—he took the clips while we were in the pre-game session with the manager—he actually made a show of this. He just dumped the clips in the garbage can. And he was chewing tobacco at the time. He just loaded up a big, big piece of chew and spit it right on top of the clips. And he'd always be the one to say, "Hey, I don't read the clips. I don't know what you wrote." But if you wrote anything that was controversial about him, he'd always call you in the next day, and he'd say, "Well, I didn't read it, but somebody told me." One time I wrote something, and he said, "Well, you know, I don't usually read your stuff, but I was in the shitter, and I had the paper in my hands." I mean, he actually said that to me.

So, yeah, what often happens in sports is you will quote players accurately and you will quote them in context, but then they'll get grief from their teammates or from the organization, and they'll come back and claim that they were taken out of context or that was supposed to be off the record. It really is smart if you're talking to a player on a touchy subject to lay the ground rules, "Is this off the record? Is this on the record? Is this on the record, but not for attribution?" Just to make sure that you've got your bases covered with the player.

For the most part, the Giants teams have been very closed in dealing with the media. I think it's mainly because in recent years the Giants have had more veteran teams. It's really the veteran players who are the ones who understand that controversy can kill a clubhouse, and that it's best to just leave things in-house, you know, not to say stuff and not to let things fester in the media. It's maybe younger or less-experienced teams where they don't quite understand that as much. The Giants, you know, they've had some dour personalities, so that's played a part in it.

The lead up to Bonds' hitting seventy-three home runs started it. We had it with BALCO when it looked like he was going to be indicted. Then we had it with his chase for [Babe Ruth's] 714. What's happened is that the Giants have become a magnet for reporters from all over the country. We had become a big, national story. And when the clubhouse is filled with dozens and dozens of reporters, then the players want to have no part of the clubhouse, so they hide in the training room, lunch room, conditioning room, their weight room, any of the multitude of places that the reporters are not allowed into. That makes it harder for me to just go up to a guy— if there's a rightfielder who has an arm injury and part of my job is to go find out how that rightfielder's arm is feeling that day—that makes it harder for me to just do that simple aspect of my job because the players aren't around. The players get upset because of all these reporters in the clubhouse. They're not happy with it. So in general, their attitude to the whole media changes and degrades. While they do recognize that we beat guys are really just there to do our jobs, that doesn't necessarily mean they're gonna run out and talk to us.

And dealing with Bonds himself, well, in a way it's easier, and in a way it's harder because through a lot of these times when he was going for something, he just wouldn't talk to the media at all. Or if he did it would only be in a press conference setting. So if he talked to one, he'd talk to all, and that in a way made it easier. But it also made it harder because you had like ESPN or MLB.com, or even reporters from the *New York Post* or the *New York Daily News* or the Philly *Inquirer*, hanging around just to cover Bonds. You couldn't really even go outside, or go to the other clubhouse, or go outside and make a phone call because you were always worried that Barry Bonds would start talking and you weren't there. Paranoia creeps in. It does make it hard when you have other things to do, but you got to just kind of stand there and babysit the leftfielder.

You didn't ask me about what it's like for the writers before the trading deadline. It's nuts because the rumor mill just goes completely wacko, mostly generated by the New York papers. They have to have stuff in every day about what's going on. It's not just the New York papers, though. They're just the biggest. They fuel it. So we spend a lot of time chasing rumors. The paranoia really starts to creep in. In fact, we had a writer who used to be on this beat who I think might have literally had some paranoia issues. He would go insane around this time. If my wife would call me on the phone and I walked away to talk to my wife, he'd think I was talking to some general manager. And sometimes we'd even play with him. He wasn't a sweet guy anyway. We'd have one reporter call me on the cell phone. I'd pick up my notepad, and I'd scribble furiously. The guy on the other line was saying stuff like, "Hey, did you see what they had downstairs at the lunch in the cafeteria? They got burgers today." So we would do that.

A lot of times, the headlines are awful. Copy editors write those. Headline writing is, you know, like doing a jigsaw puzzle. There are a certain number of characters you get based on how the page designer decides to lay out the page. Our guys are actually pretty good. It's usually at the smaller papers where you have less-experienced copy editors where it's messed up. But we get our headlines messed up, too, sometimes. And the one thing is, none of the players understand that we don't write the headlines. They just assume we write the headlines. I've had players just scream at me, "Why did you write that? That's horse-bleep. How could you write this and that?" Then I'd say, "I don't write that." They don't understand why we don't.

I'm pretty much off from the end of the World Series until the beginning of spring training except I have to follow the team when they do trades and free agent signings. I figure I work about maybe thirty days in the offseason. But for the most part, that's when I recharge my batteries. Do stuff around the house; projects which, my wife would tell you if you interviewed her, I'm not very good at getting to. Just a wife, two cats, no kids. This would be a rough life to have kids.

I'm extremely fortunate that I get to cover baseball. Two of my passions are baseball and writing. How many people get to combine two of their biggest passions into the job that keeps them alive? That's what I have, and I don't take it for granted. You know, I keep telling my wife I'm not going to do this until I retire, but I really can't imagine doing anything else.

* * * * *

JIM TRDINICH

Director of Media Relations, Pittsburgh Pirates

"You think you see everything in this game. I would compare it to Christmas, opening up presents, because every game is a present. You don't know what you are going to find unless you unwrap it. You could see a double steal. You could see a steal at home. You could see a walk. You could see a triple play. You could see a game won on a wild pitch, like last night. You can see anything."

*   *   *   *   *

T-r-d-i-n-i-c-h. Right. Director of media relations for the Pittsburgh Pirates.

Based on a seven-o-five game, the normal day for me starts around nine, nine thirty in the morning. Generally, home games are different from other games in that it's a lot more office work; a lot more phones to answer. You know, people in the office bothering you for things, coming in, asking for stuff.

There might be media requests. I handle all credential requests for the uniformed players, our owner, general manager. People from local Pittsburgh stations, Pittsburgh newspapers, or national media entities will call. They want to talk to whoever—might be Jason Bay; might be a local story; somebody coming into town wanting to do something on John Grabow. You also get fan calls. Fans might call and say, "I was at the game June thirteenth. My son caught a ball. Who hit it?" Or they want to get a copy of the tape of the person singing the national anthem that day. So I have to coordinate that with our scoreboard people to have them send a tape to these people. You never know what you are going to get—anything and everything that you might imagine.

We are in the research business too. I'm always the guy that acts as the historian during games. Say Jason Bay has a big hot streak. The media might call, and say, "Bay hit six home runs in a row. When was the last Pirate to do that?" We can look that up. So you're basically doing a lot of stuff like that.

Then, aside from meetings that I might have, we do the daily game notes. That's a six-page information sheet—anything that's happening with the Pirates—talking about the current losing streak, winning streak—whatever it might be. Who is hot; who is not. There's a whole solid page with just basic team notes. From that, you'll see stuff on our scoreboard in Pittsburgh. "Freddy Sanchez has gone 10 for his last 15," or is "currently leading the league in hitting." All that stuff, generated on the scoreboard both at home and road, comes from my game notes. The broadcasters use it. The writers use it. Also, visiting writers can go to MLB.com and download my game notes or any game notes around the league. All thirty teams put it there.

The clubhouse opens three and a half hours before every game. Usually the manager, every day, meets with the media. The media comes in the first thing in the afternoon, around four thirty. We will get with Jim Tracy, our manager, and spend fifteen, twenty minutes with him.

I'm usually in the press box after our batting practice—about an hour before the game. I'm up there working on the game notes for tomorrow. Always have to keep that going. During the game, I'm in the press box. I keep score of every game that's played for historical purposes. And if anything happens, like if someone extends a hitting streak of fifteen games, I'll give that to the home PR person. He announces it for the broadcasters.

Once the game ends, I go down to the clubhouse, open up the club-house five or ten minutes after the game—it should be no longer than ten. If we lose, we let the manager vent a little bit: "I can't believe that we lost that fricking game today." He vents to me, because I'm there. I'm his buffer before the media comes in. He will say what he can't say to the media. You know, he can't say, "Such and such a player, if he had only got a hit. He really sucked tonight. He let us down." He can't say that to the media. He will just yell. He won't yell at me. He yells, and I just listen to him. I absorb everything he says.

I've been here full time since '89. I was an intern in '85. I was here when Jim Leyland was here. He was one of the better venters. He would pace around, and shout and scream like, "Motherfucker!" From top to bottom, he would yell and scream.

Then Gene Lamont came in, and then Lloyd McClendon, and now Jim Tracy. So he's my fourth manager. They all have different modes of how they vent. Tracy will say, "Go get the media," and I will bring them in. If I feel that he needs another two, or three minutes, I'll go to the bathroom, wash my hands, make small talk with our clubhouse manager, or what-ever, and then I will go get the media and bring them in. I give the okay.

The media makes a beeline right to the manager's office, led by me. Then they come out and they look for the starting pitcher. It's not in his contract, but the starting pitcher knows to give five minutes talking about his start. And then the media asks for probably a position player. If we went up against a tough pitcher that struck out fifteen, they might want to say, "Why was Jason Schmidt so effective? What made him so good? What made Kerry Wood so good today?" Or when Jason Bay homered six in a row, they go right to him and say, "You know, Jason, blah, blah, blah, what do you feel about the game?" But a lot of the guys when we lose, they will quote-unquote hide, and go into the training room. The off-limits areas are the training room, the food room, and some clubhouses have player lounges. The media is really only allowed to go in the clubhouse changing area where the players' lockers are, and the manager-slash-coaches' offices.

The main clubhouse-proper in on-limits to writers—the media, I should say, because the media includes writers, radio, and TV personalities. After every game, we'll usually have a FOX cameraman. When we're at home, we usually have NBC, ABC, CBS affiliates there too. They'll come out and get sound bites. I usually tell the players in spring, "Win or lose, the media wants to come in and talk to three or four guys, and they are gone." A lot of the players get pissed because they see the media just waiting and waiting. Part of it's because they are waiting for the players to come out. It's like you can't piss off the players because they are my lifeblood. I try to generate as much publicity for them as I can. On the other side, I don't want to make the media mad.

I have a draw that fine line where I have to keep the media happy and I have to keep the players happy. There could be a media person that writes something negative about the player. That player might say, "Hey, I'm not talking to such and such." You know, one player can have a personal vendetta with one guy, but I say, "Hey, don't take it out on the whole newspaper staff." So I have to keep the players happy with the media.

The bottom line, I think, is winning. Winning cures all. Your marketing slogan is a little better when you win. The play on the field, the manager's moves, everything all looks better when you win. If we win, everybody is in a happy mood. The music is playing in the clubhouse. Everybody's spirits are up, even if you went 0 for 4, you don't care, because you won the game. Conversely, when you lose, it's definitely quiet in there. It's two totally different atmospheres. When you lose, the slogan sucks, the team sucks, the ballpark sucks, it rains everyday. But I think the media is very important because they get the story out.

I can't think of a guy with the bunch that we have right now that's not going to talk to the media, even if he's slumping. The toughest people are the guys in the bullpen that aren't the closer. If they blow a save—like a setup guy comes in, and he could be pitching lights out for ten straight games and nobody cares. But then that the one game he screws up, and gives up the go-ahead run, that's when the media wants to come talk to him. They say, "Jimmy T., why do they want to talk to me now? Where were they when I pitched ten scoreless innings?" Closers are tough, too, because they're a different breed. The game is usually on the line when the closers come in. You either save it, or you blow it.

I think you've got to be able to read people. We had an instance with Lloyd McClendon about three or four years ago, where I could tell he was not particularly happy because we lost a tough game. I mean, you can tell.

Before I went out and got the media, I waited because he was still pissed. When somebody asked a question, he went off. He just went crazy. Maybe I should have given him ten more minutes.

The beat writers tend to not write horseshit stuff on the players. They travel with us and they're in the clubhouse all the time. They can write that Jeromy Burnitz or Sean Casey or Jason Bay is in a long slump. They could write a fact: He is 0 for his last 15. But you can't really say, "He sucks. We shouldn't have signed the guy. He's bringing the whole club down." Beat writers tend to report the facts like, "We lost last night, blah, blah, blah," while the columnists are paid to dig up the dirt.

Columnists have their right, I guess, to write whatever they want. Even if it's an opinion, you have to be very thick-skinned. I think some of the players aren't, but the managers and the coaches and the guys that have been in the game for twenty years realize that the media has a job to do. There are columnists in every city that are going to write negative things; they're paid to be dickheads to generate more paper sales.

It goes back to that fine line thing. There was a certain columnist in Pittsburgh that actually went so far as to rip *me* one time, but not directly. Just ripped me and my assistant for doing something—drumming up support one time with Jason Bay. It revolved around taking Jason to meet with Ben Roethlisberger of the Steelers. It was purely done on our part just to say Roethlisberger is on his way to becoming Rookie of the Year. And we are taking Jason over because he had won Rookie of the Year. This was in the off-season of '04. Everybody loved it. The newspapers were there for a photo opportunity, just having, you know, this is kind of a cool thing; nothing about anything else.

Well, this columnist the next day said the Pirates are so hard up for good news that they did the lowly thing of trudging this Rookie of the Year out. I got pissed. I said I'll never talk to this guy personally. I even e-mailed him and said, "We are through. We are done."

My one big beef with the columnists is that they're never held accountable. It's their opinion. They can write anything they want in the newspaper, and they could be wrong. You know, you may have covered baseball for twenty years, but the manager knows a little bit more than the columnist of a newspaper. It makes me laugh because it's like columnists can get away with murder. It's the power of the pen.

There's another guy in town, Mark Madden, with ESPN radio. This guy is one of those shock jocks that he wishes ill upon us all the time. Why should I give this guy a guest? This guy is really dogging us over the years, so I said why give the guy that satisfaction? When they get off the air, they are going to rip us again. Well, two years ago in spring training, when he was asking for a guest for his producer. I said, "Tell Mark that he's not going to get any guests this year. He can rip us an asshole whether I can give him a guest or not." My god, for his three-hour show that day, I gave him so much fodder. He wanted me fired. He said "I will never go to Pittsburgh's press box until Trdinich is fired." He said he couldn't believe I used that language. Meanwhile he just talks shit about everybody, on the air. I know Mark, and I knew him before. I kind of talk to him now. We're not friends, but I mean, I talk to him.

But I have to realize that that's what he is doing on the air. It's all for shock, and that sort of stuff, but I didn't give him a guest for a year or two, but now this year I have. He is a big wrestling guy, so he loves Sean Casey. Seems like he softened up a little bit. I have no personal vendetta against Mark because I know that's his specialty shtick on the air.

In every press box there's an official scorer, the home PR and the visiting PR. There also are guys or ladies that are inputting information for ESPN.com, and they'll show like if Jack Wilson flies out to left. It's really interesting stuff. It's probably about a batter behind, when you are watching it live. A Pirates fan can actually go on ESPN.com or on MLB.com and watch the game on his computer.

And you have the writers and electronic media. They're scoring the game and writing their stories. Aside from their game story, they have a notebook that they write. They might talk about a guy who is on injury rehab, or if somebody might have a hitting streak going. They're typing away. Then they will start their game stories during the fourth or fifth inning. I'm within earshot of them—"Hey, when was the last time Freddy Sanchez walked?" I'm looking in my forty-pound briefcase through my scorebooks and the stat card on every player that's playing for us. I look it up, then they go back writing their stories. They get really mad when they have a story almost done and the team might score five runs in the ninth to tie. You will hear a lot of "shit, goddamnit" right there in the press box. Everyone has to re-write—they hate that word *re-write*—they have to *redo* their whole story.

I've been doing it for so long. I think I've gotten to the point where I am respected because I am up there in stature among the PR guys in the league. I'm one of the veterans now. I started in '89 as the assistant, and then in '91 I became the director of media relations. I've been doing that ever since.

My wife works for Verizon. If I go to her Christmas parties—I remember the first year, before anybody knew who I was, other than her husband. Someone asked me, "What do you do?" I said, "I work for the Pirates," and my god, everybody began to congregate around me because it's out of the norm. I mean, I'm not a player. I'm not a manager. I'm not the GM. I say I work for the Pittsburgh Pirates. It's like being a roadie for a rock and roll band, like for the Stones or for Pearl Jam. It's an interesting line of work.

*   *   *   *   *

MIKE KRUKOW

Radio and Television Color Analyst, San Francisco

Krukow pitched thirteen seasons in the major leagues, posting a 124—117 record and a 3.90 ERA with the Cubs, Phillies, and Giants. He became a full-time broadcaster in 1994 when he teamed up with former infielder Duane Kuiper as part of the "Kruk and Kuip" broadcast team. Krukow uses a telestrator to "eliminate" fans who might be using a cell phone during a game or wearing Los Angeles Dodgers clothing. He also is known for saying, "Grab some pine, meat," when a batter strikes out.

*   *   *   *   *

I am a color commentator and analyst. My job every night is to talk baseball, and to explain to the listening audience what's going on in the course of a ballgame. I think baseball is a game in which there is so much going on, every pitch—from a pitcher's perspective, from a hitter's perspective, from a defensive perspective, from a catching perspective, from a manager's perspective—all these different things are going on. We try to talk about them during the course of a ballgame to give the listener an idea of what's going on every pitch.

My idea of a perfect ballgame to broadcast is a game thrown by Greg Maddux because he has great ability to read hitters, great ability to identify situations, great ability to throw a pitch that applies to the situation based on the pitch, the umpire's strike zone, on how the ballpark is being played that day, the length of the grass, the hardness of the dirt out in front of home plate, the carry to left field, the lack of carry to rightfield, hitter's a pull hitter, hitter stays inside the ball, if he is a lefthanded hitter that sprays the ball to left field—all these enter into how that guy decides how he is going to pitch a hitter. All these things go into the equation. And all I try to do as an analyst is to describe that equation to the listening audience. I love it.

You get a guy out there who is a pitcher, as opposed to a thrower. Big difference. A thrower is a guy who is going to just try to throw stuff by a guy. Hitting is timing. What is pitching? Pitching is upsetting the timing of a hitter. So I'll watch a true pitcher, you know, a Mark Gardner who was a real good pitcher. If you watch Noah Lowery, he can pitch. Jason Schmidt can pitch. Matt Morris can pitch. You watch these guys and you know given the situation is runners at first and third, they have a three-run lead, they are not going to pitch for the strike out with less than two outs. They're going to pitch to the ground ball, throw a sinker or a hard breaking ball that's down below the knees. You get that guy to hit the ball on the ground, it's going to get you out of a jam. So you anticipate a certain pitch in a certain situation.

Plus you also identify what's working. You know what the pitcher has; you know what's working on that particular night. Matt Morris has five things he can do to the ball, and maybe only two of them are working. It's up to me, as a broadcaster and an analyst to see what is working. So I am going to tell a fan that Albert Pujols is stepping in the batter's box. Pujols is a guy who wants to beat you middle away, but he is a dead lowball hitter so you've got a window of opportunity at his hands. But you've got to be able to make a pitch in there that's got faith. You can't sink a ball in his hands; you got to run a flat ball, as a right-hander, that's going to start off at his hands, and it's going to bore in 'em. That's your pitch. Plus you also know that when he gets runners in scoring position, he'll go away from the plate. He doesn't necessarily always swing at a strike. So if I'm Matt Morris, the most scary pitch that I'm going to throw this guy is strike one. If I get strike one that's going to give me three pitches I'm going to be able to go out of the strike zone with, and I'll guarantee he's going to swing at one of them; and hopefully he's going to hit one of them off his bat, or he's going to hit one off his hands. So I'm going to explain all this to a viewing audience so they can anticipate, just like I'm going to anticipate. Then it's up to Matt Morris to execute, and if he doesn't execute—he hangs one—guess what? Albert Pujols is going to beat his ass, and that's the big leagues.

The big leagues is about making adjustments. It's about making adjustments to the stuff you have that day, to the way the ballpark's playing that day, to the strike zone you are throwing to that day, to the hitter type, swing type you are pitching against—all of it is adjustments. I played thirteen years at the big league level. You know, if I would have known that at the start of my career—with the stuff that I had—I would have had an unbelievable career. I came in throwing 93 to 96 miles an hour. I went out throwing one pitch: a 78-mile-an-hour cutter. I was an ad-lib son of a gun by the time I got out of here. I went 4 and 3 with one pitch.

To me nothing is more boring than a ten-to-nothing ballgame. Hank Greenwald was our broadcaster with San Francisco prior to me getting here. One of the things he taught me when I was just coming up—if it was a ten to nothing ballgame, I was a terrible broadcaster because I would commiserate with the guy that gave up the ten runs, which really nobody wants to hear about, but that's what I could relate to having been a pitcher. But what he taught me was that in a two to nothing ballgame, because the game is not a good game doesn't mean the broadcast can't be a good broadcast. That's the time you go you talk about a story that happened to you in 1975 in the Texas League between Shreveport and Midland, Texas, when we had locusts come in, and we had a forty-five minute rain delay— or locust delay—because the locusts were so thick you couldn't throw a ball to home plate without it hitting a bug. So I mean, you prepare going into a ballgame without really knowing what to expect, and you simply ad lib for two-and-a-half to three-and-a-half hours depending on how long the game lasts, according to the game and the situations.

I think the best audience that I could possibly have is a person that has played the game, and has seen what a four-seam fastball looks like, or what a curveball looks like, or what a slider looks like. I mean, I try and describe the difference to a person who has never seen a game, but I think it's a little easier for me, you know. Hank used to say this, "Always imagine in your mind that you're talking to one person when you are doing a game." I will do that. I will find somebody in the stands sitting below me, and I'll imagine I'm talking to him or her, and it isn't always the guy sitting there with the proper fold in his hat, with the glove that's worn out and been neatly oiled and maintained for twenty years. It could be a guy sitting there with that look in his eye like he never had a bat in his hands, never had a ball in his hand, or it could be a woman who's never put on a pair of spikes in her life. And you try and present your story accordingly to your audience. So I try to make it enjoyable and entertaining for everybody—the whole spectrum of audiences—but I think that I'm probably best suited for somebody who has played the game at some level.

I grew up in Los Angeles, in the San Gabriel–Alhambra area, which is close to Pasadena. I had a little transistor radio on my ear every night, listening to Vin Scully. Absolutely loved it. In fact, I'll tell you a story: My goal, when I was in the minor leagues, was to get to the big leagues so that Vin Scully could say my name on the radio, one time. That's all I ever wanted to do. I figured if I could do *that*, I will have arrived. In 1977, the Cubs go into Dodger Stadium. It was like "Bat Night;" sold-out crowd; 56,000 people. Then, everybody had transistor radios. I'd be willing to bet there were 20,000 radios [in the park that night]. The bottom of the first—I'm on the mound and I am listening to Vin Scully do the broadcast, and he's talking about *me*. You can hear it. It was one of the most surreal things that ever happened. I heard the whole thing. It was awesome.

[Duane Kuiper] is my best friend. You know, I sat next to him a lot on the bench as a teammate at the big-league level, talking about ball, entertaining ourselves when the game got bad. We were on some pretty bad teams. And then he went right into broadcasting and our relationship took on a different twist in that I was the player, and he was the broadcaster. And as I became a broadcaster, we came back in. There's always good chemistry there. We get to talk about something that we both love. We are really fortunate that it does work.

Frank Robinson was our skipper. And there were times when, you know, I would get in the middle of a long inning and he had to get his bullpen up and ready, and all of a sudden he would like move the hand, which was the hand sign to tell Kuiper, "Go out to talk to him. Stall." Kuiper was the second baseman; single for ten years in the big leagues. Well, Kuiper doesn't want to come out there. He's got nothing to say. I'm pissed off because number one, I'd just given up two runs; number two, the umpire just screwed me out a couple of pitches I should have gotten. Instead of a 1–2, it was 2–1. The guy gets a base hit. All of a sudden, Kuiper comes in and he's going to say something to me? I don't want to hear that. And he knows this. So he gets to the mound, and I'm there blowing snot out of my nose, and he comes up and he goes, "Section 11, aisle seat, four rows over. Check it out." And there would be a pearl sitting there; a blonde he'd already scoped out in the first inning. He never failed. He always had that.

Somebody once told us—a woman, Christine, who's in this group that sings the anthem for us a couple times a year—she said: "The reason you guys do so well is that your voices are harmonious to one another. One is a higher pitch; the other one's a lower pitch and there is a chord the two of you strike," which I thought was quite interesting. I don't know if it's factual, but very interesting. I just know that it's fun going to work every day.

Eliminating? Well, that started in a twelve–nothing ballgame where we were kind of going up in the stands, and there were a couple of guys that had phones, and nobody should be talking on the phone during a ballgame. That was an extreme rule violation. We had the telestrator right there. We thought, "We're just going to erase this guy"—we're going to eliminate him. It kind of snowballed. And in the off-season, the marketing guys call us, "Hey, we're going to sponsor the spot." "What are you talking about?" Well now, it's the Esurance online auto insurance "Eliminate Me." So now every day, we've got to eliminate somebody, which we weren't too thrilled about, but it's fun. I'd say my favorite elimination was during an intense Dodger-Giants game—and all of a sudden they go into the stands and Tommy Lasorda's sitting there. We didn't say a word. We just eliminated him. Nobody said a word. It was perfect. It's like, "See you later, meat!"

I've always believed that the story of baseball is the greatest story you could possibly tell, and I've been very blessed to work with people that feel the same way about our game. There's nobody on our broadcast team that says, "Hey, I hope it's a two-hour game." We don't care how long it lasts because where else would you rather be?

You know, I think that there is a responsibility that I have to take: approach this game with the same love that the people who are listening to me have about this game. I say this very seriously: I was arrogant when I was a player thinking that nobody could love this game as much as a player and I was so dramatically wrong. I got out of the game and I started to realize just what this game meant to people. When you see the people who come to our booth, it almost gives testimony to what this game means to them on a daily basis. We'll have Make-A-Wish Foundation come in with a child who is terminally ill and they just want to come up and see where the story comes from. You start to then realize just what it is that this game means to people. And I think my responsibility is to handle my job with the same love that the people who are listening have about the game. I try to handle that with sincerity that's genuine. That's what I try each game.

We are their eyes, talking about a game they played earlier or never played before. It's just a genuine sincerity that has to be there. You can never phone in an effort here because it's so obvious over the air that you're going through the motions. I will never do that. If it ever comes to the point where I am too tired to maintain the intensity that you need to have as a broadcaster, then I will retire.

*   *   *   *   *

BRUCE WILSON

Scoreboard Operator, Texas Rangers

"I like the atmosphere of baseball. It's fun. It's exciting. I like the people I work with. I really like everything. The years that we had the real good teams were phenomenal and stuff that I have seen has been really remarkable, like when we had like Nolan Ryan here pitching a no-hitter."

*   *   *   *   *

I'm the JumboTron scoreboard operator. This is my thirty-fifth season. I started when the Rangers came here in 1972. We had a completely different scoreboard system then with a huge outline of the State of Texas. It had like a Mylar tape machine. I used to type the "welcomes," and the batters, stats, and run it through a reader that would put all the stuff up on the scoreboard.

From 1972 until about—these dates sort of escape me—but until about the early eighties, we were in the press box. We had a little section where we operated the various scoreboard functions. Then we moved into a different booth where we had Diamond Vision until 1994.

This is the third system we've had. This system actually is keyed into all of the major-league stats. Everything that I put in updates the major-league stats, so it's all current. We start the game fresh, with everything up to date. Every play I record—hit, error, what the players' do—updates the stats. The next time up, it will show what the batter did the previous at-bat, like single to leftfield. It will update his batting average, runs, hits, errors—all of the stats I've entered into the computer goes into that database. It is displayed on the main scoreboard, the auxiliary scoreboards— in various displays. Like it might show his current batting average when he comes to the plate, or it might show on the centerfield board what he did the previous at-bat, and it will also show his batting average, his home runs, his RBIs. All those stats are updated based on the previous entries that I made. It's pretty much instantaneous.

I get here about five thirty. I eat. Then I load the lineup. Get that ready. I don't have to do a lot prior to the game now. In past years, I had quite a bit of work to do. But now it's all live during the game.

I'm positioned in a direct line with the rightfield foul lines—the second level in the press-box row. It's like a semicircle in back of the stadium, and I am over on like the third base side a little bit—over the shoulder of the batter. If you were sitting directly in back of the plate, I would be to the left. It's like a perfect view of the whole stadium with the exception of the leftfield corner. It's a little bit blocked out. If a ball hits the left field line right by the fence, I really can't see the ball. But I can see by the reactions of the runners and the umpires whether it's a fair ball. I have to watch.

When the game begins, I'm locked into the batter and the umpire. I have to watch the umpire for the signals of the balls and the strikes. Each umpire is a little bit different. They have different motions. Like if an umpire calls a strike, his arm goes out—sort of flung out to the right like a short little movement. In my particular angle, sometimes I am completely shielded. So it's difficult for me to see it. If I don't see it, I've got a TV monitor that I can look at. In most cases I can see a replay of the pitch, but not always. It used to be the umpires would give a running update with a hand signal. They would hold up their fingers, but their hands sort of blended in with the dirt in back of them. You really have to have good vision. I've got contact lenses and I can see good, but it's still a little tough sometimes to see those stubby, fat fingers blended in with the dirt.

Also, there are all sorts of different signals. Like on a foul tip, sometimes they will sort of slap their fingers together. Just a little slap, but they are all a little bit different. Some of the umpires are very delayed in their calls. Some of them are so delayed that I have to force myself to wait for his call before I look down to record on the keyboard what the pitch was. It drives the TV announcers crazy, too, because they're sitting there waiting to talk, to see what the pitch was. I'm sitting here having to record it, and if I can't see it I have to find my binoculars, get them focused, and see it. It doesn't always work.

I've got a little computer screen that if the ball's in play, I advance these runners on the keyboard, and it shows a little diagram. I have to push "in-play." He could score. He could be thrown out, tagged out, forced out. There is a million combinations of things that could happen, and I've got to unscramble and record it. Say there is a bases-loaded situation. Somebody gets a single to the outfield. The [outfielder] overruns the ball. He has an error. The runner on second advances all the way home on the error. The official scorer sitting over there has to come back and announce that's an error on the right fielder. I hear that, but the play has already happened. These things aren't necessarily determined until maybe a minute later. I've got to score these runners, and the fans out there will be sitting there going, "Wait a minute, we scored two runs and they are not up there." I really need to know how they got to the different bases by error, hit, or what.

Sometimes I have to show that the runner reached base awaiting the official scorer's decision. I've scored the runs, but I don't know how they scored—by run, hit, error. So as the game is going on, I've got to go back into that play, and I've got to redo all this stuff so it is statistically correct.

Yeah, we have had the computer blackout. It happens for various reasons. Sometimes the computer is frozen. We've had little glitches in the computer where I entered information and it didn't record. Or, say, I could enter the information and maybe not hit the enter button hard enough, and it didn't register. People start yelling at me. That's the first thing to happen. You know, "The count's wrong!" or something like that. It doesn't happen too often. Normally the umpire will look and see if the count is correct. See it's important that the count be correct because the runners may be running automatically on a full count.

You just have to be zeroed into every pitch. I get stuck with updating plays like putting runs in, updating the official scorer's decision, and going back and updating that it was an error. I can't just put in what I think it is. I might have to put, "Reached base awaiting official scorer's decision." So then the plays are going on, and he is sitting there looking at replays. The next guy hits a double and that guy scored, I'm still waiting for the official scorer's decision. Once he announces it, I've got to go back to that play, edit it, and show that that was a single. While this is happening, the game is going on.

We have other situations where we have massive lineup changes. If I don't have the lineup correct, I can't do anything. I can't do balls, strikes, runs, hits, errors. I can't do anything. Like the other night, we had a huge lead. The Angels made massive changes—about six different player changes. They were stuck in all various positions in the lineup. Until you get that unscrambled, you can't go on with the game. So my partner is sitting there helping me. He's sort of writing down who went where. And then, as you get into this, the manager comes back and says so-and-so is batting in the sixth slot, and so-and-so is batting in the fourth slot. So then you have to go back and re-change that. That's a little scary because the game's going on. They are not waiting for you. You have to scramble around and try to get the lineup right.

That is sort of stressful. I feel fine now. It used to be I would wake up in the middle of the night stressed out. Sometimes I've been in situations where the computer just flat didn't work. Like we had situations where there was a double play. You entered a double play in there, and for some reason it only recorded one out. So the scoreboard was wrong, and there is nothing that I was putting in that was wrong. It was a programming error. It wasn't recognizing something. We had to get to the Daktronics people to redo the software.

I was always a baseball fan. I had already graduated from college, and had been in the Marines. I was working at the county clerk's office in Fort Worth and I just happened to see this guy after a game some Sunday afternoon, and he was throwing a baseball around. "Where did you get that?" He said, "I was at the Rangers' game. I do the scoreboard over there." I just started drooling and I go, "Oh, man! That's what I've always wanted to do!" I just was very excited about what he was doing. He said, "Well, we need another guy." So there I was. I started the second home stand of '72. An opportunity came to do this, and I never quit. When I get into something that I like, I pretty much stay with it. I just retired from American Airlines. I was manager of reservations for thirty-one years. I did that during the day, and then come straight here for six months out of the year. It would get tiring after a long home stand, you know, doing two jobs.

Yesterday was not one of the best days. I actually ran into a giant problem, and had to try to correct it as the game was going on. I really hate to even get into it, but I recorded something incorrectly. Somehow I made the wrong entry. I recorded a single instead of a fly ball out. The whole inning was off for like a batter or so. When you see that the inning should be over and you have two outs up there, you know something's wrong. Thousands of people watching and waiting.

It's just you get into tight situations and you have to correct them as quickly as possible. I have never been in that situation before where that gross a mistake was entered. I had to go back, and basically restart the game from that batter. I had to scramble and get it corrected. It wasn't a huge problem, but I had difficulty getting the computer to go back and reconstruct the game. You really can't practice stuff like that.

* * * * *

HOWARD ESKIN

Radio Sports Talk Host, Philadelphia

Howard Eskin is a radio sports talk show host for 610 WIP in Philadelphia. Airing from 3 p.m. till 7 p.m., his show is the highest-rated afternoon radio program among men in the market. We talked in the seventh floor WIP studio, before and during his on-air broadcast. "In 1982, when I started doing TV, a guy did a story on me as a sports talk guy. He called me the 'King' of sports talkers, and then I walk in the locker room the next day and Pete Rose started calling me the King, and everybody started calling me the King. It stuck. I have like this little thing I do: I wear fur coats to the Eagles' games, and I've got my own fur coat line. Then I started wearing a Rolex with diamonds, so they called me the 'King of Bling.'"

*   *   *   *   *

My family loved sports. I was just an average kid; an average student; quiet. All I cared about was sports. I have three sisters and a brother; I'm the oldest. My father is retired now and lives about seven miles from the Phillies' spring training stadium. He loves baseball. My father had season tickets to the Phillies and 76ers. I went to a lot of games with him. Played basketball in high school for a couple of years. Played baseball—third, first, and pitcher. I was wild, but I could throw hard. Somewhere along the line, I slid headfirst and hurt my shoulder, and I couldn't throw as hard.

I started out as an announcer-late '68, early '69. Was a disc jockey on the weekends, and then an engineer at a classical music station. When I say engineer, I couldn't take apart and put together equipment, but I recorded interviews. After a couple of years, I was an engineer at two different radio stations. One was an all-news station here in town—KYW—and then I went over to WFIL spinning records for the disc jockeys. I enjoyed it. And then, I went to WABC in New York when George Michael went up there.

I used to do TV full time, five to six days a week, for ten years. But I made a decision that radio was more fun, especially with what they have done to TV in this market. I used to get four and a half minutes. Now, these guys are lucky if they get two-and-a-half minutes to do sports. How can you do anything that's fun in two-and-a-half minutes? Now, I just do a pregame Eagles show during the football season, and a half hour show on Sunday night on the NBC station.

My audience? It's hard to answer that question. Our strongest demographic is men twenty-five to fifty-four. But I'm shocked at the number of women that listen. They don't always call because they're intimidated. But they do call. It doesn't show up in the ratings, but just by sensing it when I am out in the public, the women listen. People are interested, I think, in what I have to say. Its sports, but if there are some issues going in the world, every once in a while I go off center and just talk about, you know, the lack of confidence this country has in the president; some of the problems the city has. But that's a rarity. Most of the time, I'm talking sports. I'm very opinionated, and they like it or they don't like it. Some of them say they hate—they don't hate me—they just don't like what I say, but they all listen. My opinions are very strong. Some people, not all, appreciate the honesty and keeping it real, and telling people what I really think rather than soft-shoeing through everything.

The Phillies whine more than other teams. They think when the public says negative things towards them, it's a WIP problem. They don't think it's their problem. They always blame it on WIP. A couple of weeks ago Bill Giles made a mistake in saying the people that call WIP are the crazies—he's one of the owners; his ideas and voice are what the ownership feel; he's very open. That's not really the way our fans feel, so I did a survey. Those crazies that listen and call are also season ticket holders. So their ticket holders are crazies, too.

In this town, the Phillies have not done right by the fans because they don't do everything it takes to be a world champion. They can say they are a winning team, but it's all nonsense. In Philadelphia, people really don't care about baseball anymore. I will talk a little baseball, but I am going to talk Philadelphia Eagles because, today, the veterans report for the first day. Later in this show, I'll have one of the players on. Wednesday, I'm doing this show from training camp, and Donovan McNabb is going to come on. But I will talk a little baseball because the manager came up dumb, again, last night.

I hate to say this, but most of the Phillies' people are boring. Actually, they are not all boring. Dallas Green, who was the manager back in 1980 when they won their last World Series and now works with the team, came on. He said some things which the team reprimanded him for. I found out that they called him in and told him he shouldn't be saying those things. I asked him if he would manage again if they decided to do something with Charlie Manuel. He says, "Well, I'm more like Larry Bowa. I'm a yeller and screamer." And then he made some other comments. He said, "My approach wouldn't be the way that Charlie Manuel and his coaches do things." So he, in essence, criticized what they do. He didn't get specific, but I know what some of the specifics are. They don't work on fundamentals. They don't work hard enough. When a guy doesn't do his job and starts to get a little sloppy, Dallas Green would have a meeting with the players. Charlie Manuel is just kind of nice to them because he wants to be a calm manager. This team doesn't win because they cater to the players. Dallas Green was pretty good.

Some people think that I am too hard on the players. I would take the entire team, except maybe pull four players out of a room, and the other players I'd leave in the room and throw in a bomb. Blow them up and start all over. I would keep Ryan Howard. The best player on the team is Chase Utley. It's not even close. Chase Utley, Ryan Howard, Cole Hamels—and it's a stretch to keep anybody else—but I might keep Aaron Rowand because he's a tough guy. He is an average player, but he plays hard and they need that mentality on this team. Other than Utley and Rowand, I don't think they have a whole lot of guys that play hard. I'm right just being honest about what I see in a player. I know what I am looking at.

I did the first sports talk show here at WIP when I went to the Fox station doing an hour in the afternoon, which became an hour and a half, which became three to seven in the afternoon. I've been successful for over twenty years in talk radio, so I must be doing something right. It doesn't affect the advertisers we have; doesn't affect the management here at this radio station. I think I still got a pretty good shelf life for many years based on what's going on. Management here is fine. They tell me they like what I am doing, otherwise in radio or in television if you're not doing a job that create listeners or viewers, then you don't have a job. I have a job. I'm successful according to them, and according to other people. You can't personally attack somebody, but you can have opinions about what they do. There are certain things that you need to do in terms of format and contests that I may not always like but you work within the framework of what the radio station is. But because my management respects what I do, they let me have the freedom. They never tell me before a show what to say, or they never ask me what I am going to say. If something got really hot and crazy, they wouldn't be upset with me.

You can't be great 365 days a year, but I try to approach my job as if it's the last day on the job doing the best I can every day. I think the only slumps are a day here and there. It's not weeks. You can't have slumps for weeks, because you can't. Now some days the subject matters are not always great. When the Phillies are bad and the Eagles haven't started, you have lulls. Some days aren't as good as others, but there's always something. That's the way life is, especially in this city.

Yeah, I sense if a caller wants to be adversarial. You sense by his opening comment that he either will be adversarial, or he really wants to discuss the topic. You can sense the adversarial one very quickly because he wants to challenge what I said—because he thinks he knows more than I do. I ask him what it is, and then when he goes goofy and doesn't understand the dynamics of a certain situation, I try to explain it to him. The thing that I do is I'm always down at games. I'm always talking to people. I go to football practice probably two or three times a week. I go to basketball practice a couple of times a week. It's my job. But I will call people—depending on the category they fit—either a moron, a nitwit, or a dope. A nitwit probably is at the low end of the totem pole, and then they go up a little bit to get to be a dope. It's a term of endearment. And for the people that have intelligence, sarcastically I will say, "Hey, genius."

I work because I have fun, and I enjoy it. If I didn't have any fun with any of this stuff, I wouldn't do it. I''s a big part of my life. Financially, it's helped me do a lot of things for my kids I wouldn't have been able to do. I have five kids: one is at Southern Cal; two are out of college, and I've got two other kids—a senior and a third grader. I still have expenses. Nonetheless, it gives me an excuse to work. I'm going to ride this out as long as I can. I'm fifty-five. I don't want to retire because I couldn't stop working. If I said I was retiring, I wouldn't do it.

*   *   *   *   *

BOB TAYEK

Public-Address Announcer, Cleveland Indians

"There is a baseball-rich tradition in our family. I inherited the love from my grandfather and my father, so subsequently it's in the blood. It's been passed on. I mean, I was the kid with the transistor radio under my pillow, listening to the games when I was supposed to be asleep.

I'm the kind of guy who got off a part-time job when I was in college, and would scoop down for a cheap seat to see the rest of the game. I calculate that I must have attended at least 500 games during the late sixties, all of the seventies, and into the eighties. Don't forget, those were lean years for the Cleveland Indians."

Tayek sat in the announcer's booth at Jacobs Field two hours before an interleague game between the Cleveland Indians and the Pittsburgh Pirates. This night, the Indians were honoring players from the Negro Leagues.

*　　*　　*　　*　　*

I grew up in one of the suburbs of Cleveland, and went through undergraduate school as a broadcast major. And then graduate school. Ended in various broadcast positions in radio and television. Eventually I was the program director of the flagship station for the Indians. At that time it was WWWE. Now it's WTAM. I'd been broadcasting for a long time, and I was doing some consulting for the Indians' radio broadcast, and they had an opening. They were looking for PA announcers. I was over working anyway with the broadcast team, and I said, "Well, let me give this an opportunity and see." They liked it, but my work schedule at that time wouldn't allow me to do seventy-plus games. So I became the backup, and then the gentleman who did get the job quit midseason back in '99. I said I'd fill in for the remainder of the season, and then it just snowballed from there. I couldn't give it up.

I had two kids going to private school, and I could use the money too. But it's really a labor of love. If you ask my wife, she'd say, "He loves every minute of this. Don't tell anybody, but he'd probably do it for free." I've had a passion for baseball, particularly Indians baseball all my life, so this was a great fit. It's been a wonderful blessing.

In a sense, you are a performer. I keep that in mind all day, and I get a little bit of hypochondria in that I don't want a sinus cold. I'm very careful about that, and make sure I'm not in drafts. I mean, it sounds goofy, but you just want to perform well because it's important.

It's a fairly busy day at the start of a series. There are more duties the first game of the series. It gets a little easier as the games progress. I get in here about five for a seven o'clock game. The first thing we do is open the gates at five thirty with an announcement. That triggers all the ushers and everyone else to their responsibilities. I've already pulled my scripts that give announcements inning by inning, because not only am I introducing players, but there is a lot of, frankly, retail and promotionals that's necessary in this position as well.

The in-house director, along with the marketing director, looks at what needs to be inserted at half-inning promotions. For instance, tonight there is a tribute to the Negro Leagues. There are scripts that they prepare that come ahead of time as they go through the process setting up the game presentation. I go through that carefully to see where my involvement is with the announcements. Oh, it may be anything—they might be changing a particular promotional item that will be going on between an inning. They maybe say, "This inning we are going to do the Junior Indian, or we are canceling it and moving it to another half inning." It runs like it is a live broadcast presentation in a sense, and so things have to go with the flow of what may change. Or, let's say they have a big rally after that half inning is over. They may decide they want to run on the scoreboard highlights of that inning for the fans to see, so they'll call me and ask me to move a promotional announcement somewhere else, or I may get a call that simply says guest services has a page that needs to be made for someone. You just kind of keep a heads up, and take that information down.

As soon as the gates announcement is made, I shoot up to the press area, grab the media guide for the opposing team that's in, and then check out the lineup. I have to find the media rep for the opposing team because the most important thing I have to do is get names right. I mean there is nothing that could be more embarrassing, especially if you are doing it in front of 40,000 people, than to mispronounce a professional player's name.

I love to tell this story—I hope I'm not jinxing myself: As kids, we used to take semi-obscure players and call ourselves by their names when we played pickup baseball. Back in the day, Ed Spiezio was a third baseman for the San Diego Padres in their first or second year. So I was playing third base, and I became Ed Spiezio. We followed this guy even though he was, at best, a journeyman player. And sure enough, his son Scott is playing for the [Anaheim] Angels. I'm on a headset getting instructions throughout the game, and somehow I got distracted with a request as he was coming up to bat. I'm scribbling it down and then I see him approaching the plate. I announce each player, and sure enough, instead of popping out with "*Scott* Spezio," out came "Now batting, *Ed* Spezio." The good news was he stopped, looked up at me, and started to laugh. Amen. You never know how someone may act. I thought, "Thank you, Scott, for having a sense of humor." It always was "Scott" after that. In fact I circled it on my scorecard just to make sure.

I've been observing professional announcers over the years. The best were the ones that were best prepared. They phonetically spell out every name. I spell them out phonetically especially if I am not familiar—to make sure of even little things. Like, once a game we announce the base coaches. For Pittsburgh, John Shelby is the first-base coach. I remember when he played outfield for Baltimore. The PR person said, "He loves to be called T-Bone." I said, "Are you absolutely sure?" "Yeah, that's how he wants it." Okay, it's, "T-Bone Shelby is coaching first base." It's that kind of thing you want to be accurate, and don't want to muff up.

The same thing applies even in our own in-house presentations. You get this once-in-a-lifetime thrill for a person that's singing the national anthem, or a young kid or any person, frankly, throwing out a first pitch. You don't want to blister their name. So I go through it carefully to see how you pronounce them because I figured this is their fifteen minutes of fame. You don't want them to feel like they were slighted or misrepresented.

After getting all those phonetic spellings, then I visit the umpires' room. Just stop in to check in with them at the beginning of series. It's always a new quartet. We go over the fact that I'm the timer between innings. As soon as the last out is made, I click off on my stopwatch a minute and forty seconds. As soon as it hits a minute and forty, I announce the batter coming up for the next inning, which is the umpire's cue. They also listen for that if they haven't already signaled for the batter to get into the box. They like to keep the game moving, and under Major League Baseball rules that's what we do. I make the announcement: "Leading off, in the bottom of the fifth inning for the Indians . . ." Or, let's say the pitcher gets up there late for his warm ups, we still let him know when it's a minute forty. I clock it, and when I see a minute forty, *boom*. At two-o-five, it's play ball. Sometimes the commercial breaks will be longer if it's a national telecast.

And I'm in touch with the umpires just to make sure if there is anything that they need, and I will let them know where I am seated because I look for their signal when a new player is brought in—pinch hitter, new pitcher. They always give a signal to the official scorer. I look for it, too, because that means then I can announce that player is entering the game.

Once that's complete, then I come back up and have everything in place ready to go before the pre-game show begins. I'm responsible for tying in with the video board, the visitor's lineup, the Indians' lineups.

Today we have a special public-address announcement in the pre-game for the Negro Baseball Leagues. I will read the Negro League players coming up: Buck O'Neal, Jim Mudcat Grant, Joe B. Scott. You want to make sure that's right. And sure enough, if I go through the scripts that are given, there will be typos. I try to really use my old English class grammar to go through it and correct what might be writing flaws. What comes out should come out properly.

Then we just go in order: introduce the anthem signer, the umpires, and then when the team takes the field, we punch out the players. And then the game begins. Each player gets announced each time that he comes to bat. The first time through the order—let's say starting the second inning—I will say, "Leading off for Pittsburgh and batting fourth, the left fielder, number 38, Jason Bay." I bounce around and either exchange the number for the position, or vice versa. I will simply say, "Now batting— stepping to the plate—now in the box." And I will give the name; I always give the name. I either give either the number or position; not both the next time around.

To stay in concentration throughout, that's one of the toughest things. There's a lot of conversation that can go on within the intramicrophone system with all of the camera people, the director, and everyone else. They will carry on conversations and stuff, and I just stay off-mic because I don't want to press the wrong button and say something that isn't proper. So I'm kind of the silent one up here when it comes to who talks over the intercom. I will get questions asked, but I don't join conversations just because I think if you are near a live microphone, the first rule is know what you are going to say. A couple of times things have snuck out; never anything too negative. I haven't had any major embarrassments; just a couple of minor things. That's pretty much it.

And then when the Indians are playing and are in a rally, and you know one of the players are coming up—as you would hear tonight—I know that the heartthrob of every woman here is Grady Sizemore. I really punch it, or at least for me: "Leading off for the Tribe, *number 24, Grady Sizemore!*" You know, that kind of thing; just to punch it a little bit.

I once talked to a third base coach—we were at a dinner here at the ballpark—he didn't really know me, but I knew who he was. We were talking and he said, "Nobody really knows who we are until we make a mistake in front of 40,000 people. Then they know who you are." I thought, "Boy, he is right on." If I don't hear a negative then I figure they must be happy 'cause I think the players, from what I can tell, if they really don't like something, they'll let the club know. I've never heard anything.

You are playing to the home crowd. I look at this is entertainment. They're here to see these players, and so I try to come up with at least something to give them a little more recognition, and stir up the fans. They are ready to cheer, and they want to. Oh, yeah, there is a different volume. Literally, you push a little more. I mean, to do the job right and to carry it over many innings, you really have to go to the old standard that's been taught: breathe from the diaphragm. You might push a little harder; sing it a little bit more. If you were on the speedometer, it would stay at about thirty for the visiting team. It hits fifty, or above, for the home team. That's what I try to do at least.

The difficult one, at times, is when a former star player returns with another team. That's when I try to be as neutral as I can. I don't want to downplay it 'cause I don't think that's fair to the player, but obviously I'm not going to sing it. So far, I haven't had any complaints. The fans react how they want. They're the paying customer.

[After the game] we put on the scoreboard video board "sweet play of the game." I intro that and read the tag lines. Then there's a "player of the game." Several, if you will, "commercials" that involve, you know, "AAA is here to assist you with your car." That type of thing. And there is a general closing promotional spot once they have posted the final figures on the scoreboard. Then I wait. Once the ballpark is clear, the operations director gives me a wave, and I give a final announcement that basically says, "The ballpark is closing. Thank you for attending." That's the cue for the ushers too. Depending on the size of the crowd, it could be ten minutes [when the final announcement is made]. It could be twenty minutes. It all depends. That pretty much wraps it up.

When I first took the position, I really wanted to know what it was they wanted out of this position as far as what style, because I know myself and my own voice quality. I can't do the NBA-style. I wouldn't even attempt to do the NBA-style, which is, you know, long singing, drawn out. I don't want to call it the scream, but it's really a push and a shove. I wouldn't be really capable of that. They said, "What we want from you is friendly." I said, "Friendly I can do," along with hopefully a professional sound. So that's what I continue to attempt to do. I guess it's been satisfactory.

My voice is, frankly, something I worked at for a long time. I was never real happy with it until I worked at it, I guess, like singers do. You try to lower it; bring more resonance to it, and over a period of doing that I was able to accomplish it to the point where one day I kind of said, "Jeez, I actually sound good." I think I'm finally where I want to be. You try to keep the resonance and the sound that you want. I make sure I go from the diaphragm; bring it down a little bit so that it has a little bit resonance as opposed to talking from your voice box in normal conversation. The higher the decibel, the more difficult it is for it to carry and be heard.

Baseball has been a passion my whole life. I've always lived and died with the Cleveland Indians. I think it's really a fulfillment of aspirations to be somehow connected with Major League Baseball because it's always been so much part of me. It's a labor of love.

It's a wonderful diversion from the regular work I do. I'm the director of media and public relations for the Catholic Diocese of Cleveland. I'm always working that job. It doesn't really interfere. I just scoot right out of my office at five, and get over here. They traditionally have a lady do it on Sundays. I do all the rest.

*　*　*　*　*

JOE MOELLER

Advance Scout, Florida Marlins

Moeller was the second youngest player in the National League when he was called up by the Los Angeles Dodgers in 1962. The right-hander pitched in 166 games through 1971, ending with a career 4.01 ERA.

He was eating dinner in the press dining room at Fenway Park with other advance scouts when I approached him. The Red Sox would be playing his Marlins in an upcoming series. We talked the next night, and again the following month in Philadelphia.

"With an advance scout, the joke is 'You'd better go to the bathroom before the game starts, because you're not going to the bathroom during the game.' The minute I leave, they are liable to do something I miss and then if they use it against our club, our club says, 'Hey, how come you didn't tell us about this?' You don't ever want to read in the paper: 'Our advance scout didn't tell us about that.'"

*   *   *   *   *

I grew up in Manhattan Beach, California; a little beach town. When I was twelve, I was pitching in Little League. A scout with the Red Sox talked to my dad and worked out an agreement. He said, "Here is a check for five thousand dollars. When your son graduates from high school, we have the last rights to sign him." We were a very poor family in '56. There wasn't a draft then. Whatever the last offer was, I had to go to the Red Sox. If they topped it by one dollar, we had to sign with them.

When I graduated we had clubs that came over, one at a time. I mean the *next* day after my graduation, they came to the house. Detroit came in first and said, "We'll give you eighty thousand." Then the White Sox: "We'll give you one hundred thousand." Then we called the Red Sox and said, "Here is our best offer: one hundred thousand," and they said, "No, we don't go that high."

We had also promised Walter O'Malley that we would go see him. So we went and talked to him, and he talked us into signing for eighty thousand. I was a Dodger fan, and it was my hometown. The other two offers were cash and obviously were going to be taxed at a different rate. With the Dodgers, I got it in five years. In the way it was structured it actually wasn't as big a difference.

I was with the Dodgers for forty-one years, as a player and then working in community relations and special assignments. I signed out of high school when I was seventeen, in '60. My last year was '73. Eight of those were in the major leagues.

I started in Reno. I was eighteen. I was 13 and 5 there, then moved to A-Ball. I was only there a month. I was 5 and 1, and then I finished in Spokane. I won twenty games and struck out almost 300. The next year, in spring training, I made the Dodgers. I was nineteen, the youngest pitcher ever to start a game for the Dodgers. I pitched against the old Braves, in Milwaukee. I don't think I felt a real nervousness at all. I had confidence in myself because I had an outstanding year the year before, but I was pitching against Hank Aaron, Eddie Matthews, Felipe Alou, and Joe Torre. People say, "Don't you get nervous with 50,000 people there?" You don't really because I'm thinking about the guy I have to get out. I knew what I had to do. The score was 5 to 3, I think. It was my first win. My older son was born the next day. What a thrill.

I threw hard at that time and had a good curveball. I was a strikeout pitcher, but that's all I threw: fastball, curveball. What hurt me a lot was I didn't have a changeup. I threw everything hard. I worked on trying to throw an off-speed pitch, but for what every reason couldn't develop it. Johnny Podres, who had one of the best changeups in baseball, tried to work with me. Carl Erskine worked with me. Well, the year I stop playing I was throwing batting practice for the Dodgers and working with Andy Messersmith in the outfield. He said, "Here try this." I picked it up just like that. If I had had an off-speed pitch, it would have made all the difference in the world.

I'm an advance scout for the Florida Marlins now. People don't know what an advance scout does. This is my seventh year. I started with Montreal, and then they bought the Marlins, so I moved over with them. Montreal hadn't had an advance scout for a long time. They didn't have the money. They were just so-so. In spring training in 2000, Jeff Torborg was with them working as a catcher instructor. Jeff and I had roomed together. Jim Beattie and Felipe Alou said, "We need to get an advance scout this year." Jeff, who was kind of in the conversation said, "Hey, I know somebody who would like to do that." So Beattie called and said, "Would you like to advance?" I said, "Absolutely."

I started with them and have been doing it ever since. People ask me, "What do you do?" I say, "I am a scout." They say, "Oh, I've got this kid. He is only five years old, but he can throw." I say, "I'm not that kind of scout."

I'm one step ahead of who we play next. I'm watching Boston now because the Red Sox are going to come down to our ballpark and play us next. I'm trying to figure out how to pitch 'em, how to play them—anything that I can figure out that would help our club.

In a hitter, I'm looking for changes. If the guy has a bad wrist or his back is bothering him, I would think he is going to be afraid to get beat inside because then he swings to protect that. So he is going to cheat inside. You want to pound him in there. In other words, if all of a sudden a hitter is pulling off the ball and everybody is pitching him inside, now I am going, "We've got to pitch him away." Andruw Jones is a good example. When Jones is hitting the ball the other way, you've got to pound him inside. When he starts pulling off the ball, you can throw him breaking balls away. I want to look at it so that he doesn't go into our ballpark, and then it takes us one game to realize that he's pulling off the ball.

I have a database of when I saw them last. I look at that and compare it with what I see now, and then I'll tweak it a little bit. I do spray charts. I do pitch counts: show where each hitter hits a ball, whether it's a ground ball, a fly ball, a line drive, off left handers, off right handers. I mean, it's pretty detailed what I do. Like tonight, I'll chart the pitchers and the hitters, and then I will go back to the room, look at it, and see what the common denominators are: Why are they getting him out? How are the Mets pitching against the Red Sox? And then our club takes that information and sees how it fits with our pitchers. You can tell a guy to throw a curveball or a changeup, but if he doesn't have that, you don't throw him something you don't have, or you don't throw well.

Like with the hitting coach, he wants to know everything he can about the pitchers that our guys are going to face, so if one of our hitters says, "What's this guy throwing?" he can look at my report, and say, "Fastball, slider, change. Fastball is 92 to 95; has some run to it, or some sink to it." The hitter kind of has an idea about the pitcher. They use other things too, so it's a combination of things. I'm just one part of that puzzle.

Every three days I am in a different city and in a different hotel. I usu-ally always sit within probably ten rows directly behind home plate. Every club has a reciprocal agreement that your advance scout gets the best seat. I'm watching the Red Sox. Somebody from the Red Sox is down in our ballpark watching us, you know. I'll be down there fifteen minutes before the game. Get my lineups together. Get my charts all set up. Every advance scout has different charts that he uses that to get the most infor-mation with the least amount of writing. Like the first hitter—I will draw a line where he hits the ball; what the pitch count was; how the pitcher pitched him. I watch how the catcher sets up. Good pitchers and good catchers will look two pitches ahead. How are they trying to get him out? They can't just go to that pitch all the time because the hitter's looking; he's starting to think along with them. With the pitchers, I'll look: he's not using a slider now, so he is not having as much confidence in it. All of a sudden, you see slider, slider, slider, slider. Then you look at what the counts were. You can help your hitters out—"When he is ahead in the count, he is going to throw that slider, breaking low and in on you."

What I see is what every other scout sees. Sometimes it'll take until the end of the third game to see something like guys really weak on off-speed pitches, or off-speed early and hard late. It will take a few games to see that. I mean, I've got some stuff on them already.

I never see our team. People ask me about our club. I say, "I don't know, I never see our club." Well, I saw three days in spring training. That's about it because I'm chasing the next team. They say about this job: "Either you love it, or you hate it." I love it. I like the challenge of trying to figure how to pitch guys and how to play guys. Major league [player] scouts are just watching and evaluating players. They can sit. They can go get a Coke or a hamburger. With me, don't talk to me while I'm watching the game. I always wear head phones to listen to the ballgame, just to pick up informa-tion from the broadcasters because they will say, you know, "He's really struggling, or the pitch is inside, or he is chasing breaking balls." [Don] Sutton, in Atlanta, is fabulous because he can write my report for me. He will tell me how to pitch to everybody. Chris Wheeler with the Phillies is out-standing. Keith Hernandez is outstanding. They will talk about the hitter and the troubles he is having. Or the pitchers; when they are not getting their breaking ball over, or they are falling behind and they won't throw certain pitches in certain counts. "Ah, thank you," I say, because I'm trying to figure that out, and I'm doing so many things. I mean, I send about a forty-page report every three days, so it's just a lot of information to look at.

When I get back to the hotel after the game probably at ten or eleven, I will probably have about an hour, hour and a half of work to put it in the computer, and then tomorrow I'll spend all day on the computer just kind of pulling things together. After the game tomorrow night, I'll be up until two o'clock summarizing it and e-mailing it to the Marlins. Then I get to bed at two, and I've got to be back up at five because I've got a seven o'clock flight to Washington. I've got a game Friday night.

I'm very blessed in the fact that I am extremely organized. You'd better be organized. You've got to catch the right flight, at the right time, to get to the game. If you think it's a seven o'clock game and it's a one o'clock game, you mess up. Also, I'll get to the airport two hours to two-and-a-half hours before. It's not worth it to me to cut it close.

There's kind of an unwritten rule that other advance scouts can ask me anything about any other club, but not about my club. In fact I had a call from an advance scout from another club; asked me about a guy they are going to face on Friday. I said, "Yeah, I will e-mail you what I have." So I will send him what I have on that pitcher. We share information as long as it is not about my club. I am not going to tell you how to get our hitters out.

In 2003, I worked up until the end of October. We won the World Series that year. But if we're not having a good year, and if we are out of it let's say by September first, they say there is no sense to spend the money. They will send me home. It just depends on where we're at. I might do a few series by satellite, but most likely I'm done. I will do everything I do here, but I will watch it on TV. It's about 60 percent, maybe 70 percent, as efficient. The camera is not always on the things that I'm looking at, but I can watch the hitters and the pitchers. I watch what kind of arms the outfielders have. Sometimes they don't get back in time from the commercial break and I've missed a pitch or so, or the announcers start talking about everything else but the ballgame.

I think we are twelve or thirteen games out now so as we get to September, if we are twelve games out then, we're not going to go any-where most likely. Sometimes I work six months; sometimes I work seven months. You hope you work seven months like 2003, which was one of the most exhausting years for me just because it was so intense.

*   *   *   *   *

LARRY FRATTARE

Broadcaster, Pittsburgh Pirates

Courtesy of Pittsburgh Pirates

Frattare talked to me about his 31 years broadcasting Pirates games as we sat off a stairwell behind the press box at PNC Park.

"I was one of the guys who replaced Bob Prince when I started in 1976," Frattare said. "What just totally blew me away was that there were so many people that hated me because I took Bob Prince's job, not because there was anything about me that they hated, it was that they grew up listening to Bob. Bob created a couple generations of baseball fans, and I reminded myself that if someone had been a broadcaster for twenty-eight years and they got fired and nobody cared, how sad it would be. So I said to myself, I am going to try to create my generations of baseball fans, and I would love to be here long enough that people would come up to me and say, 'We grew up listening to you.' And that has happened, and that has given me tremendous, tremendous satisfaction."

* * * * *

My job is to report the games and entertain folks that tune in. I feel very strongly about the fact that, first and foremost, people that tune into the broadcast want to know what the score is. They want a quick recap if they check into the game in the sixth inning of a 3-to-2 ballgame. How did we get to that point? I also know that each game has a theme to it, has a flow to it, a cadence, a rhythm, and I sincerely believe that the better broadcasters are those people that can sense all of those ingredients, and then impart that experience to the listener.

You prepare for the game not knowing what is going to happen, but nevertheless there are some things that can be somewhat predictable. When I first started doing it thirty-one years ago, I didn't understand that there was this flow to the game. I was just doing it. Therefore, when the top of the first inning goes one, two, three and you are off and running, then you tell yourself subconsciously all the other stuff that you prepared for the game you don't need. It's not necessary because the top of the first went quickly. You also find those games where you've prepared six or seven nuggets about a starting pitcher, and you know you are in trouble when you've used five of those nuggets in the top of the first inning. Much of doing baseball is the cake, but you also want to provide a little bit of the icing. You just don't know how much of the icing you are going to need in the course of the day.

What I have noted about preparing is I'm not sure that people appreciate how important listening is, and watching. Listening and watching are important ingredients for broadcasters because when you're sitting in the press box and you see Jeff Cox, the third-base coach, pacing the infield, I want to go downstairs later and ask him, "What were you doing?" Maybe it's not something that A, I can talk about on the air, or B, that's all that interesting. When I go into the clubhouse I very often just stand there and look to see who is there. There are times the players, coaches, and manager will give you twenty minutes, and not bat an eye. Then there are days when, if you try to talk to a particular player, he may be so busy or his mind may be somewhere else that there's only thirty seconds when what he's telling you is worth anything, if he gives you even thirty seconds.

It took me a long time to realize that some of the stories that happen in the clubhouse don't translate well to the broadcast. The old cliché about "You had to be there" is true. There are some things that go on between players that just are not the great stories that you would have hoped. I mean you sit there and you laugh seeing it happen, and then you go to the booth and try to say, you know, *"I saw Craig Wilson and Jack Wilson together . . ."* and it dies. The challenge to it is to know where those stories belong.

I do radio and television, and I have created rules for myself. For example, I believe that on radio, I am the star, and the color guy has to be in step with me. On TV, I believe the color analyst is the star, and I have to be in step with him. And then, I have to know who is next to me, what does my partner like to do and what doesn't he like to do. When I worked with Bob Walk, he is very analytical and I can play to his analysis. Steve Blass does not do an awful lot of that. It's the emotion of the game that he taps into particularly well. For example, last night Steve and I were on the air together doing television and we sensed an electricity in the ballpark that we tapped into. The game moved at a pretty good pace. The crowd stayed into it—the first-inning double play; the battle of Kip Wells and Barry Bonds and the anticipation of will he pitch to him and how will he approach him; Jason Schmidt retiring sixteen of the first seventeen batters. There was nothing that took the crowd out of it from our standpoint as broadcasters. There was that buzz in the ballpark that provided us with tremendous announcing support.

When I am on radio, my partner needs to give me enough room. There is a beginning point for every play. One thing that is very important to a good major league play-by-play announcer is the rhythm—the opportunity to get in on the play at its outset. Very often that is merely done by saying, *"Here is the windup and the pitch, or here is the 3–2 pitch."* If the color analyst on radio goes too far, then what you hear is the play-by-play guy saying, *"He swings and it's a drive to leftfield,"* but you didn't get it in the beginning. That hampers the play-by-play announcer's ability to paint the whole picture because you are now playing catch up. That's why I made the point, before the color analyst makes his point.

Also, when you get down to those critical moments of the game—the bottom of the ninth inning, the bases are loaded, and the game is tied—

there are a lot of things that you do over and over and over again because for every pitch there is the drama that needs to be reemphasized: *"Bases loaded, two outs, 4–4 game. Swing and a foul ball back out of play. So-and-so at third; so-and-so at second; so-and-so at first; so-and-so looks in for the sign, here is the windup and the pitch, foul ball out of play."* To capture the drama of it, you can't assume what you said four sentences before is going to be fresh enough to play to the drama of the moment.

I'm from Rochester, New York. I grew up listening to Mel Allen back in the time when color analysts were not a regular part of broadcasts. I'm a strong believer that my abilities as a baseball announcer are tremendously enhanced by always working alongside a former athlete. I don't think I could do as good a job if I had to worry about the things that I know my partners can provide. For example, I know about what Tom Gorzelanny and Zack Duke throw. But I don't spend a lot of time worrying about whether they been successful because their curveball or their fastball has been working tonight. I have a color analyst alongside that can help me worry about that. I can, therefore, concentrate on other aspects [of the game]. I have done games, by the way, where I have been alone for one reason or another, and I have reminded myself every time: Don't try to do both jobs. I'm not smart enough to do both jobs; some guys can. Vin Scully, in Los Angeles, can do both jobs.

Bob Prince, the longtime voice for the Pirates, came to me in my first or second year and said, "When do you give the score?" I looked at him like an idiot and said, "What do you mean?" "What are your rules for giving the score?" I said, "I don't have any." And he said, "Shame on you." I said, "Well, Bob, what do you do?" And he said, "I give the score every batter. I give the score every 3–2 pitch. And I give the score anytime I'm saying to myself, 'Have I given the score recently?'" I have followed Bob's rules for twenty-eight of my thirty-one years. I am so confident that when people call me or people write me a letter or I see somebody on the street and they say, "You don't give the score enough," I say to them, "I'll bet you a hundred dollars; you tell me the inning and the game, and I will get the tape, and I will bet you in a span of ten minutes I gave the score twelve times." They all back down and say, "Well, it must have been your partner."

Listeners tune in and out all the time. Not only turning the radio on, but their minds tune in and out. And there are times when people don't think they heard the score, but they did. Maybe there were times when you said, *"Jason Bay drove in the only run, in the third inning,"* and it's now the seventh where you just gave the score 1 to 0, but they didn't hear that. Those are the days you say to yourself, "He is not giving the score enough." I know from the times I have listened to weather forecasts on the radio, and then I hear the end of the weather forecast and I don't remember what it said. Yet I told myself I wanted to listen. So that's a reality.

I also have a rule that every time I turn over a batting order, I recap the game in some way: *"Two runs in the second; three in the fourth; one in the fifth."* If it's a 9-to-7 game, I say, *"Pirates have nine runs. Here are the RBIs: Bay, three; Jack Wilson, two; Craig Wilson, two; Freddy Sanchez, one; Jose Castillo, one."* I find different ways of doing it, but I maintain that that still provides the listener the items the listener needs to take away from the ballgame.

Another rule is: Never start a story with two outs, because you are right in the middle of the story and if a ground ball is hit, or a fly ball is hit, the inning's over. To go back to that story later, you have to recreate the whole thing again. The problem with that rule is sometimes you are a telling a story with one out, and there is a double play and the inning's over.

I have another rule: Never do ancillary puffy stuff on the broadcast when your team is hitting. Don't wish somebody a happy birthday when your team is hitting. Last night for example, on TV, I told a story about Craig Wilson buying me socks. I have this thing about colorful socks, okay. I wear colorful socks. The players have kidded me about it. Well, Craig Wilson bought me these socks, and I knew at some point last night I would tell the story because I think it is kind of a fun thing—hey, a major league player being involved. But I told myself, "Don't tell this story until you are certain it's the right opportunity." A good time to tell the puffy nonsense stories are when the pitcher is hitting because there is a good chance that nothing remarkable is going to happen. So I got to tell the story last night when Kip Wells was batting in the sixth inning. The last thing you want to be doing is telling a story, whether it's serious or not, and then all of a sudden your guy hits a three-run home run. You are caught because you couldn't jump on the beginning of the play. Your story got sent down the drain.

I think I do a better job on radio. I feel in control. I feel that I can get into my rhythm better on radio. TV is more of a color analyst's medium, and you have to be so in tune with what the truck is doing so they are not blindsided, and they need to tell you what they are going to do so you are not blindsided. We have a producer and a director that travel with us all the time. We spend a lot of time together, so it's very important that we get a sense about what they like to do; they know what I like to do. One of the things I told them was, "Do me a favor. Don't give me a lot of boat shots," because over the years that we have been playing at PNC Park, I have realized that I have nothing intelligent to say about boat shots. What do you say, *"There is a boat"*?

I also think it's absurd the obsession that baseball people have with the distances of home runs. There is no additional value whether you hit the ball 350 feet or 450 feet. Yes, I will make a big deal about a ball that hits off the scoreboard, or in the upper deck of a ballpark, but if the PR people announce it's 404 feet, big deal. I don't want to deal with that. In fact, my partners kid me all the time because we have this list of balls that have bounced into the water, and I totally ignore it because I don't think there is any value in it whatsoever. Interestingly enough, the longest ball hit here at PNC Park was hit by Sammy Sosa to deep left center field—nowhere near the water. We have been in PNC Park six years, and there's already been eighteen balls bounced into the water. That means when we have been here thirty years there will have been ninety. What's the big deal?

One of the exciting things about being a baseball announcer is that there are memorable moments that occur, and they can occur in every game, some bigger than others. The Mazeroski home run. I called the Francisco Cordova–Ricardo Rincon no-hitter, which ended with a Mark Smith three-run homer in the tenth inning. You hope that when those moments come, all of your preparation and all of your talents will come to the forefront; that they will be positively remembered. I went through a spell there where I would just brutalize game-winning home runs. I would say right center when I meant left center. I would misidentify the player who hit it, and therefore you have a double fear because you made a mistake, and you know that that mistake is going to be extracted from the broadcast and played on the scoreboard, or played on ESPN highlights. What was going on was I was so afraid that I became timid. I started finding myself a step or two behind plays. My concentration level was just terrible. That was a period when I didn't want to do it anymore because the pain was too much.

Let me be honest with you and say that four or five years ago, I started doubting whether I was any good. There were times when I said to my wife, "I don't want to do this anymore." It was too painful to sit in the chair for a nine-inning game, and then go home and sit on the back porch, and agonize over a dozen things that I wish I had done differently, or calls that I had messed up. The more I thought about it, the more difficult it became for me. My head was so clogged with the fear of failure—the fear of making mistakes—that it just added to my problem. And then two years ago, I actually took a sabbatical of ten days, and met with some people who helped me turn the corner mentally. Consequently, since then, I have fallen back in love with my job. I don't make the mistakes I once made. I don't find myself agonizing as much.

I haven't agonized for two years. I had a broadcast three or four days ago where I made mistakes that were dumb mistakes, and I shouldn't have made them. They were due, in part, to poor preparation. Sometimes when you make those mistakes, you say on the air to your listeners, *"What was I thinking?"* I'll give you an example: We were in Milwaukee the other day and I made a comment about how I wondered if the Brewers have ever had a Rookie of the Year. I quickly grabbed a book, and I mentioned that Pat Listach won the Rookie of the Year honor for the Brewers in the early nineties. And I said, *"I wonder if the Milwaukee Braves ever had a Rookie of the Year?"* I grabbed the book, opened it up, and I said, *"1948, Alvin Dark; 1950 Sam Jethroe."* Then I went to a commercial break, and I am sitting in my chair thinking. It just so happens that I was born in 1948. When I was growing up, we had an 8mm film that my parents had bought of the 1948 World Series between the Braves and Indians. It was one of the few films we had in our house. Well, I now vividly remember it was the *Boston* Braves against Cleveland, so I mean it was a dumb mistake, and I said on the air, *"Wait a minute folks, I apologize. Pardon my ignorance. Many of you probably know that the Braves didn't go to Milwaukee until '53."* Three or four years ago that would have eaten me up. I would have carried that back to my hotel room and closed my doors. As it was, I wish I hadn't made the mistake. So that night I had a drink with a friend, and I said to him, "Hey, listen to these dumb mistakes I made tonight."

One of my strengths is my voice. My dad and I have the same—I wish he was still alive—voice quality. Along the way, there were times that I fell into some bad habits. I was a disc jockey for a couple of years when I first got out of college, and I started getting real throaty with my voice because I thought that's the way disc jockeys were supposed to sound. Fortunately, I busted through that. One of the challenges that I face now is, there is a level of excitement that you want in your broadcast, but three things happen when you become too excitable: number one, you lose voice quality; number two, your mind doesn't work as quickly as your voice is working because you put yourself at a fever pitch; and number three, there is a tendency to fall into the use of words that are not very descriptive—*"Unbelievable. Wow!"* I fight with this all the time because I want there to be excitement in my voice and in my broadcast and there are times when I scream, but I am not all that comfortable with it. For example, we had a play earlier this year where I got extremely excited when Bay hit a grand slam. The ball was traveling to the left centerfield wall and I said, *"Drive, deep left centerfield, grand slam?"* And then I screamed, *"YES!"* It worked. It was okay. Better I be screaming one word than screaming a whole bunch of words. That's the challenge for me because when I get overly excited I don't find myself being descriptive. I also believe this of baseball announcers: if you do a play properly—from the minute the play starts till it ends—it's all there in the play. And I maintain that if you hear a baseball announcer going back after the play is over and recreating slightly, he knows in his mind he's missed something, and he's now trying to jump in and fix it. And that happens. But I would rather be able to know that if that play happens for thirteen seconds, that everything that I have just said in those thirteen seconds gives you where the ball went, how the runners moved, what the score is—the whole package would be right there.

I work for the club. My first twelve years I worked for KDK radio, and they treated me extremely well. But the one thing I noticed when you work for a radio station was that baseball is only a priority for them at certain times of the year, whereas, when you work for the ball club, it's a priority of the team all the time. Also, the club appreciates the fact that baseball announcers have to have credibility; that the fans are smart and they know what's going on. The club is very supportive of making sure that we call it the way it is. If a particular player makes two or three errors, there is no sugarcoating it. Ernie Harwell told me this years ago, he said, "If you mentioned that a player was 0 for 4, struck out three times, bounced into a double play, and made two errors, how much more do you have to say about the kind of day he had?"

I grew up a Yankee fan, and my favorite player growing up was Yogi Berra. No one has ever had a bigger place in my life, in my heart than my dad. Part of why I grew up to be a Yogi Berra fan was that my dad and two uncles were catchers in high-school baseball and I was a catcher in high school, so I have always had this affinity. Plus I always thought that my dad looked liked Yogi, so it was an easy thing for me to root for Yogi.

But the big thing for me was that my dad did a remarkable job of encouraging me. When I was growing up, I invented my own baseball game with a deck of cards. I was thirteen years old and my brother, who later became an architect, made me a baseball field. I took this field and this deck of cards, and I started playing baseball games. I started announcing them. I vividly remember my parents found a box of small bingo chips that had numbers on them. B8 was Yogi Berra, and B7 was Mickey Mantle. And my mother had this big box of colorful buttons, so the Red Sox were the red buttons and the Tigers were the blue buttons. I would play games down in the basement for hours, and I was announcing it and keeping score—the whole bit. My dad saw that and did everything he possibly could to encourage me.

When I first got the Pirates' job at the age of twenty-eight, some people said to me, "Boy, you are awfully young. Have you paid your dues?" I said, "I've been doing this since I was thirteen." When other people were doing certain things to prepare their careers, I was preparing myself for it as well.

*   *   *   *   *

DAN SHAUGHNESSY

Sports Columnist, Boston Globe

"My first full time job was in Baltimore in 1977, covering the Orioles. I worked at the *Baltimore Evening Sun* for two years, and then went to the *Washington Star* for three where I was a baseball writer. When that paper went out of business in '81, I came back to the *Globe* when the Celtics were very good, as a full-time writer—I did a lot of small stuff for them in and after college. I then went on to baseball in '86, replacing [Peter] Gammons who had gone back to *Sports Illustrated*. I got the column in '89. Have been a sports columnist since."

In addition to his job at the *Boston Globe*, he has written several sports books, including: *The Legend of the Curse of the Bambino*, *Reversing the Curse: Inside the 2004 Boston Red Sox*, at Fenway: *Dispatches from Red Sox Nation*, and *Seeing Red: The Red Auerbach Story*. Shaughnessy was the first interview I conducted for this book. He invited me to his home near Boston. He was in his second-floor office working on an upcoming story when I arrived.

*   *   *   *   *

I'm a sports columnist for the *Boston Globe*. That entails whatever the story of the day is. It can be high-school hockey. The Bruins and the

Celtics are not very good. I might have done eight columns on the Celtics this year, and two on the Bruins. That's unusual. If the Bruins are in the playoffs coming up, I'll be taking trips to Buffalo and Montreal. I'm writing about the marathon on Monday. But in this region right now, baseball is the flavor of the month, and it is pretty much twelve months a year. We're at a time the team is good. I do a ton of baseball. I definitely identify with that sport more than the others.

There was a time when I was a beat writer. I did the daily for baseball. There was a time when I was the basketball beat writer. Did the daily for the Celtics for four years. I didn't do any baseball when I was a Celtics beat writer. Since '89, I've been a columnist. In New England when you're a columnist and you do sports in Boston, you do a lot of Red Sox. There is so much interest in it. But there will be stretches—when the Patriots go the Super Bowl—that I'll write Patriots forty days in a row. So we do them all.

If I were in a different city I would be doing sports, but I wouldn't be doing probably as much baseball. If I were in Pittsburgh, there wouldn't be as much call for the Pirates as there is for the Steelers. You've got to kind of look at your market. In New England, you can't go wrong writing about the Red Sox.

I grew up the youngest of five children, in Central Massachusetts. I'm fifty-two. My older brother was a very good ballplayer. I went to his games. I would come back and talk to my parents about him. Kind of report to my parents what I'd seen. And I had a sister who was quite good—two years older than me. She played softball, field hockey, basketball. When I was like eight, I sort of just became immersed in all of it—playing and reading and watching, and my own dice game for baseball. Collected cards, subscribed to the magazines, and all that stuff. It was always sports.

I knew much more about baseball when I was eight than I do now in terms of who plays for who. I could tell you all the lineups. I was extremely immersed in it. And then as a sophomore I played on the high-school varsity. I was an average high-school player in a small high school. I was a fair hitter, and had fair skills. In college I didn't do it. I went to Holy Cross, and I had sort of decided on one activity: the school paper. I kind of made it the goal. I had really good role models: Peter Gammons from my hometown of Groton; Paul Brown was here; Bud Collins. They all were generous to me. I worked hard at it, had some good fortune, and here we are. This was the goal.

I have a lot of projects going at once. I've got two new books in the works. Stacks of things to keep up with. I don't have a daily column again until Sunday at Fenway. It's a day game. So I'm using today and tomorrow to work on these projects because I don't want to be doing it on the day of the daily columns.

The day games are easy. What I'm going to write hasn't happened yet on that day. You don't have to have a preconceived notion. You can just kind of let it all happen, and then just say after the game what's everybody doing.

With the night games, we need to have an idea beforehand. Like I was out there Wednesday night. It was David Wells' first game. In some cases I'll write the column at home, but I like to try and write live off the game. I like to represent the game in the first edition. So I did a running column on Wells. Talked to him after the game and kind of massaged it a little bit.

That day, I was there like at two. Clubhouse opens at three thirty. I had a lot of reading to do, and I was making calls and getting caught up. That wasn't a day I needed to do any pre-game work. What I was going to write was based on what Wells did, and that didn't start until seven o'clock. It was an obvious column. We needed a Wells story in the paper on Wednesday. This was his first start and there has been a lot of stuff going on. He called the manager an idiot. The guy had asked to be traded. There was something controversial so it made it even better.

A lot of what we gather is in groups now because there's so many of us. You can get your question out there, but you might see him the next day when he is by himself. I try to get with the guys one on one when I can. Some nights because of deadline you just can't.

There's twenty-five guys in a baseball clubhouse. They all go by it differently. Individual players no longer need good write-ups, quote-unquote, to get a better contract or to get in favor. We're just a nuisance. We're in the way. If anything, they're trying to keep damage to a minimum. By and large, they would prefer that none of us was ever there. I think they have no use for us. If we all died in a plane crash, they would be fine with it. I understand that. That's okay. They have ESPN. They don't need us anymore. I think that the teams feel they do because it's free advertising in the paper and online content. It's certainly good for selling tickets, and it keeps interest up.

The *Boston Globe* hires me to write my opinion about sports, and they stand back and just let me do that. Sure, in the assignments there's certainly some planning that goes into it. I can't say, "I'm going to the Final Four this year," but if you want something pretty badly, they'll usually let me do it. Sometimes, you know, you got to go do NASCAR. There's nobody else. I don't enjoy it, but there are days they need the boys up there. But in terms of the content, we are not told what editorial slant to take. We're on our own with that.

In my view—for the column—the idea is the hard part. I can't screw that up. It's the idea that restricts the column. You try to write as well as you can, but having a good idea is nine-tenths of it. Once you have that solved, the rest is just mechanical. You might want to strengthen something, or weaken something, or temper it a little bit. There's going to be things that you want back, you know, but you wouldn't want to be in that position nonstop. You just can't really go about it that way. I'm aware that in many cases we write something and it stays there. We move on to the next thing after that.

This is a really good town. We have four teams. We have great passion. We have really good readers and fans. Yeah, sometimes it's your day to write and there is no team in town. It very rarely comes up that you don't have something. You need to be a little inventive, you know. I got a bottle of wine sitting there from Larry Bird's winery. That's going to be a column in the next two weeks, on a slow day, because all he ever drank was beer. I know I can spin an easy column off that, and it would be a good read.

We have a big audience in Boston. For the newspaper, I think it's older people: people who go to the racetrack, or daily mass, or who write letters. Young people will read the paper online. Because of online access to sports and media, no one ever says anything about the crafted sentence, or lyrical writing anymore. Unfortunately, I feel that's less valued now. They read other fans. A lot of people have opinions. I don't want some fan telling me what happened. I can get that talking to my neighbor. I can get that listening to talk radio. I need a professional to analyze and to put this in some sort of perspective, and describe what happened. That's the whole blog culture: readers reading other readers; fans reading other fans. That's not what I got into this for.

I grew up as a Red Sox fan. I'm not a baseball fan. I'm different, though. You know, when Pedro Martinez was on the mound in Yankee Stadium in

2003, and they were five outs from going to the World Series? The Sox are beating the Yankees, leading 5–2, and the thing absolutely dissolved. It goes up in flames and flips the other way, and the Yankees win. I'm writing a page-one story on deadline that is changing dramatically at the last second. I can't be all emotionally distraught because my team lost, you know. I need to be professional. It does not matter to me. It doesn't change my life. I'm happy that it's baseball. I love the story. In my view, it's no different than if you covered the John Kerry campaign. I don't want to read a story on Wednesday, after Election Day, by some pissed off, disgruntled election reporter who fell in love with Kerry and wanted him to win, and now he's crying in his beer at midnight, on deadline. I don't want to read that guy. I want to read somebody who is telling me what the hell happened. What happened in Ohio? To me, it's the same thing in Yankee Stadium. It is not, "Woe is me. My team didn't win." It's, "They left the pitcher in too long. Matsui ripped one down the line." You see, that's what you need.

Curse of the Bambino came out in 1990. It just never went away; it's still in print. That will be in the first paragraph in my obituary probably. It was such a handy title, and then an easy theme for TV people and columnists. The New York people started teasing about it. College kids carrying signs. Then, of course, the hardcore baseball people got very furious about it and said I had violated the sanctity of what was happening on the field. It's done. I'm glad they won. Got to move on. I'm glad it's over so Sox fans can never be tortured about that again. And the idea that they won at the expense of the Yanks is the all-time joke. It was the greatest sports story of all time.

Reverse the Curse? I am really happy with it. So many books came out after that. You know, I was doing it all along. I didn't decide to do it ten minutes after they won. It was on that the night in 2003 when it blew up in Yankee Stadium. I'm happy with the way it came out. It's in my view the best one of all those books if you really want to recapture what went on that year. That's the one that will do it for you. I believe that.

One of the misconceptions was that the curse was over once they beat the Yanks. I wrote a column about that. I figured out they've finished ahead of the Yankees I think eighteen times since 1918 in one way or the other—playoffs or regular season—but you know, until you win the World Series it's there. They didn't win it in '46, '57, '75, or '86. They had to finish the job. The team's never lost sight of that. To some of the fans, it didn't matter if they won.

I go to a few places, now and then, where people know who I am. We are on TV a lot. You know it's great when I want to get a table in a restaurant in Boston, or if you go to the auto mechanic, and the mechanic comes over and spends a little more time on the pipes. That's good. It's not great if you're walking with your kids and someone says, "You suck." It's not so good then, but you know what, you take the good with the bad and you just sort of roll with it. I can't imagine what it would be like to be really famous, like Matt Damon or somebody. It's just a little bit of recognition: "There's Dan Shaughnessy." People don't know you can hear. You always hear. Yeah, that's okay. I mean, I'm not going to complain about it. It's part of it.

* * * * *

PETE D'ALONZO

Television Camera Operator, San Francisco Bay Area

"I do all the Fox Bay Area home shows for the Oakland A's and all the visitors' broadcasts for the Giants. In the winter months I do col- lege basketball and the NFL for CBS. My office is right here in the Cincinnati Reds' dugout— the visitors' dugout in AT&T Park, which is where I'm going to be tonight—right in line with first base."

Courtesy of Pete D'Alonzo

*　*　*　*　*

I work as a freelancer. The advantages are that you always work at a different venue site. We change production teams, as well. It's never the same; it's not like punching a clock. We're kinda bobbin' and weavin'.

You gotta stand normally for the duration, but you get your breaks between the innings. That's the only time you're really seated. You really have to think on your feet when all the action is really rockin' and rollin' inning to inning. You see the commercial breaks? That's our only downtime, maybe a minute and a half, unless there's action in the dugout, then we have to cover it.

We kind of key on individuals that are having a good night, and some that are having a bad night. It could be whatever spectacular play was done on the field. Normally it's the top players. Like for the Reds, it probably would be [Ken] Griffey. It could be the pitcher. He could be knocked out in the second inning; lit up with nine or ten runs. You have that kind of thing that you have to focus on. You have to really understand the drama of the game. You have to understand the strategy behind what the managers do, the pitching coaches, who's gonna come in to pinch run, who's gonna come in to pinch hit. You really have to study what's going the field as opposed to what's going on here in the dugout because any type of change that goes on, you've gotta be there to cover it.

And you've especially gotta listen to the program audio, which is the announcers up in the booth. It gives me a barometer to deal with on the field because I can anticipate a lot of times what they are going to talk about. George Grande and Chris Welsh are the announce team for the Reds for this particular home stand. I'll have the shot before they announce what exactly is being done on the field. If there's an injury, I'll be covering it right then and there. I wouldn't be shooting the managers and shooting the dugout; I would be covering whatever injuries they're talking about. You just follow a lot of the action before they talk about it. We give them information they're not aware of as well. I have to relay a lot of it to the director, and the director relays it up to them. I cannot talk to the announce team. It goes through the production team inside the truck.

There are announce teams that are more animated, as opposed to the directors who are more mundane and dry—kind of like vanilla. They only want to see certain people on the field, or they only want to see certain shots of the opposing team because they're selling their team. You kinda go with the flow and change gears when you are dealing with our type of broadcast. Eventually you know exactly where they're gonna go.

A lot of times I'm not keying on left-handed batters. I'm shooting out in the outfield, or I'm cutting away to other shots like when the announce team is talking. Last night, I was working when the ball came whizzing by my head. It was Griffey. He came around the ball too soon. In the last moment, out of the corner of my eye, I saw the ball's trajectory right towards my head. The only judgment I could make was to hit the deck. I can't hear them, but you can feel when something like that happens.

It's happened on more than one occasion. There have been times where you see nothing. If you look on that handicapped door, there's a lot of ball marks there. There used to be marks on the back wall, but they painted over it. It's hit the camera. I've been hit in the back of the legs as a ball's careening off the back wall. That's happened on more than one occasion. Knock on wood, I haven't been hit in the head yet, but who knows? In due time, my time may expire when it comes my way.

We've other elements to deal with. Like fans. A lot of people think they can come up and just start talking to us, and they can't. They'll be asking for players to come over and talk to them while you're doing your job. We can't concentrate on what they're telling me while the game is going on.

During the game itself, you can't just have a normal conversation with people in the stands when it's show time. The only time I can do that is during the break between innings.

The veterans, they will come up and shoot the breeze. They'll come up to you and remember you from the previous home stand or they remember you from other teams. But you don't see the camaraderie as much from the younger players that you did in the past. It's changed. Everything about the business has changed a lot. Today, it's more business-oriented from the players' perspective. It's more the seriousness of what they're doing, and it's more the idea that they're in the public eye. The managers and the assistant coaches are keying on if they are goofing off with us. A lot of them have been very conscientious about their behavior because they feel like they're walking on eggs.

Reggie Jackson never wanted to be shot in the dugout when he struck out or lined out, or whatever. Randy Johnson is another one. He's a real temperamental type; very sensitive for some unknown reason. He doesn't want to be shot—not only if he does badly or if it's not his day to pitch. He'll be just sitting in the dugout and he'll tell you to get the camera off of him. He'll just come after you and tell you to quit shooting the dugout. We know when we can shoot the dugout, and when you can't shoot the dugout.

Jose Lima is a character. That guy loves the limelight. That's just who he is. He likes to come up and start talking to you while the game is going on. I'm pretty sure the coaches allow him to act that way.

To me it's like riding a bike. Other times it's like riding a bike uphill, 'cause a lot of times your anticipation isn't as sharp as you thought it would be. You can't lag off a play because you find something else interesting on the bench. My responsibility is what's on the field. I got to go back to my primary assignment, and move with the flow of the production team—anticipate where you're going to go. You gotta feel the game. It should just snap into your head that you have to make adjustments. Everybody wants to jump on camera and do it, but it's the experience of knowing when to back off and find other shots that are important.

A good day at work is when you know you did a good job covering the game the night before. It's really satisfying when you come into work. You feel good inside, and you get compliments from your colleagues as well. That really sticks with you.

A bad day? The players start screaming at you, or you have a bad director, or the signal is not as crisp and clean, or the equipment is breaking down, or you got prima donnas talking over the headset. I've always felt that the way we should know when to talk to the director—it makes his life a tad more easier. They're under enough heat as it is because it comes down to ratings.

If you don't get the required sleep and diet and rest, you could come here very lethargic. You do double shows, you feel the effects the following day. I'd be shooting a day job—shooting the news, which I used to shoot for Channel 7—and come here for nine innings. I'm going to be tired if I'm going to do another eight at a local station, then come here and put in another nine or ten. God forbid if it goes into extra innings. I've been here sometimes for up to fifteen hours. I do feel the effects—like I need to recharge my batteries.

I do between 180 to about 220 games a year. I started television in 1980. It's been a very good ride. I can't complain about what I'm doing or where I'm working. Originally being from the East Coast, I love it out here, and I'm doing something that I have a passion for. I always felt that what I'm doing, a lot of people are envious. It does have its ups and downs. It's not the glamorous end of television. There's a lot of camera equipment that you're carrying. After putting in over twenty-five years, it becomes a little hard on the bones, especially when you are starting to feel arthritis in the knees. It's hard to be out here for nine innings, sometimes dealing with inclement weather, wind conditions, and moody ballplayers, and when you're dealing with producers and directors who aren't on the same page as you. So you really have to learn to change gears and become more flexible in a lot of the conditions that we work under.

I'm entertained just to come to the ballpark. When I come to a game, I want to study the ballplayers. I want to study how they prepare themselves before they take the field, and how they position themselves. I'm not a big fan of what they've done with the wide screens. Why do I need the JumboTron to entertain me? We live in this world where we need high technology to entertain us, and it's unfortunate. The art of conversation is important to me; the passion of discussing something about books, or discussing a movie. To me, that's life.

I'd say I'm still a fan of the game; not as strong as when I was in my youth. I was from Philadelphia, so I was a Phillies fan. I could name all the Phillies: Johnny Callison, Art Mahaffey, Cookie Rojas, Tony Gonzales, Tony Taylor. I remember 1964 when they took the big dive. Eleven games left and they were five and a half games up, and they lost ten out of eleven, or something like that. I remember that like it was yesterday. Some of the things that you reminisce when you were a kid are etched in your mind.

I look at this as more than a job. I look forward to the next challenges. I look forward to whatever changes in technology that could improve on my ability. I look forward to the new seasons. I'm an optimist. There's a lot of stress. But knock on wood, they keep asking me back. I guess I must be doing something right.

* * * * *

JIM FERGUSON

Official Scorekeeper, Tampa Bay Devil Rays

Ferguson worked the previous night's game between the Tampa Bay Devil Rays and the Detroit Tigers. Early in the game, he ruled a throwing error on Tigers pitcher Kenny Rogers. Several innings later, he reversed his decision. We spoke the next morning.

"The pitcher was Rogers. The first baseman was Dmitri Young. There was a Devil Ray on first base. There was a pick-off throw. The ball, when it came over, disappeared and all of a sudden it's going back to the railing, past the first baseman. I thought the throw had hit the runner because it wasn't where you could see it. It clearly hit the glove. It was totally a missed catch. So I made the call on the throw. They showed one replay, which was inconclusive, so the play stood from that standpoint. I announced that in the press box. The crowd gets the ruling when they put it up on the scoreboard—they just have a standard thing 'official scorer's decision,' and then it says, 'E-1.' The Tigers' PR guy comes down at the end of the inning and said, 'Would you mind taking another look at it?' In his view it looked like it was not a bad throw. Anytime somebody makes a courteous request, even if I feel strongly that I saw it perfectly the first time, I'll take another look at it. So I talked to the Devil Rays people and said, 'Can you show me any replays that you have on the thing?' Between innings, they put it on my monitor. They had like two or three replays, and you still couldn't see the ball directly hit his glove. It should have been caught, and all of a sudden it's passed. On that basis, because of the trajectory of the ball, it looked like it was definitely the first baseman's fault rather than the pitcher. It wasn't a bad throw. So I reversed it."

*   *   *   *   *

I've been around baseball for about forty-five years. Currently, my full-time job is director of media relations for Minor League Baseball, which in our office is similar to the commissioner's office for Major League Baseball. All of our teams are actually farm teams of Major League Baseball. We're involved in all the business activities and the league rules that come down—licensing and merchandizing, generating news releases, and so forth.

My other current association with baseball is as official scorer for Devil Rays games since the Devil Rays came to town in 1998. I work about half the home schedule, and fit it around my full-time job. The official scorers only work home games. Basically there are just two of us. We each work about half the season. There's a third scorer that does a handful of games when neither of us are available.

The commissioner's office was looking for somebody to get involved with official scoring here, and called to see if I had any interest in doing it. I said, "Yeah, I would be." I'm not on their staff; they call me an independent contractor.

The most important thing is you have to watch the ballgame and make calls on hits, errors, passed balls, wild pitches, earned runs, assists—the whole works. You have to keep a running record of everything going on, and at the end of the game there is a rather large two-page form—one for the home team; one for visiting team—you have to fill it out and then send it to the official statistician, which is the Elias Sports Bureau in New York City. As you know, baseball is a very statistics-oriented game, and those statistics all have to be recorded someplace. So that gets faxed into them after the game, every night. It's a handwritten copy. There's somebody else in the press box that has a computer that details every play, but that's not official. When I make a call, they can enter it into the computer directly to the commissioner's office, and then sideways to Elias. At the end of the game, they'll print out a form similar to the handwritten form I'm doing, and then compare to make sure they're in agreement. They've been talking about computerizing our part of it for the last two or three years, and for whatever reason they just haven't gotten to it yet.

The most important part of the job is the concentration you have to devote from the first pitch till the game's over. You have to focus totally on what's going on down on the field, and not have a lot of conversation with people around you, or wander around the press box. You have to be in your seat concentrating on what happens because, often enough, something will happen on the field when there shouldn't be anything happening. Like, there's a fly ball caught; a routine throw back to the infield. You think the play is dead, but it's not. Something happens. The ball is still alive even though there is nothing happening, but before the ball gets back to the mound, maybe an infielder has dropped it when he reaches for it, and the runner advances. All of a sudden you look up, there's a guy on another base. If you're not watching, how did he get there? I mean, it's not like you can't budge or you can't move. You have between-inning breaks all the time, and you have batter or pitching changes where you know nothing possibly can be happening, but you just have to concentrate what you are doing and not get sidetracked by anything.

I sit right in the middle of the front row of the press box, and I have a TV monitor sitting beside me. You're encouraged to use the TV monitor for replays. Like an umpire, it's important to get the call right. The difference between an umpire's decision and my decision is that I can look at three or four replays before I make the call. Or maybe make a call and change my mind after seeing a replay. When there is a borderline call, you usually wait to see if there's going to be a good replay. Sometimes the replay doesn't show you anything because the camera has moved too fast, and by the time the camera gets off the hitter and moves—like the ball's gotten to the third baseman and is gone—the TV replay really doesn't help. You have to make your decision basically on what you saw originally.

Many years ago, when I was a beat writer covering the Cincinnati Reds, an official scorer of Reds games gave one of his best pieces of advice: Usually, your first instinct on a call is the one you should go with because that's probably your best instinct. I've tried to maintain that. You know, you look at a play and in your mind—you may not announce it yet—you say, "Base hit or error?" And it's like the longer you think about it, the more uncertain you get.

You may have calls that you say, "I could have gone either way," because sometimes they are so borderline that you could really make a case for it either way. But it's pretty rare where you make a call, and then thinking about it that night, you say, "I really should have called it the other way." For one thing, if you really feel that strongly about it, you can change it for up to twenty-four hours. In other words, I could—if I worked last night's game—go out there tonight, look at a replay, and make a change in a call. It doesn't happen often, but immediately after the game I may get a call from either the home or visiting clubhouse. The PR guy, the manager, or one of the coaches might say, "Would you take another look at that play in the seventh inning?" They want it looked at.

There have been some confrontational things in the past, which is one of the reasons they changed the system of official scorer. There have been instances in the past where a player will come off the field, go in the dugout during the game, and call the press box. They call up and scream. Fortunately, that has never happened to me, but I know it's happened to scorers at various times. I haven't heard of anything recently.

It used to be, for years and years, official scorers were all beat writers covering the team for the local papers. They had some kind of rules—I don't know how vigorously they were imposed—but to qualify to be an official scorer you had to be a beat writer for x number of years, and cover x number of games so you had some experience. Obviously, other than the concentration factor, the most important things are having good judgment, knowing the rules and having the experience of seeing a lot of baseball games. I've probably, counting spring training games, seen more than 5,000 major-league games, and a lot of minor-league games. So, experience is very important in that it gives you a better idea of what a major league player should be able to do.

To get back to the history thing: Basically, it was set up by the Baseball Writers' Association, which is a very strong association. The local chapter, like the Cincinnati chapter or the Tampa Bay chapter or whatever, of the Baseball Writers' Association would say, "Okay we have four writers who are qualified to be scorers, and they will work out a schedule so that each one of those four will work x number of games however they choose to do it." That's the way it used to be, and then in the late seventies, maybe early eighties, some newspapers felt there was a conflict of interest, or potential for it, that, "I'm covering the game. I make calls as official scorer. When the game is over, I go the clubhouse and interview players. Maybe one of them is unhappy about the call I made, and he refuses to talk to me. I can't do my job as a writer because of something I did as an official scorer." You can make a case for that. And there were cases of that happening years ago.

There was one where the official scorer in Cincinnati, Earl Lawson from the *Cincinnati Times-Star*, and Johnny Temple, the second baseman for the

Reds, got into a fight. There was an error called, and a big confrontation in the clubhouse afterwards—"What you want me to do with that ball? How can you give me an error on that play, blah, blah, blah?" Well, one thing led to another and there were fisticuffs. Oh, yeah, [Lawson] could handle himself all right. So, anyway, it became more and more difficult as more papers moved to that type of an attitude. The commissioner's office then took it away totally from the Baseball Writers' Association.

You have to call the play the way you see it. I remember one time—this was several years ago—before the game, the visiting PR guy comes up to me, which bothered me. He said, "You know, our shortstop hasn't had an error in ninety-two straight games," and I am thinking, "So what?" I mean, I'm not going to *not* call an error if I see one because he's got a streak of ninety-two. I just said, "Tell him not to make an error tonight then." Well, as a matter of fact, he did. It was such an error nobody could have disputed it in any way, because what happened was a very routine play where the ball was hit to the second baseman, he flips it to the shortstop, and it's a good throw belt-high; hits him right in the glove and falls to the ground. I mean, it was an obvious error, and I called the error. But I went down to the PR guy and said, "I didn't call that error. He called that one on himself." He says, "You're right."

I don't really feel stress. I mean, you want to make sure you get every call right. You like to walk out after a game and say, "You know, I had a perfect night." But nobody is perfect all the time. You can make mistakes, but you can correct some mistakes if you're convinced it was a mistake. Because somebody thinks it was something else, doesn't mean you made a mistake, because biases always come in to play. You hear a lot—which I don't believe in—"Well, we got to get that call at home. The home team should get the benefit of the doubt." You hear that in baseball. You'll even hear players say that. Well, no! You take into consideration speed. You take into consideration if you know about an injury situation that might come into play—somebody is running different because they've got a sore foot, or something like that. But mostly it's speed. If you got a guy who has earned a reputation because he is one of the fastest players in the league, and you have a semi-routine play in the infield and he beats it out, he's more likely to get a base hit call because he put extreme pressure on the defensive guy just because knowing that if the ball takes two big hops or whatever, he is going to be across the bag. So, speed can come into play, but you still have to call what you see.

One thing, which probably is unfair in a way and yet it's not unfair, is an infielder with great range, as opposed to an infielder with ordinary range. An infielder with great range will get to balls that the other guy wouldn't have touched, and it may go off his glove and look like it wasn't great effort. It was just, the ball was hit there and he didn't field it, while the other guy might have been two feet short of even touching it because he doesn't have that kind of range. Or it may not be range as much as an instinctive move—the ball was hit, and immediately one guy goes to where that ball is, and the other guy hesitates. So in a way, a guy that has great instincts and great range might occasionally be penalized with an error just because he got to a ball that he shouldn't have gotten to.

One difficult call is a ball that is a rifle shot that hits and goes through an infielder, and somebody will say, "That was too hot to handle." You hear that phrase sometimes. There are plays like that, particularly a line drive that goes to a fielder's feet. It hits inches in front of him, with no reaction time. My thing with that is—I kind of use as a rule of thumb—if it's the second bounce, you had time to react; if it's the first bounce, maybe not. A lot of times the ball will be hooking towards the foul line and if it bounces twice—even if it is hit like a rocket shot—I'm less likely to give the fielder the benefit of doubt. I won't say that I never would, but it's like: two bounces—you should have moved a little bit. But the first bounce, you just don't really have any reaction time, particularly at first and third base. So that second bounce enters into my thinking.

There is a thing in the scoring rulebook that says, "ordinary effort." Let me see here. It's in the error section. No, it's not there. I know it's in here someplace, where it talks about base hits: "When a batter reaches first base safely on a fair ball, which has not been touched by a fielder, and which is in fair territory and reaches the outfield, unless in the scorer's judgment it could have been handled with ordinary effort." I guess an ordinary effort is up to the official scorer, you know. From my standpoint, if I see a play and my first reaction is, "That would have been a great play if he'd made it," then it's not ordinary effort. That's probably an over simplification.

The most difficult call? I would say calling whether a ball is a wild pitch or a passed ball is the most difficult because, in most cases, you're blocked out by both the umpire and the catcher. So you can't really see it. Now if it's off to one side or the other, you're all right. It's usually very clear. But if it comes straight in, and all of a sudden it goes through the catcher and out between his legs to the backstop, was it in the dirt or wasn't it? Sometimes you can tell by the catcher's reaction that it was definitely in the dirt. Basically, to me, a ball in the dirt is a wild pitch. Some of them should be blocked by catchers or be caught or stopped somehow.

Now, the other side of that is it's the easiest to correct for two reasons: Number one, almost always you get a replay immediately after from the centerfield camera, and you can see it was definitely in the dirt or off the catcher's glove. The other thing is that you can check in the clubhouse after the game: "Was that pitch in the dirt or wasn't it?" I don't go to the clubhouse. I would have the PR guy check with the manager or some coach. And then you can change it.

Figuring out earned runs can be one of the hardest parts of the job. Basically what you do is you recreate the inning as though the error never happened. In other words, if you have a case where a guy gets on base, and then there's an error on the next play—let's say there's a runner on first who had a base hit, and then the next guy hits a routine ball to the shortstop where it would have been a force out at second base but he boots it or he throws it away. It's an error. So there are two guys on. The way you *recreate* that inning is: There's still a guy on first, and there is one out. Now if the next guy hits a home run, he would have scored whether he was on first base or second base; it wouldn't matter. But if he reaches second base only because of the error, and the next guy singles, then you have to say, "Okay, would he have scored from second on that single?" Usually on a hit to the outfield the guy would score, but you might have a line drive that's a one-hop to an outfielder playing fairly shallow, and he wouldn't have scored from second. So it can get very complicated with earned runs.

I got into baseball because I wanted to be a sportswriter. That was my goal. I played baseball as a kid in a little town about sixty miles north of Cincinnati—Jamestown, Ohio. I got my degree in journalism and went to work for a newspaper in Dayton, but I wasn't really interested in the newspaper business as much as I was interested in sportswriting. My first choice would have been a player. I was a decent high school player; had a pretty good arm. I got to college; went out for the freshman team. Then I got into an automobile wreck. I wasn't going very far anyway. I probably would have been interested in coaching, but I didn't want to be a teacher, and probably in any high school you've got to be a teacher first and then you take on coaching duties. Writing always came fairly easy for me and it was something I was interested in.

I started writing for a little weekly paper in my hometown. I liked it, and was decent enough that they kept wanting me to do it. That carried on at Ohio State. I thought I would work for a newspaper the rest of my working days. After I had been at the paper for three years, I was a beat writer for the *Dayton Daily News*, covering the Reds for fourteen years. And then I got a call from the general manager of the Reds seeing if I was interested in joining the team as what they called the publicity director. This was in 1970. I just wasn't ready, mentally, to leave the sportswriting business, and I had a wife and kids, and had to move. I turned it down. I just wasn't ready to make that fast of a decision, out of the blue. Two years later he called again. I was there eighteen years. Then went to the San Diego Padres basically in the same job out there. I was there four years.

I see a lot of people that I know—scouts, writers, broadcasters, people that are with major-league front offices—who come through. It allows me to maintain a lot of contact with them. You sort of have a feeling that you're still a part of the baseball world.

It's just in your blood. I don't know how many times, like all my years at the Reds, somebody would say, "I'm fed up." When you're with a team, whether it's major league or minor league, you basically know that you're working twelve- to fourteen-hour days, seven days a week. Most of my time in Cincinnati I would come in the morning—maybe ten o'clock [in the morning] or something like that, but I knew I was going to be there till probably eleven or twelve [at night] before I'd leave. Often somebody would leave the Reds, you know, saying "I'm tired of working fourteen-hour days. I'm out of here." You knew if you saw him within six months, he was going to say, "Man, I've got to get back in baseball. I just miss it so much."

If you're with a team, you have such an attachment that you live and die with wins and losses, just like the players do. Sometimes more than the players because they can do something about it, plus they're going to get paid no matter what. If you're working in the front office with a team, you are up or down mentally, whether you won or lost the night before, and how you won or how you lost.

*　　*　　*　　*　　*

JIM FREGOSI

Player Scout, Atlanta Braves

Fregosi was a major-league shortstop selected by the Los Angeles Angels in the 1961 expansion draft. During his eighteen-year playing career, he batted .265 with 151 home runs, 265 doubles, and 78 triples. A six-time All-Star, he later managed the Angels, Chicago White Sox, Philadelphia Phillies, and the Toronto Blue Jays.

We chatted briefly at Jacobs Field, in the stands behind home plate where scouts usually sit during games. He agreed to an interview, which we did two months later in Seattle where he was scouting soon-to-be free agent pitchers.

*   *   *   *   *

I am the special assistant to the general manager of the Atlanta Braves. Basically what I do is I cover major-league clubs. I see all of them play. I'm the only one in our organization that does all thirty clubs. I write a report on every player I see. Basically it's a paper trail for trades and for the acquisition of free agents.

The importance of scouting has really increased over the last few years because of the type of money that you have to pay for young players that go through the draft, as well as the money you have to pay for free agents on the major league level. We grade out the tools of every player and see how they fit on our club. That's what it comes down to.

You can look at a player's stats. That doesn't make him a good player. Not at all. You have to see through the eyes of the scout. You have to see a player's attitude, a pitcher's mound presence, what kind of jump a player gets on a ball, how players react to situations. Baseball is still the only game in which you must get twenty-seven outs if you are going to win a game. You can't stall. You have to get outs.

Our game is a wonderful game because of statistics, but that's for fantasy-league people. That's not for major decisions as far as who can help a team and who can't help a team. Somebody that knows something about athletics can look at a young player on the field, and just by the way he carries himself you can tell whether he is a good athlete or not.

I mean, you can see a lot of times a pitcher, if somebody made an error behind them, they blow up because of the inexperience they have, and because of their attitude. They let off a certain air of negativity. There's a lot of little things that you look at that makes a player a winner. It does not always mean he's the most talented player. It's how he fits in the clubhouse, how he fits in an organization, what he can do, how he plays, if he's aggressive, if he's a hard-nosed player. I've seen players that have great athletic ability that are not really good players because they lack the little bit of extra that it takes to become a great player. I'll use a pitcher that we have in Atlanta: John Smoltz. He's got that little special extra thing: how he acts, how he handles himself, how he uplifts himself through adversity, how he is as a teammate.

Right now, what we're doing is, we take a list of all the guys that are going to be free agents—especially the pitchers. We'd like to look at the last start they had. So we have guys out that are looking at all the free agent pitchers. We want to make sure that at the end of the season, they're healthy. There's been a lot of guys that have been signed but weren't healthy. It's just a precaution that good organizations take.

Can I tell if they are healthy? Yeah. Well, you can tell by their arm angle. I've been working for Atlanta for six years. I've seen every player that's played in the major leagues during that period of time. I've got a paper trail of six years of my reports on those guys. I know their arm angle. I know if they've changed their motion. I mean, these are all things that the eyes can see. The statistics can't tell. You can see a guy's velocity being decreased. You know if a player's throwing 95 miles an hour in the first inning and he's throwing 86 in the fourth, there are some arm problems. There's a lot of little things that you can tell.

There's a shortage of pitching. Everybody knows that. You can see by the number of free agents. The first thing they do is try to sign their pitchers long term—if they've got a good pitcher—because there's just such a shortage. When you are talking seventh-inning pitchers making four million dollars a year, there is a shortage.

A lot of pitchers don't lose velocity, but they lose command. You're looking to see if his control is still there. There is a difference between velocity and command. Command to me is as important as velocity, which you can do by the numbers, but you can't see where a guy is throwing a ball on the plate. On TV you can't see anything. We only see what they want you to see. Right? You can't see a player get a jump on a ball. You can't see how a player throws the ball. You can't see his true velocity, depending on which gun the TV station is using at which time. You cannot see how a pitcher holds a runner on. You can't see him field his position. There's a lot of things that you can't see. Otherwise, let everybody do it on TV.

I sit right behind home plate. If you've happened to see a player before, you can get an idea of his mechanics. You see how he swings the bat, how he moves, if he's got command of the plate. There's such importance on hitting a home run. Guys strike out way too much. They don't protect the plate. They don't know how to hit. They don't think about hitting. All they do is think about hitting the ball out the ballpark, which I think is ridiculous. To me, it's guys that have great mechanics that are great hitters. You can see [Albert] Pujols swing the bat one time and you know he can hit.

I'll tell you, when Edgar Martinez first came to the big leagues, my back was to the cage and I heard the sound of the ball off the bat. I said, "Who is that?" I said. It's a totally different sound when guys hit the ball the right way. I saw Barry [Bonds] when he was a kid and he went to Venezuela. I was managing in Venezuela. First of all, how many hitters *choke* up on the bat anymore? Here's one of the greatest power hitters— one of the greatest players that ever played the game—and he chokes up on the bat! Wouldn't that tell somebody something?

Managers and coaches usually judge a player by how they do against them because that's a *personal* experience. They hit a home run to beat you at a ballgame. They never forget that, and sometimes the grass looks greener on the other side. But if you take out the statistics of what that player does against your ball club, he is not a very good player. But you only see it because you're focused so much on that game, where a scout may see that player at fifty at-bats during the season. The manager sees 'em four or ten at-bats. It makes a difference.

I don't think the job of the manager has changed at all. Your job as a manager is to get the best out of your players. I don't think managers win a lot of games, but good managers don't lose a lot of games. Players win the games. The players have to do it. There's nothing like being a player because managers and coaches take the game much more seriously than the players do. A player knows that he can hit a home run the next day to win a game, or he could make a great play to save a game. As a manager and coach, sometimes you don't get that. So you take the losses a little bit harder. There was a football coach that made a statement—I can't think who it was—he said, "I really miss the winning of coaching. I wouldn't go back because I can't stand the losing." It's really difficult to lose games as a coach or as a manager. But you miss it. If it's in your blood, you miss it because you miss the grind. You miss the action of the game; the interaction with the players; the teaching aspect of it. Calling room service, and if you win the game, having two scoops of ice cream—butter pecan. And if you lose the game, order four scoops of ice cream to punish yourself. Sometimes you even miss the disappointments.

The reason I am doing what I am doing, and the reason I was hired, is that I know everybody in the game. If somebody wants to know something about somebody, I can find out. If I do not know him personally, I can pick up the phone and find out. You don't always go to coaches, managers, or teammates. Sometimes you might go to a clubhouse guy: "What kind of a guy is he in the clubhouse as a visiting player? As a home player?" There's a lot of different things. That's something statistics will never tell you. To me, it's personalities. You have to have a feel for the individuals that are playing the game, and what makes them tick. I wanted a guy that cared about his teammates.

If you know something about Braves players, they don't last there very long unless they are pretty good fellows because they have to fit. We brought a lot of players into Atlanta that have had reputations of being not good fellows, but have been perfect angels the time they were there. That has a lot to do with the manager and coaches. As a manager, you always have to know what the best way to handle these players is. We can get a player and give him to Bobby Cox. Bobby's job is to handle that player, which he does a marvelous job of. We have brought people that had, quote-unquote, bad things said about them, but were never a problem in Atlanta.

There's people in the Hall of Fame that were selfish players, and weren't good teammates. I wouldn't want them on my team. The point is that, because a player is a great athlete and puts up great numbers, does not mean he is a winner. He overrides his own personal feelings and statistics for what's best for the team. They can't uplift a bad team, but on a good team they are great players. There's a lot of players that can help you win. I will give you Mickey Morandini with the Phillies. He wasn't the type of player that if he was on a bad club he could make that bad club better, but on a good team he was a solid player. Always stayed in to make the double play. I mean, it's tough to find an impact player. There are very few guys around that can take a team, put them on their shoulders, and carry them. But there's a lot of players that still play the game the right way.

Now, what comes first: good clubhouse chemistry or winning? I think a lot of chemistry comes with winning and being on a positive mode, having a feel for your team, your organization. A lot of this has gone down the drain because of free agency, but it still can be accomplished. It's a little more difficult in the era these players are playing in because they are motivated by money. They are motivated by their agents. They are a little spoiled. Athletes have been taken care of their entire life. From the time they are a young athlete in Little League the coaches baby them. There's a lot of players that I've had at the major-league level that did not know how to make a plane reservation, rent a car, or make a hotel reservation because everything has always been done for them.

But if you are going to build an organization and build a team, I think you have to find the right style of players. And by style of players, I think you have to build loyalty to the organization. I really believe that you can successfully develop a young player that comes into an organization, if he's nurtured properly and has a feel for that organization. You will see Braves players coming up and they are readily accepted on the big-league level. They are taught properly on the minor-league level. They are taught discipline. To me, discipline is the big thing. You can't teach a player discipline just on the major league level. If he has not been taught that on the minor-league level, when he comes to the big leagues and becomes successful, you have a problem on your hands. I think all these things can be done right and properly. It's loyalty to the organization that you are working for.

I get very upset sitting in the stands watching how some players react. I mean, I think it's ridiculous that a player can't run to first base. I've seen players get halfway to first base and stop. That would never have been accepted years ago. There's a lot of things that are acceptable in today's game because there's thirty clubs now, and there is a shortage of players. So a lot of things are overlooked.

I grew up in an era that if you did not play hard—if you did not play well—there was somebody there to replace you. That is no longer true. I was tough on players; probably an asshole. Excuse my language. I always felt that players got tired of listening to managers, and that when a player heard it from a peer, it went deeper. If a player was in the clubhouse and the manager jumped his ass, there had to be a player in that clubhouse that said, "He's right and you're wrong. You did this and this, and that's why he is upset with you." That's called leadership. You know it pisses players off sometimes; but I didn't care about that because the end result is there is only one way you win.

I took a great deal of pride in running balls out and running hard, and it's unfortunate that it isn't done anymore. When I was managing Philly it was very easy because if a player didn't run a ball out, the fans let him know about it right away. I said one thing to every young player that came up in Philadelphia when I was there, "If you play hard, these fans will never get on you. It's when you don't play hard that they see a weakness, and they will get on you. They will boo you."

You know what? First of all, I'm not a firm believer in rules. I'm a firm believer in motivating players to do what you want 'em to do while you are letting them think that they are doing it themselves. That's important. In other words, I sat in a meeting with all the veteran players at the end of spring training. I said, "I want you guys to make the rules: What time do you want to stretch? Do you want people on the field at a certain time? Do you want people out for batting practice? Do you want to take infield on this day? You guys make the rules. I'm going to enforce the rules that you make up." And I did. I really never had any problems that way.

I grew up in South San Francisco. My dad was a good athlete. He just never had an opportunity to play. Hell, he had to work. He had a grocery store, and he sponsored teams—Ted and Archie's. My dad's name was Archie. When the first expansion draft went to the Angels, I was signed by a veteran scout. Back in those days, scouts knew your family. He'd go into my dad's delicatessen once a week at least to tell him how I was doing when I was playing. It was a different game in that period.

True story: When my dad passed away I was at the funeral parlor, and an old Italian fellow walked down and visited with my dad for a minute at the coffin, and he walked over and looked at me in the eye and said, "You were a great player, but you could not make a pimple on your father's ass!" Exactly what he said. That brought a tear to my eyes.

*   *   *   *   *

CHAPTER SEVEN

SUPPORT CREW

CY BUYNAK

Clubhouse Manager, Cleveland Indians

Cy Buynak was an assistant clubhouse manager for the Cleveland Indians from 1961 to 1964, becoming the home team clubhouse manager in 1965. When the Indians moved into Jacobs Field in 1994, he moved back to the visiting clubhouse side.

"Last night was a quick game: two hours, ten minutes. I got a chance to be home by midnight. First time this year. My body is telling me it's time to go. We put in long hours. Like today, I got here at eleven thirty and I will be here two, three hours after the game depending on what's happening. When there's night games, you put in anywhere from twelve to fifteen hours. At the age of seventy, that takes a little bit out of you. Tomorrow's a day game. So I go home and sleep for about four hours, and come back tomorrow roughly at seven o'clock in the morning. Maybe I will just put in about twelve hours instead of fifteen."

*   *   *   *   *

I used to work for TRW here in Cleveland, off South Euclid. In 1960, I got laid off, and there was a bunch of us that always went to the opening day game, like a pack. That was our thing to do. We were sitting not too far from the Indians' locker room and an usher came up to me. He says, "I heard you were laid off." I say, "Yeah." He says, "You want to work here at the stadium?" I said, "No."

I was young. I was like twenty-five then. I was single. I'm not going to sell peanuts or popcorn because I was playing golf. This was in April. So I say, "I'd rather play golf and collect my unemployment check." He says, "Working in the clubhouse." And I said, "What's that all about?"

Because I'm short, you know, they were a little wary about me, but they gave me a chance, and I've been here ever since.

I was on the home side for thirty-two years. Now, I am on the visiting side. I had a knee replacement in 1993, and they thought it would be better for me in my final years to go on the visiting side. I didn't want to do that, but they asked. I was a little bitter at the beginning because I knew that the team would be good and I didn't want to go. But I got over that. So '93 was my last year on the home side. It's been a blessing in disguise because I lasted longer than I thought I would. I thought I was going to retire at sixty-five, and here I'm seventy and I am still here. But this is definitely going to be my last year.

I get up at six because I usually have to pick up the papers, and we will probably have donuts. Willie, my assistant, will probably be in here about seven thirty. My help will start straggling in—the batboy, ballboy, and four other helpers.

We feed the players. I always check what our needs are the night before. We were out of onions, and we needed cheese. So I left my house today and went to the grocery store to pick up the papers, cheese, onions, and peppers. The players like to read something. When they walk in here, they like to read the paper and they also like to do the puzzles, or that number thing. I buy five papers and make copies so everybody has a chance.

My wife bakes for us. She's retired. She loves to bake so I told her, "Let's give the players something they would be happy for." She makes buckeyes, cheesecakes, pumpkin squares, cherry squares, brownies, and then there's like four different kinds of cookies she puts out. She also does zucchini bread, so I'll slice that up. I put them in a couple of trays.

I also take care of the managers and the coaches, and put their coffee on. And then the coffee for the players. Some players will start coming in around one o'clock. Today, they're hitting early from two to three. I'm already set up for them when they walk in the door. They can go have a cup of coffee. If they want a pastry, they can. We also have cold cuts. They can have a sandwich or something.

After they hit, some of the players will change clothes. We take shoes that they use in hitting, and their uniforms and dirty underwear, and we wash it and have it ready for them by game time. There is some slow time when everybody comes in. We just keep an eye on and make sure the coffee is right, you know. Be visible to them. They know I'm here all the time. If they need something, they will come to me or to Willie. Sometimes during the day you might have to run back to the hotel. See, a lot of times, the players will forget something. Like when Detroit was in. They were just coming off of a ten-day road trip and Kenny Rogers ran out of socks. So last Sunday, one of my guys had to go the mall and get some socks for him so he can wear them home. He didn't realize it was ten games. No problem. We just sent a kid out and got him socks. He wanted a tie, too, so they got him both.

Once the game starts, that's when we clean up the clubhouse. I'll have a guy vacuum it, and then we will set up for after the game.

After the game, the players take off their uniforms and all their dirty clothes. We wash the shoes. The shoes have been bad this week because of all the rain we've had. We clean the uniforms right here. Everything is labeled—their underwear, their T-shirts, shoes, and so forth. They all have numbers on them. Some have initials, so you have to know their initials.

Some of them will eat before they get undressed. We have a meal after the game. It's a hot buffet. We cater it out. Last night, we had lasagna, beef tips, and fish. We try to give them three different meats: chicken, some kind of red meat, and then some kind of fish. Tonight, we are going to have Chinese. Each night is different. On getaway day, we'll have the restaurant here—Chop House—make pork chops and chicken marsala; maybe beef tenders and salmon. Once in a while the Spanish players will want Spanish food, like right after batting practice. We go out and get it. But each day we try to eat something different, so they're not going to eat the same meal twice in a row.

The media is allowed in up to forty-five minutes before the game. They usually arrive about three thirty for a night game. After the game, it's up to the manager. It depends on what kind of day they have—if it's a winning or losing situation. Sometimes they let them in right away, or it takes any-where from ten to fifteen minutes before they let them in. If they have a bad game, then it could be longer. Like Lou Pinella, when he was with Seattle, his thing was to close the lunchroom after the game, and then the players couldn't eat for ten minutes. I guess he wanted them to think about the game they just had a little bit, and then go eat. Then he would let the press in about fifteen minutes after that.

A lot of players, if they don't want to talk to the press, they go into the training room. Instead of making it obvious, they will pretend they are get-ting treatments, or maybe they are getting treatments, but that's how they get around it. See, the media is not allowed in the training room. In fact, nine out of ten teams will close the double doors to the training room. If the media wants to wait till he comes out of the training room, they'll wait if they really want to talk to the guy.

When Cal Ripken was playing, he would go into the training room or he would go to the weight room, and sit there for a while so the press couldn't get after him. But he was good to the press. He would talk to them. If there was something special that he did that day, he would talk to them and then go into the training room. But once he talks to you, he's done. Sometimes you get reporters that like to get a one-on-one deal, but once he talks to the group of them, he will go into the training room.

We have a stereo system. If they win, they will put it on after a game. And if they lose, it's very quiet. There's a difference. You can hear a pin drop. Before the game, there's a lot of music. It's up to the managers. When Jimy Williams was with Boston, he made them get headphones because everybody used to argue about what music to put on, what tape to put on, what disc. They told me he started it in the spring training. If you don't have a set of headphones, Jimy said he would buy you a pair. But then you get some teams, they blare the music. It seems like whoever is pitching that day, he gets his choice of music. David Wells used to play hard metal, and it would be blaring.

I think the manager that's probably the most difficult, at times, is Buck Showalter. He's very much baseball-intense. We've got to make sure everything is the way he wants it and just sort of stay out of his way. He's always looking for a place where he could have a meeting with the players, without us around. We have a room downstairs that we turned into a weight room this year. I tell him he could take the players down there. Sometimes, they think we're spies. We're not.

I like Jimmy Leyland. I've known Jimmy since he was the Marlins in '97. My wife knew he liked upside-down pineapple cake because of all that pastry we had for the Marlins in that World Series. He said, "I don't see any upside-down cake." Mary—I didn't even tell her—she knew that Jimmy Leyland was with Detroit. She reads the paper too, you know. Keeps up with everything. One night I was home just before Detroit came in and I said, "What are you doing?" She says, "I'm making Jimmy the upside-down pineapple cake." Mary made it from scratch because she couldn't find a box. Jimmy was really surprised that Mary remembered. Jimmy really liked that. It was nice.

When I was on the Indians' side, I enjoyed Buddy Bell. You get to know these players. You become friends with them and you just enjoy them. If they are losing, like Kansas City was, then Buddy was frustrated because he was out of it and it bothers them. I understand what's happening, so I just let them be. I sort of don't say anything. Sometimes a player will get frustrated, and he'll throw things. We don't say anything. If we have to pick something up off the floor, then we just do it.

I get a salary from the ball club. I'm sure every equipment manager gets a salary from their ball club. It is not a big salary compared to, maybe, somebody in the office because they know that the equipment manager also gets money from the players.

Everything you see in the clubhouse that is edible, I pay for it. All equipment managers do. I'm talking about any kind of food or drinks before the game and after the game. We spend from fifty to seventy thousand dollars on food and everything. The players pay clubhouse dues. It sort of takes care of what they eat, plus they give you a tip. It's not automatic. I think the players just know. First year players usually don't pay as much as the veterans. The veterans will tell the rookies what to pay. It's just like an unwritten law. They all know that the cost of living has gone up. They know they have to take care of equipment managers because he's buying the food for them. I don't think I want to get into how much. I think that's private business because I don't ask people what they are making. The players eat well, and they take care of the clubhouse guy pretty good. Like tomorrow, Pittsburgh, before they walk out of here, they will pay me. Sometimes they will give money for my help, if they like the help. They will tip Willie, too. Yeah, it covers the cost. I wouldn't be in business this long if it didn't cover the cost. In all of the years, I have been lucky. I only got stiffed once.

I have been here so long, a lot of people call me "the Legend." Peter Bavasi gave me that name. I look back, I can't believe it's been forty-five years. I enjoyed the job. I always tell my young guys, "Don't look for money. Look for a job that you can enjoy." There's tons of people that wake up and dread going to work because they look at the clock. I don't have that. I wake up and I know what I've got to do that day, and I go out and do it. I'm very blessed that I have this job. It means the world to me. Baseball has been good to me.

*   *   *   *   *

COLLEEN REILLY

Public Affairs Assistant, Boston Red Sox

Reilly and I sat and talked in Section 27, along the third base line at Fenway Park before a night game.

"My middle name is Maggie," she said. "It was Margaret. That made me scrunch my face up a lot when I was little, so my mom had it engraved on a charm bracelet as Maggie. Margaret, I learned, means pearl, which I love. Right now, Maggie is my preference. I am sure when I am ninety, if I am blessed to live a long life, I will have people call me Pearl. I will be demanding at that point."

*   *   *   *   *

It's been an unstructured path to arrive here. I suppose everything is based on faith and trust, and I've been blessed with the opportunity to work from the spirit of idealism. I don't want to lose the love for that.

In Baltimore, there was a tradition of a base sweeper, Linda Wareheim, who would dust off the bases with a broom when the grounds crew would be out in-between innings, and then she would banter with an umpire or a third-base coach. It was an evolved routine. After I had been here for about nine months, Charles [Steinberg] said, "Would you be willing to do that?" I said "Sure." Really, I didn't have an image of what Linda Wareheim did or what I would do. It just sounded spirited, and at the time it was the sixtieth anniversary of the All-American Girls Professional Baseball League, so in an effort to honor that, I wore a uniform and they called me "Maggie the Base Sweeper".

I would banter with, you know, the policeman or the third-base coach. I was so self-conscious because I was wearing a skirt that was definitely shorter than anything I would ever have on. I didn't even want to [do it] unless I had these baseballs we had in the office that I threw out into the crowd, because I did not want to attach that image to anything domestic. I wanted the athleticism represented because the women of that league were so awesome in the true sense of the word; just wonderfully inspirational. So, anyway, Maggie fit into that little routine. I would sit at my desk, work away, work away, and then at the end of the fourth inning, I would run, change to that uniform, run out to the bases, run through the crowd, and then head back in to work.

I started out in fan services as a Fenway Ambassador. That was in 2002. I'm twenty-eight now. I'd just moved home from China. I wanted to sell hot dogs here. That was my plan. I was teaching English right out of college. I went to a small liberal-arts school in upstate New York—Skidmore College. My plans initially were to study elementary education, and then by the end of my sophomore year I just fell in love with English, and then met this professor who looks just like Shakespeare. He was telling everybody about this program in Qufu, which is in Shandong Province where Confucius was born, and I said "I'm gonna go."

I called my folks, and said this is what I want to do. I probably had about 350 students, and lived in a rural old setting, rode a bicycle, and loved it—ten months.

When I was in China I really missed anything attributed with home, and Fenway Park was a part of that longing. I lived in a really dirty area where they said, "Don't take your shoes off; always have sandals on." That was so constricting. I came home and I wanted to delight in everything ordinary. I was so excited to be barefoot again. I was delighted it was July. I was so happy to see my family. I love water. I love getting in the ocean. Everything was refreshing. I said I'm going to just celebrate these blessings.

Come fall, 9/11 affected everybody. I decided to go to Harvard Extension and take classes—religion, international politics—and I was volunteering at an after-school program, and then joined an improvisational comedy troupe. There was a point when my parents said, "Colleen, you are the busiest unemployed person that we know and there's got to be a point where you need fill your car with gas." I said, "I would like to sell hot dogs at Fenway Park," and keep doing these other things. "They said, okay, go for it."

Then, just as I was starting to look into it, this ad came up for Fenway Ambassadors. It said the Red Sox were looking for folks with a theatrical background and compassionate hearts. The description was appealing. The glamorous reasons for working for the Boston Red Sox was not the draw for me. I knew that if the name "Red Sox" was attached to *anything*, then a lot could be done in the community, in a classroom, in a home. *That* was appealing to me: to know that there was an arsenal of gifts that could be given to folks, so there will be a new prism for the community work I was doing—the prism of baseball. That was exciting for me. Now, it's four years later and the array of causes is only more immense and more real to me, as well as the need to respect and give to each other—anything from raising money to taking care of a family who just lost their home to a fire.

I'm from Boston, and not a rabid fan by any means, but I could identify with the love. I guess if you want to overlap with people, that's where you can do it.

The chronology is this: I became a Fenway Ambassador, and then was blessed to become a member of the community-relations department. Charles said, "If you are one of my assistants, you can have the flexibility to continue with micro-marketing, television, and video production." It wouldn't take any sort of constraints away, and allow me creative freedom.

Micro-marketing? The way I would describe it is when you are—I'm sure this is not original—in a plane at 30,000 feet, the entire country is a quilt of states. When you are micro-marketing, you drop down, and you are in the homes; you are in the classrooms. No longer is Red Sox *nation* about masses; but individuals, and treating people the way that you would want your own mother treated.

They always put quotes around [micro-marketing] when they say it. That word "marketing" is very funny. Even calling my work a job is very funny. Of course, it is—it is work—it is a job. Surely, anytime you're committed to arriving at your desk at a certain hour, instead of jumping in the ocean, seeing your mom—I mean, it is a job to show up. A responsibility is there. There are job aspects, believe me. You know, even throwing on high heels, for me, is a job. That's some difficult stuff right there: walking on an extra inch and a half under your heel. I grew up a tomboy, and I didn't grow out of that. I think that lots of us ladies, here, appreciate the fact that we can wear a ball cap to the office.

I think that overall, it says that we should never forget to whom we are grateful. The Sox will never overlook that these people in these stands are the reason the Sox are big, and even when the record is bad, and the loss column is packed, you say "thank you." You never stop saying, "thank you." I mean, growing up, didn't your mom or dad always say, "Say thank you"? So we are never too big to say "thank you." These guys on this team, the franchise, the park—if people feel forgotten or are not appreciated, then that very sad thing happens, I think, to us as we evolve into adults, has happened in baseball too. "Oh, you got bigger. You got famous. You got expensive, and once again, you disappoint, you dishearten." I don't think that these folks want to ever let that happen.

I believe in the individual, and I believe in surprising folks with a goodness that adults would say doesn't exist, for no reason except that I appreciate how good you feel. I know people love the Sox. There are people who actually, I think, have a chamber of their heart that fully beats for the team.

My aunt Susan is an immense Red Sox fan. She had a seizure in the ocean and was in a coma, and then woke up and asked about the Red Sox. She said, "How did the team do?" You know, it's that kind of—I don't have to love the *team*—I mean, it's a different kind of love. It's not the kind of love that would distract me from doing my, quote, job. It's the kind of love that appreciates all these seats being full and what it is to feel the roar of a crowd when Ortiz hits a walk-off. It's love that seeps with richness that it brings to people's lives. That's what I adore. I know what it is to love that. I love my brothers that way. I love music that way. I love Bruce Springsteen that way. Those are the things that make my heart pound, the way the Red Sox do for fans.

The greatest part of my day yesterday was listening to two kids who are receiving Red Sox scholarships discuss what it means to them to be Red Sox Scholars—to listen to them articulate gratitude for the opportunity for the education. The sixth grader that spoke last night thanked the teachers and his parents, and then he thanked the boy that told him, "Hey, you should check out the Red Sox Scholars program."

We're investing in another class. In June, we had twenty-five kids stand out on the field with a player, hand in hand. Their loved ones looking on. There's an appeal there that if you're too young to understand what the money means, you're not too young to understand it's very cool to walk out onto the first baseline with Coco Crisp, David Ortiz, Manny Ramirez with their arm around you—like you understand the concept of reward to some extent; that you have achieved something great. The Sox, I've got to say, I love how smart they are.

It's impossible not to recognize who we celebrate in society. We're celebrating people on TV, on stage, on the field. Even though there is a guy who will sit in this row tonight, in this seat—who's probably done something tremendous and is not acknowledged for that, because he's not in any of those mediums. So if you celebrate kids with someone who is celebrated, then their self-worth increases.

These guys all have voices, and in one way or another the kids hear them, and the Red Sox scholarship program is about meeting the needs of the future with these kids. And inspiring people: inspiring people in the stands, inspiring parents at home, inspiring kids in school to actually believe. I think the big word is *believe*.

A woman by the name of Alice, who is 102 years old, from Brooklyn, Connecticut, is coming to the park today and throwing out the ceremonial first pitch. Alice was in a nursing home. It burned down. She was displaced along with some other folks. The news station covering the story found Alice and uncovered this passion for the Red Sox. They interviewed her; broadcast the interview; sent it to the Red Sox. We called Alice. Invited her to head up here and throw out the first pitch. She's a firecracker, without a doubt. We taped my call to her, and the TV station taped her at the other end. The purpose of the call was to say, "Thank you." Always gratitude. I mean, that's what everything is: gratitude and inspiration. "Will you come pitch?" She said, "Yes." We talked for about ten minutes. She was so cheeky and wonderfully refreshing. You know, at 102, you don't mess around.

So I took everything that she said, and I try to carry that stuff with me at twenty-eight. I don't want to waste any of my days, or any of my moments. This is it. It's easy to forget. Some really beautiful things are overlooked.

I think that's why I was telling you about Jesse. Jesse is this young fella from New Hampshire that I met a few years ago. Fourteen. He loved the Red Sox. He had this very quiet, humble, refreshing passion. There's a lot of ways that people express their passion, and sometimes in someone's quiet presence it's even more powerful than it is in someone's hollering, ranting, sign waving. I'm not judging that, but there is something about Jesse that inspired me. It renewed my passion for the job.

Jesse was losing his sight and his hearing and did not let that deter him from playing ball, or any other pursuits in his life. Something I loved about his company was his genuine delight in the *now*. He came to visit the park a couple of weeks ago with his fellow classmates, his beautiful mom and grandmother, and his terrific teacher.

So we went out to home plate, and we felt grass, dirt, and took a tour of the ballpark. We were filming it because I wanted to Jesse to be on "Red Sox Stories" for two reasons: One, I wanted to honor how special he was, simply; and two, I believed in the inspiration that he would be to other people.

It was glowing. It was morning—a gorgeous June summer morning. June has a feeling like no other month. The way the grass smells after it's watered, or the guys run their laps. The thing about my presence that day was I wanted to let go of my vision—like the wind that's moving through the park right now. It sort of kisses your skin. I was trying to tune into those things. That day, if you said, "Give me one word," I would have said, "Light." I remember his hands. I remember holding his hands and feeling immense gratitude and relief. A calm, grateful, serene breeze. There was not a ballgame that day. There's this calmness over the entire neighborhood if there isn't a game.

I was invited to attend his class that Friday morning, and was going to see his room where it was decked out in Sox gear. His mom was going to bring down his collection of twenty-eight bobbleheads. The night before, I was in bed reading *The Five People You Meet In Heaven*, which I've read and recently have been revisiting things I've forgotten that have enchanted me. Things like the movie *It's a Wonderful Life*, or my favorite book from fifth grade; things that seemed magic beyond magic to me at one point in my life. Before things got really busy.

So I was re-reading this book to remember what I loved, and I had this feeling. I put the book down. I actually felt fear. I'm just being candid with you because I think we're both here because we both appreciate humanness. This spirit, voice, tension—I don't know what to call it—in my body that feels awkward actually talking about because I can't articulate—it's beyond me. It was an impending death feeling, and I was scared. Then I had a dialogue with whatever was moving through, and it was out loud. A few minutes later, peace.

The next day, my mom called early in the morning looking for her raincoat, which I had stolen. I ran to her apartment with it. We had five minutes. It was like hearty hugs, and a little bit of conversation. I said, "You should come to Perkins with me today if you feel like being inspired—Perkins School for the Blind." She was actually heading north, to say the rosary with stellar women. So we were both going to be in great places at the same time.

Then she gave me a bathing suit as I was heading out the door. I ran upstairs, threw it on—a bikini. I mean, *this is my morning*! I threw on a teakettle, and music. I was just excited to be alive.

And then the phone rang. Ten minutes before the phone rang, that feeling came back that had moved through while I was reading that book. This time, rather than have a dialogue with it, I shrugged it off and said, "Don't be scared," and it kind of moved on, which is so easy to do. We can preoccupy ourselves with a million things.

It was Jesse's teacher calling to let me know that he passed away. I felt like I needed something to grab me physically, to match this stunning feeling. My heart pounded. I just cried and cried. I think that to have watched him with his mother a few days prior—for someone who adores her family, my own family—my immediate response to anybody in any situation is the effects on the family. I am a sister and a daughter. That's where I will arrive emotionally. I felt for their loss, but also for his. I so believe in process, and in the world's unraveling as it should despite the immense pain that we experience individually, and as masses.

When I went to his wake, there were 600 people in line. One was wearing a Red Sox jersey. David Ortiz. Big Papi.

I think that when it comes down to the big lesson, what separates folks from the highest good is ego. And that's, I guess, what was missing: his. There was just this very pure, kind, appreciative soul that moseyed through the ballpark that didn't feel he had less than anybody else.

*   *   *   *   *

MICKEY MORABITO

Director of Team Travel, Oakland Athletics

Copyright Michael Zagaris

Mickey Morabito was wearing a World Series ring from the A's 1989 sweep of the San Francisco Giants as we talked near the press box. Morabito had to speak loudly into the voice recorder in order to be heard as the crowd cheered wildly throughout the early innings of an A's thrashing of the Baltimore Orioles.

"I think you've got to probably be pretty calm, and not get too stressed out over things," he told me. "If everything is falling apart around you, you're going to have to stay cool because you got this fifty-person traveling squad that you got to get from here to there. So I think the biggest thing is maintaining your composure when things go wrong. I think I'm pretty calm."

*   *   *   *   *

Mickey is a nickname for Michael. I've been called Mickey all my life. I like to tell people that I was named after Mickey Mantle, but I was born in 1951 and that was Mantle's rookie year. I don't even think my father could have predicted that Mickey Mantle was going to be that great a player.

I'm the director of team travel for the Oakland A's, or traveling secretary. They keep changing the name. In a nutshell, my responsibility is kind of like a road manager. The areas that I handle would be booking all the airline flights; blocking out all of our hotel space; the buses that pick us up and take us from the airport to hotels and hotels to ballpark and back again' booking the equipment truck that picks up all our luggage, takes it to the hotel, takes the equipment to the ballpark; and all the logistics of moving the team from city to city. That's the basic premise of the job.

There's a lot of other things that get involved with it. I occasionally take care of the players' tickets on the road and at home. I hand out their paychecks. Any special requests that the players might have for their family or friends, and stuff like if they need extra rooms on the road. It's a lot of areas. To simplify, I just call it "hotels, planes, buses, trucks." It's all the road arrangements for the team.

I started as a batboy for the New York Yankees, back in 1970. I wrote a letter to the director of stadium operations. I was seventeen. I didn't get hired. I got called back in for another interview when I was eighteen. I talked to the director. "How is school? What do you like to do? Are you a Yankee fan?" You know, just general stuff trying to see that I was a good-mannered young man, I guess. I mean, they're not going to ask if you know how to put pine tar on a bat. I was hired, and worked my way up in the organization in the public relations department.

The PR director left, so his assistant became the head PR guy, and I got put on as the assistant PR guy. Two years later he left, and so after the 1976 season, I got elevated to the public relations director. I got hit right away. It was a lot of on-the-job training because the Yankees hosted the All-Star game in '76, and then after not being in the playoffs or World Series for a long time, the Yankees went to three straight World Series—'76, '77, '78. I call it the "Reggie-Billy-George period."

I became very friendly with Billy Martin when Billy was managing the Yankees. Then Billy got fired, and he got hired here by Charlie Finley in 1980. I was in spring training with the Yankees, and he called and asked if I would like to go to Oakland with him. Martin said, "There's no front office out here. Charlie said I can hire whoever I want." Out here, there were five or six people in the office. The Yankees had that many in their accounting department!

I was trying to figure how I would do this, so I went in and asked George Steinbrenner for a raise, which I knew he wouldn't give me—I give George a lot of credit because when he gave me the PR job, I was the youngest PR director in baseball—so when I went in to tell him that I had an opportunity to leave, I think he knew what I was doing. He knew Billy and I were pretty close. He put his arm around me and said, "You know Mickey, we are going to evaluate raises at the end of the year. You are still young and this is what you are going to get." What made me upset was that the Mets had just hired a PR director from a small school in New Jersey and he was making $27,000 more than I was making at the time. I told George, "I've been through an All-Star game and three World Series, and you've always said that you wanted the Yankees to be the first-class team in New York, so why are the Mets paying their PR director more than me?" He said. "Well, we're going to evaluate it at the end of the year." I said, "Mr. Steinbrenner, I appreciate it but I have another offer." I ended up resigning and flew out and started work with the A's. It was a big gamble to take. My family and friends were all in New York. I felt maybe I was ready for something different, so I made the move and twenty-seven years later I'm still here.

I think Billy and I just hit it off right from day one, and forged a nice friendship. I think he appreciated the way I was able to help him with the New York media, and it was just two Italian guys bonding there. I always tell people Billy did the two best things for me: One, he got me out of New York; and two, when he got fired in Oakland and went back to New York, he didn't make me go back with him. So I was able to stay out here, and it's just a great place to live. It was a great move. I love the Bay Area.

I was hired as public relations and traveling secretary the first couple of years because Charlie Finley didn't want to spend a lot of money on employees. When the Haas family bought the team, we divided the job up. I just do the travel stuff. I think I wanted to get away from dealing with the media on a day-to-day basis. With the travel, I felt that I was more involved in baseball operations and a little closer with the players. I enjoy doing that. For example, we've got a tentative schedule for next year, so I'm in the process of calling all the hotels, getting rates, seeing what's going on in different cities with hotels, blocking space as soon as the schedule gets finalized. Then I will start sending it out to our airline and getting some bids.

That process starts now, and then it continues through the off-season. Once the season starts, you've really pretty much got everything set, and it's just a matter of following through. Three weeks out, I will send a rooming list to the hotel, and will make changes as we get closer. I'm in contact with the bus and truck companies. I'll always call them the day of travel to let them know we are on time or we are going to be a little late because, as you know, baseball doesn't have a clock on it so you don't know how long the game is going to take. So a lot of the preparatory stuff is done in the off-season, and then during the season you're constantly following up on it.

We travel with about fifty people. Basically, it's the twenty-five players, six coaches, the manager, two trainers, the equipment manager, our public-relations director, a video coordinator, a strength-and-conditioning coach, our radio and TV broadcasters, and myself.

One of the things the union negotiated in their last agreement was that all players get a single room. They used to double up, and lot of the veteran players would take a single room. They would pay the difference between the rate. It's a little bit more costly if we have to get everybody a single room, but I don't have to sit around and try to figure out who is going to room with whom. It makes life a little bit easier for me. Our range is probably from a low this year of about $105 in Anaheim, to a high of, I think, $239 in New York.

You are at the mercy of things that can break down—airplanes, buses. Last year, we were in Cleveland and the power unit, which powers all the lighting and electrical stuff on our airplane, broke down and it was kind of iffy if they were going to be able to get it fixed that night. We're all on the plane ready to fly, and it looked like we might not make it. So I'm calling the hotel to see if we can get back in to stay, if need be. Turned out that our hotel was sold out after we had left, so I'm on the phone trying to find fifty hotel rooms at eleven o'clock at night. Luckily they got the thing fixed, and we were able to take off.

Last week, we had just left Texas, and one of our buses broke down. We had to pile everybody on one bus, rather than have two buses like we usually do. I mean, those are the things that can happen to you. It's a little nerve racking. You try to stay on top of things. You can't anticipate those things; you just have to be able to react to them. Hopefully, you make sure you covered your bases and make alternate arrangements if you have to—another plane, another bus—these things are machines; they're going to break down.

A bad day at work is when I get a call saying something broke down. That's probably the worst that you can hear. You're ready to travel on a get-away day, you get a call and there a panic on the plane—they're working on it. That's probably the worst nightmare in this job. It's stressful because you're constantly being in touch with everybody. Like if I know we're leaving that day, I'm calling the hotel and giving them any last-minute changes. I'm in touch with the bus and truck companies to make sure they know where they are going to pick us up as soon as the game is over. I'll be in touch with our airlines to let them know we're leaving the stadium so they can be ready for us when we arrive at the airport.

We charter an aircraft with a company out of Phoenix. We have two planes, and they fly us, the Arizona Diamondbacks, and the San Diego Padres. It's working out well for us because it's a first-class configured aircraft. One is a 737 and one is a 757. They've got card tables, seats that face each other to form a club area for the guys who play cards. It's very comfortable. We enjoy using that type of aircraft over a just a normal regular-configured commercial aircraft. We just got next year's schedule, and for a third year in a row we are traveling more miles than any team in baseball—about 52,000 miles.

I would say probably from the early nineties every team is pretty much 100 percent charter. There is almost nil commercial service after a night game and you are playing in a different city the next day. That means if the game runs late, staying in that town, getting up early in the morning, traveling, and then playing that night. For us to get out after a game, you need to charter. You try to go in a comfortable way so that when these guys get to the next city, they are well prepared to play. You want to get them on that plane and get them to a hotel so that they get at least half a decent night's sleep.

I've had some guys that just don't enjoy flying, but it's part of their job. You've got to do it. When I was with the Yankees, Phil Rizzuto, one of our announcers, was petrified about flying. He hated it. He would drink some hard liquor, put a pillow over his head, go to sleep, and wake up when the plane landed.

We have about 3,000 pounds of personal luggage and about 6,000 pounds of equipment. Each player has an individual duffel bag that has his uniform in it, his spikes, his glove; and then in addition to that, we've got bags for the bats, balls, the batting helmets, all the catchers' equipment, video equipment. Our trainers have their trunks with all their medical supplies. It's pretty extensive the amount of stuff that we travel with.

Guys are constantly leaving cell phones on planes and buses or leaving things in their rooms. I've had guys leave sport jackets, suits, pants, shoes, in their room. You just call back and hopefully the maid picked it up and returned it. I've been fairly lucky about finding most things.

Each player is allowed six tickets. Major League Baseball, they have this comp ticket system where the players go on a computer and click on the game they want to leave the tickets for. They put in their name and password, how many tickets, and it prints up a report. Then we'll fill the tickets for them, print out labels, put the label on the envelope, stuff the tickets for them, and send them out to Will Call. Basically, it's about two hundred tickets for a game. Most teams give the players fairly good tickets.

Our accounting department, on the fifteenth and thirtieth, will give me all the paychecks and I will hand them out to the players. If we're on the road, they will FedEx the checks to me overnight. A lot of the players do direct deposit, but they still get their check stub. There is no need to have a live check in the amounts that some of these guys are getting. The least somebody is making is $325,000. Jason Kendall, our highest-paid player, is making about ten million dollars a year. Divide it up, and figure it out.

I've worked in baseball all my life. It's basically the only job I've had. I'm fifty-three years old now, so that's pretty good stretch working in one industry. I enjoy it. I know a lot of people would probably love to have a job in baseball. I guess I wouldn't be doing it if I didn't enjoy it. I still enjoy the travel. It can wear on you a little bit at times, especially if you're in a losing season. I think towards the end of the year, in August or September, you just want it to be over with. You get tired of being around these guys for six months, but luckily for us over the last six years we've been in the race till the end, and it's exciting playing games in September that mean something. I think that keeps me going.

*   *   *   *   *

LUKE YODER

Director of Landscape and Field Maintenance, San Diego Padres

Courtesy of Luke Yoder

"The grass in the infield is three-fourths of an inch, and the grass in the outfield is five-eighths of an inch. This is a pretty big outfield. Maybe there is a ball hit, and somebody is running to home plate. We would like it to get to our outfielders a little bit quicker. You have to give them a better chance to make an out. Like last night, it was tied up in the ninth inning against the Mariners. Two outs. Trevor Hoffman was pitching and Richie Sexson was on second base. There was a hit to right field. It was bouncing and rolling through the outfield grass. Brian Giles was able to field it in enough time to throw Sexson out at home plate. Now, I know Sexson isn't the fastest player out there, but had our outfield grass been taller, thicker, slower, Giles may not have made that play. He was able throw him out. Maybe that's one thing our management looks at, and that's why they want the grass that tall. I just do what I'm told."

*   *   *   *   *

My name is Luke Yoder. I'm thirty-four. My title is Director of Field and Landscape Maintenance; better known as head groundskeeper. I maintain the PETCO Park playing field, as well as all exterior landscaping. The primary focus is, of course, the playing field and making sure that the players are happy and safe; making sure the field looks good. We draw 40,000 fans every night, as well as a national TV audience whether it is on ESPN highlights, or a nationally televised FOX game, or even a locally televised game.

The way I kind of look at my job is there's three things that I've got to achieve: Safety on the field—it's got to be safe for the players that run around out there and take ground balls; consistency—it's got to be a consistent playing field day in and day out, eighty-one games a year, so the players get that home field advantage and learn the way it's going to roll; and aesthetics—we've got to keep that field looking good all eighty-one games.

I grew up in a little town called Mauldin, South Carolina. As a kid, I was the neighborhood lawn boy. I started probably in sixth grade cutting my dad's lawn for a couple of bucks, and the next thing you know the neighbor said he would pay me six bucks to cut his lawn. About the time I was in high school, I had purchased a riding lawnmower. I would tow behind a little push mower for trimming. I had twelve to fifteen lawns, per week, in the summer, so I wasn't doing too bad for a high-school student.

I never thought I would cut grass the rest of my life because I didn't care for it. I figured I would go to business school or something. Well, as I was figuring out my major and what to do, I visited my uncle in Ohio. He is a superintendent of Scioto Country Club, a very elite golf course. I saw what he did, and I was amazed at how he could manicure turf. He told me, "Luke, you can major in horticulture turf grass management." He said you get to work outside the rest of your life; it's really not that bad. So I figured I would attempt it and see if I liked it.

I got accepted at Clemson University. After the first year, I kind of fell in love with it. I said, "This is great. I think I will be doing landscaping for the rest of my life." South Carolina's got a lot of golf courses, so I was working at the local country club in the summer and I'm working at the turf grass research plots at school. I was all set to be a golf course superintendent. Before I graduated, my advisor suggested to try working for the Greenville Braves. I kind of chuckled and said, "The Greenville Braves? You mean that team down the street?" He said, "Yeah, just try. See what you think. You can always go back to golf."

I worked one summer for the Greenville Braves, and when I graduated in December '94, I sent some resumes out and got a few small offers from teams. I got one decent offer from the Sioux City Explorers, a little independent league team. They weren't affiliated with anybody. I took that job and went up there. I left South Carolina in February '95 and it was 60 degrees. I drove into my first blizzard in Omaha, Nebraska on the way up to Sioux City. I spend one year there. Had a successful year, and then what I feel is the biggest move in my career was, after that one year, there was an opening at the Iowa Cubs, in Des Moines; Triple-A for Chicago. So I took that head groundskeeping position and worked there for four years. My third year there, I started feeling around the big leagues. In the fall of '99, I flew out twice for interviews with the Pittsburgh Pirates. I ended up getting offered the position and accepted the job.

In February of 2000, I moved out to Pittsburgh as head groundskeeper. I went there when PNC Park was still being built, so I was able to get in and get my hands dirty as far as construction and design, and all that. I was there for three and a half years.

Then I heard about San Diego building a new ballpark and I said, "You know what? I bet you they don't have to pull the tarp out there as much as in Pittsburgh." We were averaging sixty-five tarp pulls per year. That really puts a lot of stress, mentally and physically, on you. It makes the job a lot harder when you have to pull the tarp to protect the field. It's 170 feet by 170 feet; weighs approximately 2,300 pounds. Some of my guys have had back injuries and knee injuries. You can get caught up in the tarp. If it's windy, and if a couple of people let go but a couple of people hold on, you can leave the ground. So if you get somebody who's really dedicated and three people next to him get scared and let go, then that dedicated person is going to leave the ground. I've left the ground before. I've never broken a bone, or anything, but I have seen people go ten feet off the ground and just go flying. It's very dangerous when it's windy. Sometimes you've got to put it on when there is lightning. That part of it is stressful, but more than anything it's the mental part of making the decision to put it on or not to put it on.

Once the game starts, it's in the umpires' hands. The umpires make the call. Any other time, it's up to the general manager and the groundskeeper. Most of the time, the groundskeeper decides, "Am I gonna put it on overnight, or not?" If we have a chance of rain overnight, and you don't cover the field and you get to game time and your infield's too sloppy to play—but it's not raining—then you lose the game, and it's the groundskeeper's fault. You don't want that to happen to you. You could lose your job whether it's in the minor league where you might have five thousand dollars at risk, or whether it's in the major leagues where you have over a million dollars at risk. So that's always on your mind.

People say, "Luke, why don't you put the tarp on every night just to be sure?" Well, if you do that, the grass will die. You've got to really manage it properly. When you put that tarp on, especially in the summer, it's creating like a big incubator dish for disease, and the next thing you know you've get a big square dead spot out there that's 170 feet by 170 feet. My rule of thumb was: If there was a 30-percent chance of a quarter inch, or more, I would put it on; if there was a 20-percent chance of an eighth of an inch, probably not. That was something that I was used to, but always dreamt about the Southwest and how those guys didn't have to pull the tarp much.

So I ended up applying for this job, took a chance, and it worked out. I was fortunate to be able to come out and be involved in a totally different part of the country building a second new major-league field. I started work here in June of '03. The first season was all field construction. The field was put in by September. I maintained it throughout the off-season, and opened it up in '04. We've got about 97,000 square feet of turf out here. The entire playing field—with the warning track, infield skin, and all that—would be closer to 130,000 square feet total.

The neat thing about the baseball field is that you can create more of a home field advantage than you can in other sports like soccer or football. You can actually have an effect on how fast the ball rolls through the infield to get to the infielders; what it's going do on a bunt; things like that. The only rules that Major League Baseball sets for us are the dimensions of the bases, the height of the pitcher's mound, the [distance from the] rubber to the home plate. For example, in front of the plate, we can make that dirt soft or hard. If we make it hard, it's gonna go against the sinkerball pitcher. We're going to get some choppers that could possibly go over the infield for a base hit, whereas if we have a sinkerball pitcher throwing tonight—and my manager communicates to me that he would like it soft—then after the game last night, I would flood it out; flood it again in the morning; flood it again at lunch. Let that water really soak in. When you walk on it, it's almost like Jell-O. Then, ideally, a sinkerball pitcher comes in low, and you get a chopper off the front of the plate. It's going to die; make for an easy out. So a long story short: There are things you can do to make for home-field advantage in baseball versus football.

Most of the work goes into the dirt. We probably spend 70 percent of our time on the skinned area—meaning the mound, home plate, infield skin—and maybe 30 percent on the grass. That's where the game is played, and that's where the greatest potential for error is: the dirt.

Anything to do with the way the field plays is communicated to me through the manager. At the beginning of every year, we talk about how he wants the field, and then there will be a few times during the season where things will change, or where he will make a few adjustments. He would communicate to me on the softness or hardness of the dirt, or maybe the way he wants the ball to roll on a bunt. You want it to roll foul? You want it to roll fair? How do you want the base paths sloped? That's a call that has to come in the off-season because you are talking about sloping the field.

This field is built like a big golf green. You could compare it to a big flowerpot, as far as the way it's set up for drainage. It's got the turf on top. The sprinkler heads are at grade. There's eighty-one sprinkler heads that are about the size of a silver dollar with a rubber cap that sit flush, at grade. You can't find them unless they come on. When they come on, they pop up a couple of inches, water the turf, and then go back down, so they are safe. Underneath the turf, there is twelve inches of speck sand—the United States Golf Association certifies this particle-sized sand—it's got 90-percent sand; 10-percent Dakota peat moss. The Dakota peat mosses are there simply to hold some moisture and some nutrients for it to feed on.

Underneath the twelve inches of sand is four inches of pea gravel that serves as the choker layer. It's kind of like the gravel at the bottom of a flowerpot. It allows the water to move through. And then underneath the gravel is the subgrade. There's French drains cut in that flow to the main drain, which allows all the water to move through very quickly. After it's all filtered out and everything, then it goes into the city sewer. We do not use reclaimed water in here. We use potable city water.

This is Bull's-Eye Bermuda grass, overseeded with perennial rye grass. It gets overseeded in the winter in order to be nice and green for opening day. The Bermuda grass is warm season, and the perennial grass is cool season.

The height of the mound is supposed to be ten inches above the plate. The rulebook calls for a one-inch drop in elevation for every foot off the pitching rubber. Major League Baseball goes around once a year and checks every field—the dimensions of the bases, the bullpens, the mound and elevations, and stuff. If you get into the playoffs, they check everything again.

This warning track is a combination of decomposed granite and cinder. Cinder is a volcanic lava coated with a polymer—kind of a waxy coating, which makes it dustless and mudless. It's something that just about every team in the Southwest is using now. This prevents dust from flying when we're dragging it. It keeps the ballpark cleaner, and it also prevents us from having to hand water it to keep the dust down.

Thank goodness we have a lot of really good security here. The fans don't leave much on the field. They behave themselves pretty good, and security keeps an eye on them. On fields in the past that I've been on, I've found plastic beer bottles, caps, money, paper airplanes, but that was in the minor leagues years ago. I don't find much from fans on the field here.

From ballplayers, it's mostly chew, sunflower seeds, pumpkin seeds, and big wads of bubblegum. I hate to say this, but I would rather have them chew than do sunflower seeds, pumpkin seeds, or bubble gum. The chew, we can water it in, it disappears, and doesn't kill the grass. Bubble gum sticks to the mowers, sticks to our shoes. We've got to pick it up. Sunflower seeds create litter. It looks like little white specks out there. Pumpkin seeds? It takes forever to get those off the field individually. You've got to vacuum them off the field every day. We go out there to suck up the sunflower seeds and pumpkin seeds, just so you don't see all those white specks on the field. That's something more players are doing these days because more players are not chewing, which is a good thing for them, but it doesn't help us.

Pests? We have chinch bugs, pill bugs, several types of grubs. There's some cutworms, and some webworms. Nothing too terrible. That's not one of our biggest challenges. We only apply insecticide once a year—as a preventative measure—around June first. We don't kill all of them; we just keep them at a minimum in order to maintain our turf grass. It would be overkill. I mean, there are some beneficials too. I don't want to kill those. We just make sure we don't go past the threshold level, and make sure that we're able to grow good turf while still putting up with a few insects.

Diseases are something we really have to keep an eye on. We've get certain diseases like Pythium, Gray Leaf Spot, Rhizoctonia, which is like a brown patch. Some of these diseases, especially Gray Leaf Spot, could really take over a good 30 percent of the field in a twenty-four-hour period if you are not careful. You've really got to be on top of that.

We do everything we can to keep the players happy, to keep them safe, to keep them feeling comfortable about taking ground balls off the field. We drag right before they go out there, and between the third and the fourth inning, and between the sixth and seventh inning. It's something they like, and it's something that helps the field, and gives us an advantage. We do it right before the home team goes out there so they get the fresh infield.

Our guys seem to be pretty happy with the surface that we put out for them each night. They like the way it is. They haven't asked us to make changes, but at other places, infielders might say, "This is too hard, add more water," or they might say, "You need to make it hold together better." Most of the time their complaint would be that it's too hard. If you have a poor infield, wearing spikes can cause it to be really choppy. Let's say you've got a big player running around the bases in spikes. If the infield is brittle or not holding together properly, he could leave a footprint or a hole everywhere he runs. Well, you figure after five innings of that, you're going to get a choppy infield. A ball rolling across the field at 80 miles an hour isn't going to roll smoothly. It's going to hop. That's what you have to prevent. Ideally, what I like to see is when the players run around the field, I would like to see just the cleat marks, and not the shoe marks, meaning all you see is a couple of little holes. That's not going to create a bad hop. So what I'm looking for in a good infield is to be able to walk out, put my thumb in it make an indention, and then do what I call "a key test." Take a key, put it in and out anywhere in the infield easily without it breaking it apart, and it just leaves a hole. That's what I am looking for in a good infield. The challenge is to keep it being consistent for eighty-one games times nine innings, day in and day out. Easier said than done.

On your average game day, I work thirteen hours. I start at ten, and finish about eleven. You work the whole season like that. During the season, you don't have too much of a life. When the team's out of town, you can take some half-days off on the weekend, but somebody is here every day. We don't ever just leave this field. I've got two full-time assistants, a couple of interns, and then I've got eight people that show up on the night crew every night for the games.

I love my job, and I love San Diego. I could see myself doing it for quite some time. Maybe I will say five to ten more years. It depends on how long I can keep working these hours, and you know, see what happens in my life.

*   *   *   *   *

CHRIS LONG

Director of Entertainment, Philadelphia Phillies

"The other nightmare I remember is we had a gentleman who had sung numerous times. He was a cameraman for one of the local TV stations. From the minute he began singing—it was almost like a delay in my head—I kept thinking he must be singing the second verse. What is he singing? By the time I was 100 percent sure that I knew he was not singing one word correctly, the crowd began to boo. I was going to cut him off and go to the organ at that point, but he was so far into the song, I just let him complete it."

*　　*　　*　　*　　*

This is my thirty-sixth season with the Phillies.

I'm the Director of Entertainment, and my responsibilities are primarily the on-field events: people throwing out the first ball, people singing the anthem, coordinating with our sponsorship, community, and events groups for different things—photo day, fireworks, the Phanatic's birthday—promotional things that we do. We have check presentations. For example, last night, one of our sponsors was doing a fund raising program with the Boys and Girls Club of Philadelphia. So we did a check presentation on the field for that.

I started out as a secretary in the promotions department, and each year I would take a few more responsibilities on. I didn't have really any interest in baseball. I didn't play sports that much. It just looked like an interesting job. Eventually I did become interested in the game. The job kind of grew around me, and in 1978, we introduced the Phillie Phanatic, our mascot. I took on that responsibility—the booking of the character, the coordinating with the performers, and helping them get to appearances. There are only two that do it here in the ballpark, and then we have backups because the character began going to outside appearances: store openings, sponsorship events, and a lot of community events. I had done the booking for the players who went out and did appearances, so it was a natural thing for me to take over the booking of the Phanatic.

It's interesting; the majority of your crowd will arrive relatively late, almost at game time. At six o'clock you have a fairly empty ballpark for a seven o'clock game. By seven o'clock, or even seven twenty, you have more of the crowd coming in. It's just the habits of people these days. Part of it is [attributed to] hectic and crazy lives, and getting home to get families. I don't think a lot of the average fans come even to watch batting practice anymore. There are your die hard fans that are always going to watch it, and there's some families that will bring their kids because they try to get autographs and catch a ball during batting practice.

One of the things that we found is that by the third, maybe the fourth inning, people begin to get out of their seats and walk around the ballpark, whereas before, people would sit in their seats and watch the game inning by inning. You find people now, adults as well as people with kids, will sit only so long. Then, people will go back to their seats and sit, and then you will see them get up and walk around again in the seventh or eighth inning, or leave depending on how long the game has been. We found that you would see people walking the concourse, so we began to look at what we could do to entertain them, or to make that experience more entertaining; perhaps to teach them a little bit about the game. Once we identified that, we knew that we had to make sure that we did things to keep their attention and to make it fun to come out to a game because, although the baseball game itself is the primary focus, you need all those ancillary things to bring people back; to keep them coming back. There always has to be something going on. We call people the "MTV generation."

Yeah, we do get requests to throw out a first ball. We have so many and it's also hard to choose one fan over another. I honestly feel you can't say yes to one and not say yes to everyone that says, "It's my dad's eightieth birthday." I so respect that, but if we already have first balls committed to people who have a program with us, we have to be true to our programs. The majority come through either our sponsorships or our community-corporate night programs. There are some additional ones. For example, tonight we have a woman by the name of Stephenie LaGrossa. She was the two-time TV program "Survivor" contestant who evidently is recognized as being one of the best athletes on the program. She happened to be in town, and was coming in to sign autographs.

It's like any other job. There are days when it's wearing, particularly with the hours we put in. I'm here at nine in the morning, and I don't leave most nights till ten thirty. And it's not just me. When the team leaves, it's a little more manageable. I'm still here till six, seven—sometimes eight o'clock at night.

Generally, one of the first things I do is pick up messages and then go through e-mails, follow up on what we are doing for this evening, do a timing schedule for each game. I will work on a little script that I have to write: introducing the first ball, introducing the anthem; introducing any of the programs that we do on the field. If there is another one of the offices here that will have more information on it, I'll ask them to write something up for me. I may edit it. I give a copy of it to our scoreboard person so that he can follow along. I also give it to our PA announcer.

Once we get closer to game time, I will make sure everybody has what they need. I go down on the field usually around six thirty for a seven-o-five game, and begin doing whatever it is that we are doing on the field. I want to make sure that the field has been cleared, and if there is a problem that we are going to have the time that we need.

Once the game starts, I check in on a group of performers we have who go out and sing happy birthday to people in their seats, and then they go perform throughout the ballpark. They will do little trivia questions, have little skits, and give away little tattoos or something like that. They're called Phanstormers. They're dressed in retro jerseys, and khaki pants, and shorts. If we have something going on in the fifth or seventh innings with the Phanatic, I am generally down with that to make sure those people are where they should be and that everybody has what they need.

And then once the seventh inning comes, I collect the moneyboxes we have in the concourse. We have an area called "broadcast dream" where you can actually broadcast half an inning to an inning of the game, and then we put it on a CD. It's not going out over the air. A fan can sit at a desk with two microphones—two people can do it at one time—they have a monitor in front of them just like they would if they were in a broadcast booth. We have speakers so that fans going by can actually hear them doing it. It's ten dollars each half inning, and they get the CD. So I check on that group and make sure everybody is okay.

There is also a moneybox at the birthday desk. The birthday program consists of wishing them a happy birthday on the scoreboard. For a birthday, it's eighteen dollars for what we call the Phanstormer Package, with somebody coming and singing, and ten dollars if they just want their name in lights and a birthday cap. And then we have a package for people who celebrate their anniversary. They get a frame and their names on the scoreboard; that's twenty-five dollars.

Games around the ballpark are free. We have what are called Games of Baseball—all of them relate to the game in some way. There is a speed pitch. If you are trying to see what it's like to throw 98 miles an hour, it gives them an idea of how difficult it is for players on the field. We have Ballpark Pinball, where it's a big pinball machine and you can get points—hit it, first base, second base, third base. We also have the Phun Zone, which is the little climbing areas that young kids can go into. And we have Pitch'em and Tip'em, which is a game where you throw and knock things down. It's like a carnival game.

What do I worry about? Any of the hundred things that can go wrong. Equipment can fail. Somebody doesn't arrive on time. Something will happen with the mics. We improperly introduce somebody. We had a lovely woman once. When she began to sing [the national anthem], she got through, "Oh, say can you . . ." I don't think she got further than that, and she looked me right in the eye and said, "Oh, lordy, I forgot the words. Can I start again?" I said, "Just begin to sing." She started to get herself together and began to sing. I knew she was struggling again. I could see her fear. I started singing with her. So did the crowd. People just supported her. It was a beautiful moment, even though I was dying at that second. This was kind of when we shifted more towards groups as opposed to individuals.

We ask people to send us audition tapes. Our preference is actually to book choirs of fifteen or more, for two reasons: There is less chance of a snafu, and it also becomes a good way to sell tickets. We also get some groups through our community-night program. These are groups that buy up large blocks of tickets to make it their night. It might be Bowling Night, Hamilton Township Night, or something like that. They will send us an audition tape, and if it works in the schedule, we will schedule their group.

If we don't have a group booked, or if we get a last-minute cancellation, we will schedule individuals to sing. We have had many successes, but I stand relatively close when it's an individual. I kind of stay in the general area and I sing with them as they are singing. You have to be careful. You can" just jump in because then that throws them off completely, but there were times when I had moved slightly to the front of them. I just kind of do it slowly so that if I feel that they are getting in trouble, I am there to kind of support them.

One of the things people always ask is: What do you do in the winter? People feel that once the team leaves town in September or October, you don't come back again until April. We prepare. There is a large group of us that meets, and we have to decide what the promotional items are that are going to be given away. We have to put the promotions on our calendars— the staples: the fireworks nights, the photo days, the Phanatic's birthday, opening day, fan-appreciation day—they all have to plotted in. And then there's groundwork that you have to do for preparing for the season. We have a winter tour that goes out to malls and to dinners throughout the area where we take players out to meet people to remind them that baseball is coming. You know, to get people thinking about baseball.

We work very hard to encourage families to come out to the ballgame. Even the youngest ones can't wait to see the Phanatic. You can bring your young child, and it builds memories with the parent or grandparent or godparent or just a friend. You don't always get that two-and-a-half-hour time period when you can share time without it being totally interrupted. It's memory time. How many people will say, "One of my earliest memories was going to a ballgame with my dad, or going with my mom." Or, "Oh my gosh, I remember going with my dad and my grandfather." And it's boys going with moms; sharing something that sometimes you don't necessarily get with some of the other sports.

One of the things about baseball that I feel, and I think that many people feel, is that it's so different than any other sport because of the pace of the game, which is criticized a lot. What it allows is for you and your family to come to a game, and be able to converse while things are going on. To relax and enjoy the company of each other while still being able to follow the game, whereas, in hockey and some of the other games, you can't do that.

I guess it's become so much ingrained as part of my life. I basically grew up here. I started out at twenty years old, and I met some of my best friends here. Most of the time we are making people happy. How many people can say that about their job?

*   *   *   *   *

KURT SCHLOSS
Director of Merchandising, Cleveland Indians

"The good thing about Indians baseball, and baseball in general, is you really don't have a hard time selling. I mean, they're going to buy a pin. They're going to buy a jersey. They're going to buy a hat. They might not buy all three, but they're going to buy something because they want to remember their experience here, either at Jacobs Field, or the fact that they saw Len Barker's perfect game, or that they were here for the '95 or the '97 Series. It's a sense of community when a team does well. People want something to have from that time they remember."

*   *   *   *   *

I was recruited to the Cleveland Indians in 2004. I was living in Franklin, Michigan, working for the largest wholesale distributor of wearables in the United States. The company I had worked for had been bought out, and when this opportunity knocked it seemed like a good thing. A head-hunter called me and said the Indians were looking for a director of merchandising. Strangely enough, I get six degrees of separation: My godmother's husband's family—the O'Neill's—used to own the Cleveland Indians.

I grew up in Cleveland. I moved back to the street I grew up on. I lived there from 1969 to 1986. My kids get to play on the street I grew up on. All the old neighbors are still there. They are happy to see a Schloss come back—you know, little Kurt Schloss coming back to the neighborhood. And they know I work for the Indians.

I manage the buying and selling of all Indians product, both in our six team shops that are located throughout Northeast Ohio, and in the ballpark here in our fifteen concession locations. The buyers and the ballpark merchandising operations people report to me. We are one of the few organizations in Major League Baseball that is responsible for running our entire retail operations, from front end to back end. A lot of the thirty teams outsource to a third party, similar what they do with their food and beverages.

Number one, we think we can do it better. Number two, it's profitable. When the team does well, we do very well. People, like myself, who have a retail background and have grown up in retail know how to probably do it better than people that get into it for six months, and then get out of it for the other. We're in it 365 days a year.

We've been in malls since 1992. It's an extension of the ballpark. It's taking our trademark—our brand—out to the customers. I mean, we are in business eighty-one days a year here in the park. There are Tribe fans from January first to December thirty-first. Like most retailers, we do a large amount of our business in the last quarter of the year, so we're continually selling Indians product.

We sell everything from shot glasses, keychains, pins, plush blankets, throws, T-shirts, hats, foam fingers, pens, pencils to three- to six-inch Grady Sizemore and Travis Hafner bobbleheads. We carry authentic merchandise for authentic fans. I mean, you can go to any other retailer and find a T-shirt or a hat, but you can't go there and find a set of poker chips and playing cards, or golf balls. You can't find vintage pieces like a Satchel Paige figurine in motion, where he's actually throwing the ball. We pride ourselves on doing the things that are outside the normal retail chain.

We're going through the licensing process right now with our attorneys for a T-shirt graphic called the GRADY BUNCH that shows nine players on a T-shirt all looking at each other, just like they did on the original Brady Bunch series. It's a parody of the Brady Bunch. Grady Sizemore is our key player. Grady is a young single player, and because women want to be married to Grady Sizemore, one of our best-selling shirts is a HELLO, MY NAME IS MRS. SIZEMORE T-shirt. It helps his image because of the stature that he currently has. We have to get his permission because it goes to not only Major League Baseball Properties, but also to the Players Association because all the players are, obviously, managing their images.

This is an entertainment business. We are a lot like Disney World in that we really don't want you to know who we are. We want you to enjoy the experience here at Jacobs Field. We want you to feel good about the purchase you've made. We want you to *see* our concession stands, but we don't want you to really *notice* our concession stands. As you'll notice, there aren't a whole lot of bright pink and bright blue concession stands out there in the ballpark. We want you to come here, enjoy the game, enjoy the product that's on the field, and then take something away that says I was here at the game today; I had a great hot dog; I got a great beer; and I got a great T-shirt. It's not about us; it's the people out here having fun. When we engage them in a positive way, we have all the financial measurements that we use to gauge whether we are capturing the highest amount of people that come into the park. If we have a great product offering and we convert a lot of those people into transactioned customers, we see it in the bottom line.

The purchasing patterns change over time, and a lot of that is driven by the team. We are basically in the third year of player popularity growing—people figuring out who these young guys are. We went from having a team that sold out 455 consecutive games here at Jacobs Field, to the slow decline of our team. Our last financially significant year would have been 2002, and then we performed poorly in the playoffs. In 2003, we traded away a lot of key players, or we didn't re-sign key players.

For example, Coco Crisp was traded to Boston. We had his name on everything. We had his name on jerseys. We had it on T-shirts. We had it on baseballs. We had it on pins. We had it on everything. Trust me, our general manager doesn't call me, you know, "If I trade this guy, what's it going to do your business?" I found out pretty much the same time everybody else did. We came out at Christmas with a lot of Coco Crisp product already in our stores. My reaction is, "How much Coco Crisp liability do I have?" We take a markdown right away because he is no longer part of our organization.

The people had lost an identity with the players—new players; transitional players. So they're not as interested in buying somebody that is not going to be here tomorrow. Our retail business collapsed; took a dramatic step backwards from the glory days in the mid-nineties when we were selling out every game.

It was a slow decline, so maybe we lost a million or two in revenue in the merchandising side of the business. When people aren't coming to the park, my revenues follow that same trend. We bottomed out as far as attendance and merchandise sales. But as you start to build a solid base of players, and the team really starts to perform, you get more and more people interested in the product, and it makes it a lot easier for me to do my job and for our people to go out and sell the product. The more interested they are in who we are as a ball club, the better my business is going to be.

In 2004, we took another step forward as those new players started, and people started to know who they were. And we do a lot on the retail side working to help promote these young players. We bring them to our stores. We do signing sessions. Slowly, over time, they build up a presence in our customers' minds, and our business starts to take off from there.

Thinking back to the original question of why things don't change that often on certain pieces, I think a lot of that has to do with the tradition of baseball. It's good to change some things, but not all things, and a gradual change in some cases. There's a bank of 1948 logos that we use—what we call our "Copperstown Collection." Those are from the bygone days—the classic Chief Wahoo, which may be seen as more offensive today to some of the baseball population. It's a two-sided coin. There's a lot of people that love Chief Wahoo because of what he stands for—the history that he represents here in Cleveland; of the club that they remember and the team they grew up with. How Chief Wahoo became a part of the Indians, I'm not sure. I don't know the entire history, but a lot of fans want it because that's the team that they grew up with. There are a lot of fans that don't like it because it's kind of derogatory towards Native Americans. And there's a lot of Native Americans that don't like the campaign of getting rid of Chief Wahoo because it's perceived as trying to wipe out the Indian, again.

The retail selling price of an authentic jersey is between $180 and $200. The "authentics" would be products the players wear on the field—what the fans want to wear: the road jersey or the home jersey, or the home hat or the road hat; the dugout jacket that the manager wears. Those are the pieces that are always going to be there because that's what the players are wearing. The last significant change was the dugout jacket, which was changed for the 2005 season. They want to keep the game fresh in the fans' eyes, and they want to keep merchandise fresh and to keep selling products. Who would want to still see the Houston Astros wearing those rainbow jerseys? If they were still wearing those rainbow jerseys after all these years, people would be bored of it.

I would say the majority of our fans are in the twenty-five to fifty-five age range, which is probably pretty similar to the rest of Major League Baseball. I would say 50 percent of the business is done under the men's category, which means we have women buying men's product, whether it is an authentic jersey or a T-shirt or a hat. The women's business, 10 or 15 percent of the total, is a growing category in that we're able to introduce product that's more tailored to the female customer, whether it's different fabrications, different treatments like crystalline looks, rhinestone looks, pink colors, powder-blue colors that you typically wouldn't find in hats. The novelty item, which is everything from baseballs to the foam fingers, represents probably another 40 percent.

You get a little riskier with some of the women's product you carry—change some fabrications; make the looks a little smaller; more junior looking. The averaged-sized woman in the United States is size fourteen. That woman wants to look like a woman. She doesn't want to buy a man's shirt, so you have to find the right supplier that can get you a woman's shirt that fits the size fourteen without making it look like a men's over-sized T-shirt.

You always take a risk with novelty items. It could be plush piece where maybe you do a plush pink dog to see if the girls will want it when they come to the game, but you know our mascot, Slider, is really what the fans want. Maybe it doesn't turn over that well. So you take the markdowns and you move on. You find the next item that, hopefully, will be the home run.

We did a bubble coat this year—sort of look like the Michelin Man. Basically it's a down-filled parka that comes down just above the knee. It had a big ol' script "I" embroidered on the left chest; "Indians" across the back. We probably bought a couple hundred, and were selling them for ninety dollars. We couldn't give it away. We're now selling them for twenty bucks, and not many at twenty bucks. There's a threshold where people will buy anything, just to get a bargain. It's cheaper to buy an Indians coat at twenty bucks, probably, than it is to buy another coat somewhere else.

We get a lot of requests for uniforms from the eighties, which people saw in the movie *Major League*. You know, when they were a kid or when they were a young adult watching the Indians, watching the movie helps them remember what they remember about baseball. Or, the old time players or the Hall of Fame players—that helps them remember the '48 championship, or the terrible years in the seventies and eighties. The old uniforms help people mark a place in time. The new uniforms help them move on, and yet, sometimes there's a resistance to that change.

One of the things we are always constantly reminded here at the Indians is that you have to continually improve, continually grow, continually do new things, make changes. If you don't, then your product becomes stale. If your customers see that as a stale product, they lose interest. Our job, as entertainers, is to continually provide a new show, a better show—that's on the field, that's in the park, that's in the people we hire. It's in how we approach each one of those aspects of the game.

I am located on the second floor of the executive office here at Jacobs Field. I don't have a view of the field. I look out to what I call my Japanese rock garden. We have a game tonight, so I'll be in and out of the park all night long. I walk the stands to make sure that we are set up properly. On a game like tonight, with 30,000 people coming, we'll have probably fifteen locations open. I'll walk to see they are signed properly with our promotional signing. We like to put as many price point signs on the products as possible so when a customer walks up and they see an item they like, they don't have to ask somebody how much it costs. It helps them make the decision process easier.

We want to make sure the sales associates are wearing their name badges, are dressed appropriately—shirts tucked in, no excessive earrings, no cell phones, no hats. The idea being is we're here to help our fans enjoy the game. We don't want to be recognized as a distraction from that enjoyment. I make my rounds up to the first inning making sure that if there any issues, they are resolved quickly before the first pitch. We want to engage our associates so that they are in the right frame of mind for entertaining fans.

I spend a lot of time walking around being a casual fan to see how fans are experiencing the atmosphere. I'm also checking what the fans are wearing and what they are not wearing. Are they wearing old product? If you see a lot of women in the park, are the women wearing men's clothes, men's T-shirts and jerseys, or are they wearing women's product that we are carrying. I'm looking to see if there are kids in the park. Do we have what they want? Our fireworks night is on Friday nights, and this year we're carrying the flashing blinking toys that you would see at a circus. They immediately catch the kids' attention—every parent's nightmare, but every child's dream is to get one of those. So we're capturing that dream, as well.

When the game's over, we still sell. There's a lot of people walking out of the park that didn't want to make that purchase early, so we try to sell them on the way out, "Thanks for coming to Jacobs Field. Would you like to buy a hat?" The park clears pretty quickly. Then we start to close our locations. If it's nine thirty that the game's over, it's almost ten o'clock by the time everybody is out of here and we stop selling. It will be another hour and a half for shutdown, so you're talking eleven thirty by the time we get out of here.

*　*　*　*　*

CHRIS FERNANDEZ

Video Coordinator, Tampa Bay Devil Rays

"I go by Chico more than I go by my real name, which is Chris. It came years ago from a coach for the Reds. My last name is Fernandez. He started to call me Chico, and it just stuck. I don't speak any Spanish. There is no rhyme or reason to it. I guess it's because of the last name, so I guess it just seems right. This game is funny. Everybody has a nickname. Like, his nickname [pointing to another Tampa Bay employee] is 'Killer.' Our trainer years ago nicknamed him Killer. It's not for any reason. They call him Killer, and it just stuck. The hard part is if you ever go into the real world and ask somebody for a reference, and you use your real name, they would be like, 'I never heard of the guy.' 'Never heard of the guy?' 'Killer? Oh, yeah, I know him. Great guy.' That's the downside of it: There are so many nicknames in this game, people forget your actual real name."

*　　*　　*　　*　　*

I'm the video coordinator for the Tampa Bay Devil Rays. I guess the title is misleading. Actually, I am responsible for the video coaching material that goes on around here. We capture all the video for each game, as well as scouting opponent's games. I create spray charts, pitch-location charts, steals, bunts, how often they bunt, what counts they bunt on; just about anything you can name—basically everything you are going to need to do to help a player get better. I give everything to the coaches, and then they determine how they want to play a guy, or pitch a guy. That's all created out of this room right here.

I'm in between the dugout and the locker room. There's not even a sign on the door. In feet—I'm not the best at measuring—I would say I'm probably thirty feet away from the dugout. I used to be right inside the locker room. I moved my office to a little bit bigger space; a little bit closer to the dugout.

We have a very enhanced computer system—a workstation with three laptops—that allows me to log a game pitch by pitch. When you see a pitcher throw a ball, everything's logged: the location of that pitch, what type of pitch it was, the result—strike, ball, hit, double—where was it hit, line drive, was it hit hard, soft. Each video clip attaches that information. It's all instant access.

We take the regular broadcast feed from our home station, which is FOX, or the Rays' network. The centerfield view is from the television, just like someone sitting at home. We take the centerfield shot from that, and then we have our own cameras that I can control. We take a side view of the hitter, or the side view of the pitcher, depending on if we are on defense or offense; then behind the home-third angle, if we want to see some fielding of a certain fielder. They're all captured and viewed at the same time.

A player can come in right after an at-bat. He can sit down and watch just what happened so they can evaluate instantly, or the next day they can come in. We do our games, as well as scouting opponent's games. We have all that video logged in our system so, with the click of a mouse, today's starting pitcher can be pulled up the last time we faced him if you want to see just that, or his most recent start. We produce all that here, as well as cataloging years of video on DVDs. We go back three years now, and eventually will go back five years. From that point, most guys will have moved on or retired.

We have an advance scout that sends me his report. It's e-mailed. First day of a series, I print out this spray chart, which shows over the last eighty at-bats where they were hitting the ball versus left-handers and right-handers. Then I take a pitch location chart. There's over 900-at-bats worth of data that's collected. That shows us on certain counts where a guy likes to swing; where we can go to pitch to him—that he's not very good on a fastball in a certain location on an 0–0 count, so that's where we attempt to go. Then my next step is I will print out a stolen base chart, which gives us the batter, the pitcher, the catcher, the runner, what count it was, and when that opposing manager likes to put the steal on. Then we do a hit-and-run chart, which—same thing—it's the batter, the pitcher, the catcher, the runner, what counts, and who they like to hit and run with. Then we do a bunt chart.

Those are all printed out and given to the coaches. That's on their chair when they get in. They are in about one, one thirty, two o'clock for a seven fifteen. They have a meeting. I don't really know exactly what kind of meeting.

I was in by probably eleven o'clock. A lot of stuff I'll do the day before: the charts I know that the data won't change. What I will do is, usually about an hour before the game, I'll put a videotape together of the starting pitcher so that the hitters can watch that in the clubhouse. Last night was Kenny Rogers—Detroit Tigers. So there was a tape of Rogers in his last start. Then right behind that, tape of the last time we faced him, since it was fairly recent. I try to keep it as recent as possible. If it gets too old, we change. That pretty much sums it up until game time.

Players come in before the game; players come in during the game. Before the game, Jonny Gomes came down to look at the last time he faced Kenny Rogers, even back to 2005, which is also in there to see. He told me that he was 5 for 9, or something. Carl Crawford was probably here by one thirty. He was looking at how he did the day before in New York—just to look at some things—and then he also pulled up the last time he faced Rogers. Damon Hollins was in. Josh Paul came in and went over all the hitters for the Tigers, and how to pitch them.

During [last night's] game, Rocco Baldelli was up. Jonny Gomes was up. Jorge Cantu was up. I'm trying to think. Russell Branyan came up. Most of the guys are going to come up. Some guys come in after every at-bat. It's all instant access; so when an at-bat is over with, you can come right up and watch that at-bat. There is no delay time.

Some guys are going to feel more comfortable with little information, and some guys want all the information. I couldn't really say generation makes a difference because I've had young guys that don't want to really look at a lot, and I've had older players, or veteran players, that live off of it. I mean, they thrive off it. I think it's the player himself. An older guy that we had here years ago, that thrived, was Greg Vaughn. He was in every day, at a certain time. He was a veteran guy that was religious in using it. He came in, but he only looked at positive things. He never looked at negative. I thought that was interesting. I learned something.

A couple of years ago, we went through a slump, and instead of showing the opposing pitcher before the game, and maybe how successful that guy was, I put a highlight pic together of our hitters hitting well, and showed that. I think, you know, maybe seeing something positive is better to see right before you go out. I always thought that was an interesting outlook on how to use things just before a game; just look at a positive build-me-up–type thing.

Jose Canseco was a big user of it; used it quite frequently. As a DH, after each at-bat, he would come in and look. He could tell where his swing went wrong, or maybe he'd make an adjustment.

I'd say I somewhat grew up in baseball. My mom was a big baseball fan; took me to games. She actually dated a gentleman that managed in the minor leagues. So I was always around the ballpark. I became a Cardinals fan.

Got my first job working in the clubhouse; kind of a like a batboy working in the clubhouse. Back in '75; maybe, '76. It was with the Cardinals' minor-league team—the St. Pete Cardinals. Yeah, down here in Florida. Then just kind of rolled on from there.

From there, let's see, I don't remember where I went after that. I went to school, and took a job with the Reds working in the clubhouse. I was a teenager. And then went to the Blue Jays, and worked in their Triple-A visiting clubhouse. Then went and coached high-school baseball for a while, and came back to professional baseball with the Devil Rays in '98. First job here, I worked here in the umpires' room. Then the next year, this job came open, and I have been here ever since.

It takes some time, but it's not as difficult as it seems when you first look at it. It's just being able to log a game. I mean, it's no more than keeping score except you are adding a lot more into it, and you need to be accurate. But it's basically using a computer, trying to keep score, capturing video, and being able to break it down.

When we go on the road, we bring everything with us. We have this portable system; it's packed away in trunks. It's all laptop-based, so it's packed away in a trunk, and just like everything else, it goes. Set up, and print out the same stuff for the next series.

There's been times on the road where the feed was on a satellite feed, and because of inclement weather, it was cutting in and out. Actually, this year when I was in—I don't want to say what city because I don't want to get anybody in trouble—but about four or five weeks ago, there was no feed available. I walked into the dugout for a couple of innings.

There's been one other time, and that was in Baltimore. It was a day-night double header. The first day game was a makeup game, and neither team was televising, so there was no TV. I went and sat in the dugout for like four innings. That's the only other time that I have actually seen a game on the field, other than watching it through a TV monitor every night.

I am a one-man show. I mean, there are many places where there are two, three, four guys—it just depends on the scale of what goes on. To be honest with you, there are ups and downs on every job, but every now and then you have to look at it: I am one of thirty people that get to do this for a living, which is pretty exciting, and it's a privilege. I'm blessed to be able to come to work at a ballpark every day.

*   *   *   *   *

JOHNNY PESKY

Instructor, Boston Red Sox

Courtesy of Geoff Coe

The right field foul pole at Fenway Park is called "Pesky's Pole," a name given by a broadcaster after Pesky won a game in 1948 with a home run that hooked around the pole. Pesky played from 1942 to 1954, missing the 1943, 1944, and 1945 seasons while serving in World War II.

The locker nearest the door to the Red Sox clubhouse is reserved for Pesky, number 6. He talked while getting dressed into his Sox uniform, an hour before batting practice. Johnny is eighty-eight years old.

* * * * *

The new owners have been great. I can't say enough about them. Mr. Henry and the general manager and the others, they kept us here—Jim Rice, myself, Luis Tiant, Dwight Evans. I am one of the few guys that they kept on. These people here have been wonderful, and I've got no complaints.

I got a very fine job. Well, I represent them publicly, sometimes. I do a little bit of, you know, talking to the players—how important baseball is and what it means, because you only have so many years you can play. If you're a good player, you can you can do quite well. Some guys take advantage of it and some don't. It's like any job: If you like your job, you are going to do it well. And the better you are as a player, it's going to be better for you down the road.

I was raised in Portland, Oregon. When I was about nine years old, I was working in a clubhouse. We would get out of school at three or three thirty, and a bunch of us used to go watch the last couple of innings. Then we got to be a nuisance, and the groundskeeper—an awfully nice man—gave us jobs us to do: clean the bullpens and stuff like that.

I signed right out of high school; just a kid playing in school, and getting scouts coming around looking like they do. That happened to a lot of kids. We played on semi-pro teams in little towns around the area. A catcher got $40,000 from the Detroit Tigers to sign. This kid was a fine player. I wasn't in that category, but I did get a little bonus. I just wanted to play. My mother picked the Red Sox for me to join. That's one of the best things that ever happened.

I had two years in minor league ball—class B to Triple-A to the big leagues. I had finished the year at Louisville, Triple-A, and then they were bringing me up. I thought that when I got there, they would option me out, but I made the ball club. I got a contract before the season started.

In '42, I joined the Navy like a lot of us did—the only thing I did that I am quite proud of. You know, the war come on. I went in with Ted Williams, Johnny Sain—who was with the Braves, Joe Coleman—with the A's, Phil Rizzuto—with the Yankees, and lot of others. I went in with all those smart guys. Being a high schooler, they kind of looked out for me. A guy out of Dartmouth had set up all these interviews for us, and we could make a choice to go into what service we wanted. I knew I wanted to go into the Navy. Ted did too. And then this guy Dominic DiMaggio went into the Navy. Christ, there was a thousand guys. Bob Feller was another one—a captain in the Marine Corps. He threw so hard. He was a hell of a pitcher. Ted Williams loved him. He thought he was the best pitcher he ever saw. I'll agree with that.

That's the way it was in those years. When the war come out, it kind of threw things out of whack for a while. You were worried about your own well being, and we were all single; in our early twenties. We did our bit. We served our time. We did the regular Navy duties, and we had to cope with what was going on. We made it all right. And then they dropped the big bomb and that ended everything. Mr. Truman did a fine thing, and we got back to playing. I missed three years of baseball: '43, '44, and '45. Come back: '46, '47, '48. '49, '50, '51, '52. I've done a hell of a lot of things for the ball club.

I was a middle infielder—shortstop; I played a little third. I was a decent player, but I played with great players: Dominic DiMaggio, Bobby Doerr, Ted Williams, Vern Stephens, and those guys. You could name a hundred guys that were great players in those years—Joe DiMaggio, Luke Appling—oh god, there were a lot of great players. We were contenders. We were close a few times. If you could play a while, you hung around, and it was fun. I mean, I was lucky to get through school. Baseball has been good to not only me, but to a lot of us.

Dom DiMaggio led off, and I hit second. I wasn't that good of a hitter. I hit in front of the best hitter that ever lived: Ted Williams. Oh hell, I got to hit a lot of good pitches. They weren't going to walk me to get to him. He was not only a great hitter, but a good instructor, had great eyesight, knew the strike zone, and was just a wonderful man. God created the perfect hitter. He was one of the brightest guys that I have ever been around, baseball-wise or anything. He was the top of his class. When he was here as a player, he understood hitting and tried to help a lot of guys out. Williams was the greatest hitter. He still is as far as I am concerned. I haven't seen anybody else like him.

Williams would always preach to us about what to expect and that sort of thing. When you are talking about big-league ballplayers, sometimes you could be really wrong because it's just so unpredictable. With every series, you have a list of their players, and what this guy can do, and you have a meeting about how you prepare and how you want to set up and play against him. You talk about their strong points, or weak points. Now they've got photography, which has become very big. And you get a lot of ideas from your coaches and your people that work on the road come in with reports. A lot of times in baseball the guy hitting might be in a little bit of a valley. You would like to get him when he is in a valley because you want to get his butt—you want to get him out. It's not a very complicated thing. It's really like going to school. You learn things about other players. When you're on the field, all those instructions go down the drain, but it's nice to get an idea.

I managed the Red Sox in '63 and '64. Not too well. You know, this was something that you live for, and I wished I could have had a better team. The general manager, Mike Higgins, and I never hit it off. He didn't want me, and he fired me. He didn't like me for some reason. I must have irritated him. But I had the job for two years. I wish I could have kept around a little bit, but I had a good time. It was fun. I got no complaints. I understood. I was glad to get the hell out.

Then I started coaching. I wanted to stay in the game because it was the only thing I knew. I wasn't a great player. I never got big money when I played, but I have managed to survive, and married a great little gal— Ruth Hickey. Married to her for sixty-one years. Ten more days, she'll be gone a year. She is up there. We had a good marriage, and we have a wonderful boy. God treated us very, very well.

I've been in the game my whole life and I've never done anything else. That's the way baseball is, and that's the way life is. It all depends on what you want. I've been really happy with this. I've never done anything else but baseball. And I'm not in bed. I don't know how much more I got. They might have to put me in the jitney and take me off.

* * * * *

ACKNOWLEDGMENTS

This book is about people who work in major-league baseball. It's about their jobs. Producing a book is a job, too, but I have to say: this has been fun—from the first interview to the period at the end of the final sentence.

When friends heard about this project, they often would say, "So you're writing a book?" I replied, "No, I'm collecting stories." The only way these stories could have made it into print was through the generosity of a lot people; some mentioned here, and others who helped even when they didn't know it.

First on my list of thanks are two guys: one I met, and another I haven't. Dan Shaughnessy, the talented sports columnist with the *Boston Globe*, graciously invited me to his home for the first interview. He politely told me I wasn't the first fella to produce a book like this, but he kindly answered my questions anyway. Two days later, the Houston Astros became the first team to grant clubhouse access, after Astros Chairman Drayton McLane read my letter to him, which explained what I was doing. Thank you, Mr. McLane.

I am indebted also to the many overworked people who let me pester them about acquiring media credentials and scheduling interviews. Without them, this book wouldn't have happened: Randy Adamack, Seattle Mariners; Rob Butcher, Cincinnati Reds; Shirley Casabat and Matt Hodson, San Francisco Giants; Cathy Davis and Donald Muller, MLB Commissioner's Office; Bob DiBiasio and Bart Swain, Cleveland Indians; John Dever, Washington Nationals; Greg Eklin, Texas Rangers; Luis Garcia and Jeff Overton, San Diego Padres; Mike Herman, Minnesota Twins; Sherry Clawson and Avery Holton, Round Rock Express; Carmen Molina, Tampa Bay Devil Rays; Gabe Ross, Sacramento River Cats; Larry Shenk, Philadelphia Phillies; Jimmy Stanton and Todd Fedewa, Houston Astros; Dr. Charles Steinberg and John Blake, Boston Red Sox; John Steinmiller, Milwaukee Brewers; Bill Stetka, Baltimore Orioles; Mike Swanson, Arizona Diamondbacks; Jim Trdinich, Pittsburgh Pirates; and Jim Young, Oakland A's.

I am especially grateful to all the men and women who let me stick a voice recorder before them and their willingness to talk with this stranger. I interviewed more baseball people than those who appear in the book. Their personal stories were compelling. Unfortunately, because of space limitations, their words are not included. Please know, though, I sincerely appreciate you sharing with me.

The heavy-lifting duties of transcribing hours and hours of the interviews were handled initially by Kim Murdoch, Erin Sales, and Kathi Myers. Later, Sanjay Kedambadi, with Bharathi Mediscribe Pvt. Ltd. in Bangalore, India, expertly completed transcriptions, even when background noises from batting practice, clubhouses, and stadium music almost obliterated some recordings.

I am honored that my agent, Bob Diforio of the D4EO Literary Agency, had confidence in the book and worked hard to peddle it. Thank you, Bob, for not bugging me by asking, "How's the book coming along?"

I am indebted also to Mark Weinstein, the superb Senior Editor at Skyhorse Publishing, for his guidance, vast baseball knowledge, and faith that these stories are worth telling. And to Amanda Bullock whose keen and meticulous copy-editing was invaluable.

My sister, Beverly, works for a major airline company and is entitled to choose one person as a "companion flyer." I'm the lucky brother she listed, for it allowed me to travel on the cheap around the country. Thanks, Bev.

And thank you also to three couples that boarded me when I was on the road: Krystiana and Andrew; Christine and Jason; and Abby and Gil. I appreciate your kindness and hospitality.

And a special thank you to my loving daughters, Sarah and Megan, and their athletic husbands, Scott and Brian, for still being willing to play catch with me and for listening as I told them repeatedly about the progress of the book. And to Greg for being a special brother and an avid baseball fan.

Above all, I could not have produced the book without the advice, encouragement, and patience of my loving wife, Sher.

A final thanks to Jerry Zimmerman, Wisconsin State Fair Historian, who provided the correct spelling of mascot Willy B. Bacon's name.

ABOUT THE AUTHOR

Courtesy of S. Jones

Tom Jones lives in Sacramento, California, with his wife. He plays third base for the Yankees in an over-forty-eight adult baseball league that uses wood bats. His .588 batting average in 2007 led the team.